JUL 2022

Praise for *Fighting against the Odds: An Insider's Life in UFC, Boxing, and Entertainment*

"Fiaz Rafiq and I bonded over Bruce Lee. His interview-heavy books on Lee, Muhammad Ali, and Arnold Schwarzenegger and pioneering coverage of full combat 'cage' sports was impressive. However, I didn't understand him before *Fighting against the Odds*, his moving memoir that doubles as a self-help book. He's the Islamic Horatio Alger. With a high school education, while adhering to his religion, he's become a well-regarded entertainment writer and sportswriter, among the first to identify MMA-style combat sports as a phenomenon. As a shy, introverted kid, he fixated on Bruce Lee, hiding it from his strict parents. Like Lee, he was a small-boned kid and saw martial arts as an avenue. His passion became his life's work as a writer. No one else covers MMA with such insight. Now, he spins out his unlikely life story with entertaining energy, verve, sincerity and passion."—**Alex Ben Block, former editor of the *Hollywood Reporter* and veteran showbiz journalist**

"An inspiring story of a kid who discovered his path in life—and success—through his passion for Bruce Lee and the martial arts. Highly recommended."—**Matthew Polly, *New York Times* best-selling author**

"[Fiaz] studies his subjects and does his homework so much that he can't go wrong. Fiaz studies the person—like he studied about me, Bruce Lee, Muhammad Ali, Arnold Schwarzenegger, and all those guys. And he knows more about the person than the person knows about himself."—**Royce Gracie, three-time UFC champion**

"The story of an obsessive individual who drew inspiration from his boyhood idol, Bruce Lee, to follow his dream and shape his life. It reflects how his passion forged friendships and taught him to roll with the blows that journalism can throw at you."—**Simon Jones, *Daily Mail***

"Fiaz knows exactly how to get to the heart of every story seamlessly—and telling his own is no different. A must read for fans of combat sports, MMA, and Hollywood."—**Ellie Henman, *Sun***

"Gripping memoir that doubles as an insightful deep dive into the world of entertainment and sports by a journalist who identified the phenomenon of MMA fighting as well as one man's journey to discover who he really is."—**Halina Watts,** *Sunday Mirror*

"My old friend Fiaz Rafiq has released a fascinating book about his experiences (as a journalist) in the world of MMA (combat sports) and beyond. This lovely soul is very impressive, winner of the *Sunday Times* Book of the Year for a previous title *My Brother, Muhammad Ali*. You can be sure that this book is equally insightful."—**Geoff Thompson, world's number-one self-defense expert and** *Sunday Times* **best-selling author**

FIGHTING AGAINST THE ODDS

An Insider's Life in UFC, Boxing, and Entertainment

Fiaz Rafiq

Rowman & Littlefield
Lanham • Boulder • New York • London

Published by Rowman & Littlefield
An imprint of The Rowman & Littlefield Publishing Group, Inc.
4501 Forbes Boulevard, Suite 200, Lanham, Maryland 20706
www.rowman.com

86-90 Paul Street, London EC2A 4NE

Published in the United Kingdom as *To the Top: Enter the Octagon, the Ring, and Entertainment.*

British Library Cataloguing in Publication Information Available

Library of Congress Cataloging-in-Publication Data Available

ISBN 9781538154830 (cloth : alk. paper) | ISBN 9781538154847 (epub)

♾️™ The paper used in this publication meets the minimum requirements of American National Standard for Information Sciences—Permanence of Paper for Printed Library Materials, ANSI/NISO Z39.48-1992.

Contents

Foreword   ix

Preface   xi

1   Crazy Obsessions   1

2   It's a Man's World   9

3   Feeling Despondent   15

4   The American Dream   24

5   Enter the Gracies   34

6   Returning to Los Angeles   42

7   Enter the Journalist   50

8   UFC Assignment   59

9   More Real Than the UFC   66

10   The Giants   70

11 Hollywood, Here We Come! 77

12 Home Sweet Home 88

13 The Sport of MMA Hits the Mainstream 93

14 Ringside and Brock "The Beast" Lesnar 101

15 UFC 105 Encounters 107

16 Boxing versus UFC: The Tyson–Gracie Challenge 115

17 UFC, Royals, and Rich Arabs 124

18 Mike, Managers, and Me 132

19 Muhammad Ali Encounters 138

20 From Martial Arts to Movie Magic 147

21 I'll Be Back 152

22 From Hospitality to MMA Chaos 160

23 Adventures in New York 169

24 Las Vegas 174

25 Canada: MMA Mad 180

26 The Massive MMA Fiasco 185

27 I'm No Terrorist 189

28 From Racism to Road Rage 200

29 Mr. Rocky 205

30 Bruce Lee: Enter the Ring 211

31 Enter the Octagon   216

32 Old School Meets New   220

33 Challenging Conor McGregor   227

34 Tough Man Tales   235

35 Notorious   242

36 Meeting with an Underworld Figure   250

37 The Perils of Sports Fame   256

38 Michael, Matt, and Martial Arts   261

39 A New Direction: New World   267

40 Flying High   276

41 A Tumultuous Year   285

Epilogue   293

Afterword   295

Acknowledgments   299

About the Author   301

Foreword

I've known Fiaz for a long time, for more than 24 years to be precise, since 1996 when he first visited the Gracie Academy in Los Angeles, California, as a 20-year-old and became my student. That's how far back we go. Subsequently, whenever he visited Los Angeles, he would occasionally take private lessons with me on a one-on-one basis. I don't believe in good students and bad students, but I do believe in good teachers and bad teachers. If I'm a good teacher, then a student will learn.

Despite Fiaz's long-term enthusiasm for the martial arts and UFC, he eventually gravitated toward and forged a professional career in journalism, focusing on combat sports and entertainment in the literary world. He's been around the arts for a long time, particularly as a sportswriter dedicated to promoting the sport of mixed martial arts (MMA), professional fighters, and world champions.

MMA has been labeled the fastest-growing sport in the world, and it has certainly presented endless opportunities for different businesses, gyms, fighters, fans, judges, and magazines, culminating in the mainstream media taking a keen interest in what was once labeled "human cockfighting." Fiaz has been a part of the effort to legitimize MMA from the outset and always helped publicize my seminars and anything I was promoting via coverage in the press. "Hey, Royce," he would ask me, when barely anyone knew about MMA. "Is there anything you would like to promote in the magazine?" He has always supported me—I can't say enough good things about that.

Another thing Fiaz brings from martial arts is a strong work ethic. He creates work of a high caliber because he's utterly resolute in his approach. He always researches his subjects with devotion, and by putting in the time and effort by doing his homework, he can't go wrong. Fiaz studies the person—just as he studied me, Bruce Lee, Muhammad Ali, Arnold Schwarzenegger, and all those guys—and produces commendable results.

Ever since I've known him, he has invariably spoken with great pride and optimistically about the late Bruce Lee. He would say to me with great conviction that if Bruce Lee, who was already researching MMA, was alive today, he would have embraced Gracie Jiu-Jitsu. Fiaz devoted an inordinate amount of time researching Bruce Lee's life; he knows everything about the man. He literally knows more about him than the late master knew about himself. I remember joking with him, saying I can't stand the fact I'm number two on his list of heroes after Bruce Lee. I told him I should be his number one.

We never fail to inject a dose of humor when we get together, especially whenever he's in Los Angeles or we're talking over the phone. He had a tendency to complain about being subjected to terrifying ordeals at American airports because of his religious background. Consequently, I used to tease him about that all the time. Recently, I was showing some of my students in America one of the videos Fiaz sent me of him praying in the street. They all thought it was amusing. They were like, "Man, that guy's crazy." I said, "He doesn't care, he just dropped down in the street and started praying."

Indeed, these days, it's very hard to find individuals who you can call real friends because it's not out of the ordinary for people to have ulterior motives—they are looking for something in return. True friendship is not easy to find and sustain. But Fiaz has been a good friend of mine for many years now. I know that if I need anything, I can count on him day or night. I'm very pleased he has written his memoir showcasing his journey as a journalist because, having worked with, been around, interviewed, and written about a plethora of fascinating figures, he has compelling insights to share with the world.

Royce Gracie
UFC legend

Preface

When I first began my career in journalism, never in a million years did I envisage that one day I would be writing my memoir. Even a few years later, when I had already had the opportunity to explore and write about the colorful lives of some of the world's biggest sporting and Hollywood action heroes, it never really dawned on me that I would share my own journey. It was only after almost two decades in my chosen career that I started to consider myself alongside other notable journalists whom I saw releasing their memoirs and autobiographies—many were from the political fraternity, but a few had written their own acclaimed and award-winning combat sports–related memoirs. Matthew Polly (a Bruce Lee biographer and martial arts enthusiast) and Davis Miller (a Muhammad Ali and Bruce Lee biographer) were huge inspirations on my own writing but also made me consider whether other people might find value in reading about my life, just as I had read about theirs.

Before embarking on the project of encapsulating my life experiences, though, I asked myself, *Why would I want to write and share my story?* This wasn't a hard question to answer, for two key reasons. First, having worked closely with many famous individuals, I have a great deal to share, from the anecdotes they shared in our interviews and personal conversations to the details of their lives I've never had the space to recount before. Second, coming from a humble background where facing prejudice was a daily hurdle, I felt that my story of beating the odds to become a successful writer and reach the top could inspire others facing their own struggles.

For almost as long as I can remember, my ultimate aspiration has always been to become a professional writer and author, but the forum I found to explore my craft came from another place, too. My voracious appetite for the written word developed alongside an almost unhealthy obsession with the fighting arts, something I pursued for much of my youth. Eventually, my interest led me to holding the prestigious position of chief columnist and features writer for the number-one martial arts magazine, *Martial Arts Illustrated*, a position that gave me unprecedented access to many warriors and athletes and helped me forge friendships with some historically significant names in combat sports. And eventually, my dream of working alongside some of the UFC champions was one that I made a reality through motivation, obsession, hard work, and resilience.

I was able to eventually break through into Hollywood when I came on board the now defunct *Impact: The Global Action Movie Magazine* and subsequently the national tabloids. When it comes to the glitz and the glamour of celebrity life, the majority of us only ever aspire to getting an autograph or selfie from our favorite stars. We never really have the opportunity to sit down with them and discuss their lives or rub shoulders with those closest to them. For me, though, being up close and personal with these people became a part of my regular routine.

It was never a smooth ride, however. On my journey, I experienced hardship, rejection, and harassment, including discrimination in America airports and a disturbing visit from the United Kingdom's Special Branch, which suspected me of being a threat to national security. Somehow, I made it through to write this book, which I started in 2015 but shelved as I focused on other projects. It wasn't until five years later that I decided to finish the book. It's a fascinating odyssey in the form of a personal journey through my own coming-of-age story where I share the struggles, triumphs, and low points as a journalist, alongside hundreds of behind-the-scenes anecdotes and stories of UFC, boxing, and entertainment stars and my personal experiences working with the best. I hope you enjoy the ride as much as I enjoyed the drive.

1

Crazy Obsessions

As a young kid growing up, I was profoundly influenced by the late great Bruce Lee. The King of Kung Fu has had an everlasting impression on my life. No, I didn't grow up in the 1970s at the height of the kung fu boom. I was a child of the 1980s, a decade that saw great socioeconomic change due to leaps in technology and advances in globalization. The world was rife with conflict: the Cold War, the Falklands War, the Iran-Iraq War, and the Soviet-Afghanistan War. Pop sensations Michael Jackson, Madonna, Prince, and Wham were selling millions of records. Action heroes Sylvester Stallone and Arnold Schwarzenegger were competing for the number-one spot at the box office. And Mike Tyson was obliterating every opponent put in front of him. It was a time where larger-than-life heroes were the norm, but I became obsessed with a small, ultra-lean Chinese guy who'd died almost a decade before.

I first encountered Bruce Lee when I was 10 years old. I remember the day vividly. It was 1985, and I was at a family friend's house with my brother and two neighbor friends. To keep us kids entertained, the family friend's nephew slipped a videocassette of *Enter the Dragon*, Bruce's only Hollywood action film, into the chunky VCR. Back in those days, there was no such thing as DVDs, let alone a streaming platform that instantly granted access to hundreds of films from Hong Kong or China. It was the era of the classic videocassette, chunky silver and black video players, and going to the local video shops to scout out something that looked promising. As a matter of fact, many TVs were made out of wood, and today's teenagers would have been appalled by the size of the screen on which we had to watch Bruce's dazzling choreography. But still, what I witnessed that day was just totally mesmerizing.

Never before had I been exposed to such an amazing depiction of the human body in motion. Bruce himself looked almost unreal, stripped of all fat and as lean and dangerous as the praying mantises that fight early in the film. By the finale, he's dispatching multiple fighters with deadly fists and feet, looking utterly believable in contrast to the slow-motion choreography of most action films and the telegraphed punches of Rocky.

I was hypnotized: I had just been introduced to this phenomenon and was eager to learn more, but to my dismay, I was quickly told that this diminutive-looking guy who beat the hell out of 20 fighters at once had vanished from the face of the Earth. *What?* I thought to myself. *No, he can't be. I've just had the most remarkable experience of my life, and you're telling me this deadly fighting machine is gone!* It was beyond belief. Sadness tinged the exhilaration I felt at seeing Bruce's balletic performance, but from that day on, my whole life would change completely. Things would never be the same again.

Not that it was easy to get my kung fu fix. After my first introduction to this different kind of action hero, whenever *Enter the Dragon* was playing on TV, I would have to sneak down from my bedroom to watch it, as my own family hadn't yet bought a VHS player. This was problematic because this all-time classic was always on late at night at around 11 p.m. and had a few scenes that most parents would have doubtless thought of as inappropriate viewing—for me it was more than that because watching movies late at night wasn't something we could do. I was supposed to be in bed by 10, and so, to overcome this barrier, I would slowly sneak down the squeaky stairs to get my fix of the Little Dragon.

This was no easy task, believe me. It would take me about 10 minutes to get downstairs because I didn't want to wake anyone up and get caught in the act by my parents, and I'd want to get downstairs as soon as possible. The epic opening fight scene with Bruce and Sammo Hung, a skinny guy and a fat man battling it out in what resembled an MMA setting, was one of my favorite fights in the film. You have to understand that one of the consequences for breaking rules at home included my getting a good hiding. Still, I was prepared to break the rules over and over if I had to. Another key thing I had to do to prevent getting caught was to keep the volume level low—just loud enough so I could detect what the actors were saying. Take into account that back in those days, there were no remote controls, which was always a pain because you had to get up from the comfort of your seat to adjust the volume level. Fortunately, I had pretty good ears, and so, somehow, I got away with it every single time. Whether or not my parents were aware that I was sneaking down I will never know because they never mentioned it or questioned me.

As I've mentioned, we never had a VCR in those days, and so, though I was itching to watch the handful of other movies Bruce had made, I had no access to them. Instead, I would find solace through conversing with a friend in school who understood my Bruce Lee obsession. As others played soccer or talked about who won the game over the weekend, my friend would relate the story lines of Bruce's other films and how the kung fu master would kick ass as I eagerly hung on his every word. I needed more Bruce. It felt like being deprived of something. I felt like a drug addict wanting to feed a habit.

Eventually, I found a way to get my fix. On weekends, I would go, along with another friend who shared his enthusiasm for the martial arts master, to the house of a friend whom we coaxed into sitting through the films. Renting a Bruce Lee video, which at that time cost only 50 pence, became a weekend ritual. I had specifically taken out a video club membership at a local video rental store just to do it. And if you checked my rental record, you'd find that other than *Enter the Dragon*, *Fist of Fury*, *Big Boss*, *Way of the Dragon*, and *Game of Death*, I never rented any other film from the store. Sure, I occasionally enjoyed other Hong Kong kung fu flicks, but most if not all of these were cheesy with laughably trite scripts, compared with the intensity of Bruce's output. No other actor on the big screen, no matter how popular, came close to the persona this fighter possessed, a feeling that's never been replicated.

I'll be honest, there have been times throughout my life when I've thought, *What if Bruce Lee had never existed? What would the world be like? What direction would have my own life taken?* I have actually thanked God for creating this man, the man who brought joy not only to my life but also to millions of people's lives around the globe. He was the epitome of cool, a symbol of male vigor and hope to people who couldn't hope to compete with traditional jocks. No matter what problems you were facing in life, watching Bruce was a sanctuary for you as you took delight in watching him take on endless obstacles in the four and a half films he had churned out in merely two years in his truncated career. We all need something in life that helps us forget our problems for a while, and for me, it was Bruce.

‿2‿

Growing up, I never particularly had an affinity for reading in school. In fact, I never was inclined to study much at all. However, once Bruce Lee came along, I developed an interest in literature relating directly to the martial arts. From the age of 10, I would religiously visit the local library in town with my brother and my next-door neighbor and borrow books relating to the Oriental arts. Bodybuilding books—specifically the ones written by Robert Kennedy, who was a well-known Canadian bodybuilding author—also caught my attention. Eventually, I developed a voracious appetite for the written word. Being a young teenager finding a path in life, in my "reading sessions" I took delight in the mini step-by-step pictorials more than the text. Some kids grew up reading superhero tales that helped them cope with adversity, but the antics of Batman and Superman never invoked my interest. I got my thrills from learning everything I could about my hero and martial arts when I was growing up via the medium of print.

In my second year of high school, in 1989, when I was 13, it dawned on me that martial arts and bodybuilding magazines existed. I remember coming across *Combat* magazine and its competitor *Martial Arts Illustrated* on the shelves of WHSmith in town and being immediately entranced by this new source of information. I would religiously save my bus fare so I could purchase the monthly *Martial Arts Illustrated*, which at that time cost £1.25. I say that, but sometimes it was financially beneficial to stand there and flick through the pages, read, look at the action pictures, and shove the copy back on the shelf, often placing it in the wrong pile. This strategy was seemingly implemented by many like-minded people—at least from the mismatched nature of the shelves.

Bruce was more than a martial artist, too. His mind and intellectual side (he studied philosophy at the University of Washington) eventually influenced me to a great degree. He once wrote, "Many people live only for their image. That is why whereas some have a self, a starting point, most people have a void because they are so busy projecting themselves as this or that. Wasting, dissipating all their energy in projection and conjuring up a facade rather than centering their energy on expanding and broadening their potential." Similarly, he told an interviewer, "It is easy for me to put on a show and be cocky and then feel pretty cool. Or I can do all kinds of phony things and be blinded by it. Or I can show you some really fancy movement. But to express oneself honestly, not lying to oneself, that is, my friend, very hard to do." He believed that imitation was not the path, and he advised his students to find their own way and not be blind followers. Certainly, this concept of finding your own way was derived from the writings of the great philosophers he read about, but he implemented the philosophies into his art and teachings and, as he advised others to do with his art of jeet kune do (literally translated as "the way of the Intercepting fist"), added what was specifically his own.

One of the core tenets of his philosophy was to know yourself. Why would Bruce pursue philosophy? This is a question I wanted answered for my own personal satisfaction ever since I came across this as a young man. "My majoring in philosophy was closely related to the pugnacity of my childhood," Bruce once said. "I often asked myself these questions: What comes after victory? Why do people value victory so much? What is glory? What kind of victory is glorious?" With the assistance of his university teacher, who advised Bruce when he was in the middle of selecting a subject, he chose to study a subject that he believed would explain what man lives for. "When I told my friends and relatives that I had picked philosophy, they were all amazed," Bruce said. "Everybody thought I had better go into physical education since the only extracurricular activity that I was interested in, from my childhood until I graduated from my secondary school, was Chinese martial arts."

In time, you came to realize that the late kung fu master, the man with a physique to die for and an iron fist, was an extremely intellectual human being. He perceived a direct application of philosophy to a physical art form. Furthermore, he was an ardent follower of self-help writers, Napoleon Hill and Norman Vincent Peale being two of the more prominent ones to influence him. When I learned about Bruce's reading habits, I wasted no time in collecting more books from his inspirations as I strove to train my mind as much as my body, emulating the late kung fu master.

Flicking through martial arts periodicals, the ads for clothing, equipment, and tomes caught my attention as much as the images of photos of martial artists performing high and flying kicks. The martial arts was an industry in itself, I would soon come to realize. I got in the habit of ordering goodies from the mail-order ads. Mind you, literature wasn't cheap, and as a young teenager, I didn't have a lot of money.

I would also have to have my purchases delivered to a friend's house instead of my own address. I had a tendency to keep my hobby and passion a secret, like a scared little boy. For some odd reason, I found it a taboo subject to broach. In my house, even asking to stay out late could prove troublesome. We grew up in a disciplined home where extracurricular activity was not on the menu. Telling my parents I'd become obsessed with this strange man from Hong Kong would have been like being in an Italian restaurant but asking for Chinese noodles. It seemed that other kids' aspirations were supported by their parents, but I was deprived of that privilege. It can have an indelible impact on a kid's development. It feels likes the other kids have been given an edge, the head start in a race, and you can't start your run until they're halfway to the finishing line. How are you going to triumph against someone when you're way behind because you are being held back? It's a feeling that stayed with me into my adult years, but later it would vanish.

Still, if you look at this from a more optimistic angle, if you lack support and encouragement while growing up, it can boost your motivation. And as a consequence, you're determined to prevail in life. So it can work both ways. Some people have things given to them on a plate, but they lack commitment and that all-important relentless drive, and so they never make it, they never achieve their goals. Whether I had support or not, I feel I had a natural tendency and passion for pursuing what I wanted in life, sure that nothing was going to hinder my progress. No one was going to extinguish my dreams because of my sheer tenacity.

There are countless success stories about successful people who had it hard but still had their dreams manifest into a reality through sheer force of will. These are the kinds of stories and lessons that offered me inspiration. I'm a big believer in making your own destiny. I find it rather disappointing when I hear people say, "Well, it's not going to happen to me." In life, no matter what you pursue, I'm a firm believer that it doesn't matter where you come from—whether it's a small village in some part of Asia, like the one my parents came from, or a big bustling city in the West. You've got a brain, two arms, and two legs just like anyone else, so you can pursue something in life and achieve your goals.

◦⌒◦

As I immersed myself obsessively in my hobbies and cultivated a penchant for the martial arts in particular, taking things to the extreme was nothing unusual for me. I believe I was born an extreme, obsessive person. Eventually, it would become my biggest asset in life, but my obsession did get me into trouble several times. In English class, for instance, I was once caught reading a bodybuilding magazine under the table. My teacher threatened to bring my interests to my parents' attention, which scared me more than you might think. I don't think my parents would have understood why I was reading about scantily dressed men and women in a magazine. Fortunately, I was let off with a warning. Many years later, I consoled myself with the fact that even the great Arnold Schwarzenegger had his fair share of arguments with his parents when he was growing up obsessed with a sport that nobody really cared about. Still, I was always careful to hide those periodicals under my bed at home.

More serious was the fact that I took to regularly sneaking a nunchaku into school, which I tucked into my trousers above my belt and under my sweater. I was very lucky one day when I got into an altercation after English class that my friend had my pair of "chucks." I beat up a boy named Craig, who had to be hospitalized because of a broken nose and broken ribs. The fight lasted only under 10 seconds as I hit him with multiple head butts and round kicks to both his ribs. He couldn't do anything. Had this illegal weapon been found on me, there would've been grave consequences. By the way, I had all the justification to fight and would never fight to hurt anyone unless it was for self-defense. He had been giving me attitude for a while and was provoking me for no reason.

Martial arts and physique personalities were undoubtedly famous in their own worlds, but even the mainstream general public, who didn't follow these sports, had some sort of reverence toward these alpha males and females. At the same time, bodybuilding and its adherents more often than not received negative press from the mainstream media because of the stigma of drugs attached to the sport and its athletes. Steroids were part and parcel of the iron-pumping game and of course still are. These glossy, colorful publications were littered with supplements and nutrition ads aimed at convincing readers to part with their hard-earned cash by claiming that the overmuscled athletes featured next to them used nothing else. Whether these products worked is another story, but those well-placed ads certainly caught my attention.

Suddenly, I was enticed into trying out natural supplements. I kept it simple. I was an advocate of vitamin C because Bruce Lee consumed 1,500 mg of vitamin C on a daily basis. We had these purple-colored multivitamin tablets prescribed from the family doctor for free. My whole family was on them. So I had this pill every day, thinking it would make me invincible and strong. Protein is essential in building muscle, and if you're an athlete, you should consume plenty of protein, the experts claimed. I did for a while, but then I stuck to natural milk, drinking three glasses daily in the vain hope of becoming a Superman.

It wasn't long before I was put off supplements (or should I say "magic pills") after I had a near-death experience when I was in my mid-teens. I had ordered GABA capsules from a company via mail order, which was one of the main avenues you used to buy supplements in those days before the advent of the internet. Now they are stocked in Walmart and TESCO, too, but back in the day, things were a lot tougher. Anyway, after gulping down some capsules one day, it had an adverse effect. I became extremely ill. Worse than that: my whole body felt "dead." A doctor had to be called. I felt like I was on the verge of leaving this world. I had an allergic reaction to the pills, and my brain and my body felt like a sponge. I was hallucinating. The doctor said I had one of the most severe allergic reactions he'd ever seen to the capsules. After that unfortunate episode, I took an oath that I would never take something like this again. And I never did. I was relieved enough that I was going to live. I became very wary of supplements. I valued my life more than any amount of muscle I might put on. Stories of bodybuilders dying after taking steroids had been circulated in the specialist press, and it was petrifying. But I never took steroids and was never tempted to experiment at any cost whatsoever.

To be honest, although I ventured into the world of supplements, I never seriously continued taking them on a long-term basis—one reason being that they were too damn expensive. How could a kid afford them? And as for how some people could sustain their habit on a monthly basis, throwing their hard-earned cash away on the hopes of muscle, was beyond my comprehension. So it was short lived for me. At the time, one big company was publicizing their products like no one else. They seemed to have caught on with consumers and attracted a loyal following, even breaking into the mainstream in terms of customer base and distribution. The martial arts and bodybuilding bug had hit me hard by now. It was infectious. And nothing and nobody was going to cure this infection.

2

It's a Man's World

Most young teens played and watched soccer in our community—when I say "community," I mean the South Indian Asian one—but hardly any teenagers hit the gym. And it would be a miracle if anyone actually pursued the martial arts of the Far East. You would be hard pressed to find an Asian kid with an interest in the Oriental arts serious enough that they would even take part let alone pursue it on a serious level. Of course, like anything, there were the exceptions.

Perhaps one of the most striking aspects of Bruce Lee is his trademark physique. This 135-pound frame is revered by his fans, and I was no different as a youth, admiring his onionskin definition and razor-sharp cuts. In 1989, at the age of 13, for the first time ever, I stepped into a weight training gym in an attempt to emulate my hero.

A lot of the gyms in those days were housed in old orange-bricked mills. These gyms would often be referred to as "bodybuilding gyms." Most of these facilities have become extinct now as big modern-day franchise facilities have mushroomed all over the world, but back in the day, it was grim and gritty. Every Saturday morning, along with a friend, I would religiously walk to this gym for a workout. It was an old-school facility, full of big, burly, sweaty men pumping iron, with physiques that were built on years of hard-core training, proper diet and nutrition, and, in some cases, steroids. We were just two young teenage kids who thought we could one day make the drastic transformation to look just like the stars we admired. Black Box's *Right on Time* would be blaring as we pumped our tiny teen muscles, inspired by the bodybuilding stars. The atmosphere was electric, aggressive, but friendly.

I vividly recall that the walls of the gym were plastered with posters of Serge Nubret, Franco Columbu, Dave Draper, Bill Grant, and Chris Dickerson—some of the greats whom I would interview decades later when I became a sports journalist.

I stuck to the iron for a long time. In my youth, I had contemplated whether I should take the martial arts or bodybuilding route as far as dedicating time to a physical pursuit is concerned. It's difficult to jump between two disciplines—one can't ride two horses at the same time. Even though I continued pumping iron, martial arts were my first love. Training with weights became a form of supplementary training. My bedroom became my training space. I'd stretch out my legs, throw high kicks and hundreds of punches into the air, and try to mimic Bruce Lee in my bedroom. My uncle, who had moved to the United Kingdom from Paris several years earlier, was a martial arts enthusiast himself. He would teach me moves in our living room, from high kicks to painful stretches and some kung fu moves. We shared a mutual appreciation for the arts, and he became very close to me, encouraging me to further pursue the martial arts.

Moreover, as soon as I had discovered that Bruce had developed his own form of combat, jeet kune do, I was immediately drawn to it like a moth to a lightbulb. How could I train in Thai boxing or karate when Bruce Lee, the man I idolized, had created his own system? This motivated me in my quest to learn more about the man. I embarked on a fascinating journey of discovery, delving into his art and the art of those who were directly associated with it, such as his personal students. I would accumulate any information I could get my hands on about the system.

To put things in perspective, I was a small-boned kid. I often suffered from asthma, and physically, I believe, a lot of kids were stronger and healthier than me. One of my best childhood friends, "Big" Ash, was always stronger physically and a lot bigger in stature. I wasn't one of those types of people who took up martial arts because they had to: to defend themselves because they got into fights or were bullied. To be honest, I really didn't perceive the martial arts primarily as a means to defend yourself if someone attacked you. That was pretty far from my mind. To me, it was about learning to fight and enjoying a hobby.

In hindsight, it's funny, but when "Big" Ash and I were making our transition into high school at age 11, we proclaimed to ourselves that we were going to be the toughest in the class (or maybe the best soccer players). We were eager to stand out and garner respect. Nope, it didn't happen—at least not for me. "Big" Ash unleashed his potential early and did make a name for himself.

Growing up, some kids are blessed with a big mouth, something I never did have. It's a double-edged sword. Being all talk can get you what you want, but often bullies or people with the gift of gab develop a somewhat false sense of confidence. They are of the belief that they are tough, as they can "act" themselves to the top, with intimidation often playing a key role. Lack of physical development and suffering from asthma was my worst enemy, alongside my childhood shyness, which didn't help. It's believed that most shy children develop shyness because of the type of interaction they have with their parents. Parents who are authoritarian or overprotective can result in their children becoming shy. And I fell into this category. I would come to learn in life that if you're a diffident individual, it can have an adverse effect on your life and how people perceive you, while those who are extroverts are often seen as "better" people even though you might be better and more capable than them given the opportunity. In general, and in particular within the community, if you exude confidence socially and are talkative, you are perceived as someone who knows the world, someone with whom others feel very comfortable, which seems to garner respect from peers and those around you. There's value placed on you. It's a system that rewards extroverts, and I was never comfortable in it.

As a kid, I was involved in an average amount of fights but never got beat badly—and every single one I beat I did so with a degree of ease. Every single time, it was the other kid or individual who would provoke me with attitude, as they would perceive me as unimposing. They would find out the hard way that this wasn't true. Trouble would always come to me; I never went out looking for it. I was able to hit hard as a teenager. There was always the frightening prospect of losing, which to my young mind would be more mortifying than getting hurt. An overwhelming fear would grip me in the gut just thinking about it. I was never afraid of getting hurt.

Eventually, I would tally 10 altercations in my youth—losing two. My first loss taught me a lesson. I learned that if you decide to fight, don't go in halfheartedly. In my early teens, I decided to get into an altercation with a boy from school who had been giving me some attitude for no reason whatsoever. Because I had put another boy (whom I mentioned earlier) in the hospital, I decided to avoid punching this boy in the face or doing serious damage, instead hitting him on his shoulder of all things. Wrong move! He took me down and totally controlled me, sitting on top of me in what modern MMA fighters call the "mount." My being "nice" in a fight led to my getting my ass handed to me. *Never will I ever do that again*, I thought to myself. In fact, this boy used to watch WWF and was quite solid.

⌒⌒

Our teenage years are such a vital time in life, and making the right choices can have a profound effect. Sometimes, teens are influenced by, to whatever degree, someone they know and are in awe of. For me, I grew up in a mainly Asian community. If there was anyone who influenced me, it was a local boy named Affy. Some other young teens growing up in our community who, by the way, won't admit to it now also revered Affy. He was four years older than me and was the epitome of cool and toughness and someone I looked up to. He is one of my best friends now. You could say that he was like a local celebrity in our little community.

I remember reading an autobiography of the unlicensed famous boxer and street fighter Lenny McLean, who said that when you could fight in school, you were treated like a celebrity. He was somewhat right. In my school, being tough and fighting meant respect, and you were treated like you were famous in your own little world. I mean, every kid wants to be liked and appreciated, and some are willing to do dumb things for attention.

Now, there are always people who perceive themselves as "hard" when they were, say, 12, and it's something they carry on their backs to completely define themselves for the rest of their lives. It is an attitude that was rife where I grew up. Many times, these "hard" kids are actually hiding their weaknesses and playing down their faults while highlighting their strengths—more often than not, strengths that they don't really possess. Honestly, many people, especially young people, are insecure and just crave acceptance, often just putting up a fake front.

One of the foremost lessons I learned in life comes from achievers of the highest caliber—fighters in particular but also sports athletes and other well-known personalities. I came to learn that it's okay to highlight and reveal your weaknesses openly, accept them, and come to terms with them. As a young boy, I was reluctant to expose my shortcomings, but it eventually would sink in as I understood the professional fighters' backgrounds and ways of thinking. If you are secure and content, then you won't mind exposing and talking about your deficiencies. So the lesson I learned from some of the toughest men in the world has been this: never hide your deficiencies; instead, embrace them. When you're a kid growing up, you can eventually unleash your potential and find yourself. And this is what I would eventually do as far as challenging myself.

⌒⌒

Eventually, I was curious to find out about the childhoods of famous fighters and champions. I went on to study and write about some of the most notorious fighters in the fight game, which gave me an extensive background on their lives and childhoods. Bruce Lee, as I mentioned, started training in the wing chun kung fu system in Hong Kong at an early age but didn't use it much. William Cheung, his close childhood friend, personally told me that he and fellow students wouldn't let Bruce fight often in the infamous rooftop matches that took place when they were young. Bruce was a child actor, and William said it wouldn't look good if his friend fought and his face got battered and bruised. As much as I am an ardent follower of Bruce and his legend—many sources are often biased and can more often than not be accused of highlighting the more positive sides while neglecting to elucidate the weaknesses—over the decades, certain stories have circulated about Bruce being super-invincible as a teenager taking part in rooftop fights. These are often sugarcoated, so it's tough to tell where the truth lies.

Then there's the notion that had Bruce not made it and went to America, he would have become a gangster. I find that implausible at best. In fact, I surmise it may be best to dismiss these thoughts altogether. Moreover, at the wing chun school, there were some seniors with more knowledge and skill than Bruce. He would have had to cultivate humility.

Recognized as the biggest draw the pugilistic world has had to offer since the retirement of Muhammad Ali, the mighty Mike Tyson, who became the youngest heavyweight champion in boxing and earned the moniker of "Baddest Man on the Planet," was a timid kid and was a victim of bullying. He started to develop at the right age, just before he turned a teenager, and by the time he was in his mid-teenage years, he was so ferocious that he'd beat you before the fight even began. "When I read the stories about myself, people keep saying that I was a tough kid in the streets," Tyson revealed in an interview after capturing the heavyweight title. "I used to get into a lot of fights, but they didn't know that I used to get beat up all the time. Maybe I had a lot of fights, but I always got beat up. They say I was street tough and that I used to go beating up everybody in the street. But it wasn't really like that till I started fighting in the ring; then it became a whole different story."

Speaking of boxers, Sugar Ray Leonard once personally told me when and why he pursued the brutal sport of boxing. "I pursued boxing because I was such a shrimp and a nonathlete," one of the all-time greats recounted. "My brothers Roger and Kenny were basketball players, football players, and track stars, but I couldn't match them until I started boxing. I was the type of young kid at 14 that was never really athletically inclined. They were real athletes. The same reason my brother Roger encouraged me to come down to the center and get involved in boxing." He went on to become pound for pound the best pugilist in the world.

You want other examples? Jean-Claude Van Damme, a bespectacled skinny and weak teenager, transformed himself into an Adonis, earning the nickname "Muscles from Brussels." And I will never forget what Bill "Superfoot" Wallace, the greatest kicker in the world and world martial arts champion, revealed once in an article I read as a teen: if there were 37 kids in his school class, he wasn't in the first 36 toughest people. My good friend Ronnie Green, five-time world Thai boxing champion and the best ever to have come out of his country in this brutally punishing sport, was a victim of bullying and racism. But after taking up the arts at age 13, he was fighting professionally at age 17.

Another close friend of mine, Joe Egan, Mike Tyson's sparring partner who earned the title of "Toughest White Man on the Planet" from the notorious boxing legend, was also a victim of bullying as a kid. He suffered prejudice because of his Irish descent and accent, which resulted in cruel bullying. Then you have one of the best fighters ever to step into the Octagon in the brutal sport of MMA, UFC welterweight champion Georges St. Pierre, another victim of bullying as a kid. From the age of 15, he was training and fighting and beating full-grown men. He once told me when I first interviewed him, "I had a lot of anger and pride in me when I was growing up. I didn't want to tell nobody about my problems. I had pride and a big ego, so I wouldn't tell anyone because I thought they'd say I'm like a baby or a kid who cannot defend himself."

So what do all these legendary fighters, alpha males, and notorious men have in common? They had that natural potential within and at the right developmental stages unleashed it to the max. It's all to do with timing—it's all about when it will kick in. All successful fighters have endured hardships and obstacles in various shapes and forms. When growing up as kids, a lot of the self-proclaimed tough guys aren't prepared to suffer—hence, they are never able to unleash their potential when they become men.

3

Feeling Despondent

I was still at school when I came across a small black-and-white ad in a national newspaper offering a writing course. The home learning course, as it was called, was offered by the Writers Bureau and would set you back £25—a decent amount of cash at that time. I wasted no time filling out the little coupon, as you did back in those days, and slipping the cash in an envelope to mail it. I had made up my mind to become a writer. Whether I thought I would succeed is entirely another story. I always held the belief that I should go out and grab what I craved in life. I was determined enough, there's no doubt about it, but I'm not sure I was confident that I actually had the skills to carve out a career.

I eagerly waited for weeks and weeks for the course work package to appear at my doorstep—but nothing. The Writers Bureau was based in Manchester city center on Dale Street. Disillusioned with the "goods" not arriving, I decided to take a bus and pay the bureau a visit to squeeze some answers out of them.

The office was on the second or third floor. As I walked into the dimly lit office, it looked as if it had been ransacked, with tons of papers, folders, and cabinets spilling out everywhere. It wasn't exactly a modern-day visually appealing setting as far as ambience goes. It resembled more of the kind of 1930s newspaper office that I had seen in countless old black-and-white Humphrey Bogart gangster films. You could actually smell the paper.

I was greeted by a nice well-mannered lady, which was a good start. Keeping myself composed, I told her that I had ordered the writing course but was still waiting for it to appear. In those days, 14 to

28 days for delivery was the norm. Now when you order something from the internet or over the phone, your item is likely to be mailed the same day or the next day. But back in those days, you were lucky if you received that kind of prompt service. So you had no choice but to play the waiting game.

Anyway, I provided the lady with my details and explained to her that I had placed cash in the envelope as a means of payment, only to be told you're not supposed to send cash through the mail and that checks or postal orders were the safest method of payment. As it happens, there was no record of my order. It was obvious that whoever got their dirty hands on the envelope had stolen the money and thrown away my order form. Protesting to my helper, I told her that someone had stolen the money and that I wasn't pleased about the situation. Still, there was nothing either of us could do about it, as there was no record or proof.

She was apologetic, but that wasn't going to bring my money back, nor was the company going to, out of sympathy, give me the course for free. So I had to hand over my hard-earned money again—actually, it was my life savings, as I was still in school and not working or on benefits. She gave me a big turquoise cardboard box, and I walked off, maintaining my polite demeanor with the box glued to my chest in Manchester's Arndale shopping center.

That box was damn heavy. I was never a heavy lifter in the gym and was somewhat frail then. Struggling and out of breath, I walked into a clothing store to ask for a bag, but the sales assistant declined to assist me. I'm sure she thought I was carrying a suspicious package. At the time, there was no Middle East–related terrorist activity like the current situation—even though it did exist notably in Beirut—and the Irish Republican Army (IRA) would succeed in bombing the Arndale only several years later. In fact, whenever the word *terrorists* was uttered in the news back in the early 1990s, it was usually geared toward the IRA. So I guess she was being sagacious.

Being a really young, aspiring, wannabe writer who often fantasized about one day having a book on the shelf with his name emblazoned across the cover, I scoured through the course, not really paying close attention to detail. It wasn't long before I drafted my first-ever writing piece—on none other than my hero Bruce Lee. I wrote it or, should I say "scribbled" it, on A4 paper with a blue Biro pen. Back in those days, that's how most people wrote articles—in pen. Or they would type it out on a typewriter. At one point, I purchased one but couldn't get the damn thing to function properly. That typewriter was a pain in the ass, but I was never great with technology. I'd surprise myself if I could screw a clothing hook on the wall, never mind get a typewriter working. These days, I've had no choice, I must admit, but to embrace modern technology. But compared to most people, I'm still living in ancient times.

Drooling with excitement, I sent the scruffy handwritten piece to the *Daily Mirror* of all people. Looking back now, I was thinking big right from the start. Scribbling an article, a first attempt, you'd expect one of the major national newspapers to dismiss it and refrain from even responding. I mean, looking back, I'd have chucked it into the nearest trash can. But to my great surprise, I received a letter back, which I still have in my possession, dated May 19, 1993.

"Dear Fiaz, thank you for letting me see a copy of your article on Bruce Lee," the features editor wrote in my first rejection letter, which, by the way, would be only one of few rejections I would ever receive as I progressed in my martial arts magazine writing career later, which lasted 15 years. "Sadly, it is not suitable for publication on this occasion and I am therefore returning it to you in the hope that you will meet with success elsewhere. Again, thank you for getting in touch." Although this was my first rejection in the literary world, to me it was a win to just have had a response from this prestigious redtop giant. Furthermore, it was encouraging and had a rather optimistic feel to it. I had just left school eight months earlier, so life was just beginning. I could handle rejection, no problem. Unbeknownst to me, this would be the beginning of a life-altering experience.

A relatively recent study revealed that the most desired jobs in Britain, according to the *Guardian* in February 2015, are not what you might think. Instead of actors and musicians, it seems that an aura of prestige still surrounds the quiet, intellectual life enjoyed by authors. Being an author is the most desired job in Britain. Moreover, according to a September 2002 *New York Times* article, in America a study was conducted by pollsters to find the number-one profession people aspired to—and, as it happens, more people (81 percent) wanted to be authors than pursue any other profession.

I guess I was on the right track. Now, I knew it wouldn't be easy. Everyone knows that writing is among the toughest professions to make a career in. And, some people would probably tell you, the odds of being published if you write a book are extremely low. The chances aren't much different from becoming a professional athlete, a well-known actor, or a famous musician. There is no guarantee of success—it's almost the exact opposite.

⌒

Speaking of school and careers, it's undeniably odd how after we leave school having completed our education, we are suddenly catapulted into the "real" world. In the final year, suddenly you've got career counselors talking to 15-year-olds to get them to decide what they want to do with the rest of their lives. For me, I felt it was just too early to absorb what these real-world adults had to offer. So the classic careers lecture went in one ear and immediately out the other. I didn't pursue further education or go to college. What was I going to study in college? I was over the moon that school was over.

Not everyone was on board with my plan, of course. Every parent wants their child to have a good education and do well in school, which will prepare him or her for the outside world, and mine were no different. My brother, who is a year older than me, always had an edge over me in schooling and was one of the more intelligent kids. My IQ level and academic tendencies were nowhere near his standard. If I were to rate myself, I would say I was in the middle ranks—not near the top but not with the bottom bums who didn't even try. My brother was in the top pack. But what I lacked in educational qualifications I made up for in abundance in the form of motivation and ambitious nature. This gave me a certain edge that I felt was absent in many others.

Regarding schooling and education, now that I am more mature, I by no means stand by my original philosophy, one that basically assumed that education is not important. If anything, I am an advocate of kids getting a good education and investing in their futures. Yet I can say with great conviction that if they lack the academic side, it's not the end of the world because they may have a talent in sport or an artistic endeavor. The key is to nurture what you're good at and interested in. Furthermore, I'm a firm believer that if you have determination and are very persistent, you can make it in this world without that piece of paper that they call a "degree" that seemingly confirms your credibility. Besides, employers today are looking for experience.

After leaving school, I enrolled on a "Youth in Business" course. It was a government-based course funded by the Prince's Youth Business Trust. What business was I going to pursue? It would be martial arts related of course! I believe you should do what you love in life, and this is true relating not only to a hobby but also to a career. Numerous studies, in particular one conducted by Gallup reported by *Forbes* in November 2011, found that 75 percent of people are in jobs that make them unhappy, and that's no way to spend a third of your time on this planet. Anyway, there were more than half a dozen youngsters who were in this course. Music was often blaring—Gerry Rafferty's "Baker Street" would pump you up and motivate you—as we cracked on with our work, though I wouldn't exactly call it "work."

Personally, I set out to learn about setting up a martial arts mail-order business. Inspired by the mail-order ads in the magazines, I decided that selling martial arts goods via mail order would be fun and the right career move. If I remember correctly, we received about £30 a week for being in this course. This would be paid in cash at the end of each week in a brown pay packet. Getting your hands on that pay packet was what it was all about for most of us.

With the business course coming to an abrupt halt—after a year, the funding ceased, so the course itself became bankrupt—it was time to be supported by the government for sitting on my ass. In 1993, freshly on benefits and signing on with the green logbook they gave you and with no real direction and career prospects, I eventually got a job and started to work in a lamp factory nearby. This job lasted only a few months, and then I worked at a socks factory. Again, I was out of there after a couple of months. It was slave labor that tortured you like the Romans did to their captives rowing the ships. *Is this what life is all about?* I thought to myself. It soon dawned on me that it's bloody hard to eke out a living. Things were looking bleak.

Then there were family associates poking their noses in. I remember there was an older "uncle" (friend of the family) who had his son slave it out for long shifts in a hanger-manufacturing factory. The son had to hand over the pay packet at end of the week to his "master" dad. This "uncle" also brought the factory to my dad's attention to get me slaving away, too, but I never pursued it. I may have had certain harsh restrictions put on me as I was growing up and hard rules to abide by—because I had strict parents—otherwise, I got clobbered at home, but my parents never in my life asked me for money or forced me to work. I was cognizant that some youth my age were made to work and had to give their wages to their parents. I was lucky in that sense. I was never used in that manner. There's no right or wrong, and by no means am I saying that handing your pay packet to your parents is wrong. All I'm saying is it never happened to me. So, although some other kids had certain privileges in life in general, there was some leniency on me at home.

↝

Disillusioned with life, I was looking for an avenue that would let me both make a living and achieve peace and harmony—or at least not hate my work. Almost three years after leaving school, I finally ventured into the mail-order business in 1995 and placed a small ad in a boxing magazine advertising *Tao of Jeet Kune Do*, the best-selling martial arts publication, which was compiled after the untimely death of Bruce Lee. An eclectic and hybrid system, this tome is a compilation of Bruce's notes and thoughts on his personal expression of combat, philosophy, and life. One-third of this tome is littered with boxing concepts and theories, so I thought I'd introduce this product to a new market.

If I remember correctly, I paid £35 plus a value-added tax to place a small ad in the periodical. I ordered copies from a wholesale martial arts supplier in London and filled orders, which I received at a mailbox I rented. So, this was the start of my first martial arts venture. Further ads followed in a couple of martial arts magazines. You couldn't miss the gimmick ads in the martial arts periodicals selling courses like "How to Become a Black Belt in a Year" or other gimmicks promising all sorts of rubbish and nonsensical material, such as "Become a Deadly Fighter in Three Months." Needless to say, these types of deadly courses weren't everything they were hyped up to be. These ads influenced me, as I thought that running a business selling products relating to your hobby was fun. Moreover, working from home or office fulfilling orders and cashing the checks and mailing packages was a simple, straightforward process. I thought you could laugh your way to the bank eventually.

Looking to expand further, I decided to add a mail-order video club as part of the same setup. I was looking to find a much more solid avenue to eke out a living.

When I was scouring through martial arts magazines five years earlier when I was 14 in 1990, I had come across the fascinating Gracie family of fighters, who possessed an invincible aura. I'd seen two graphically violent videos, from the *Gracies in Action* series, which had raw street-fight footage and was shocking to me as a young man. It featured members of the legendary Gracie family taking on all comers, fighting them with almost no rules, often on floors with no mats or pads. The Gracies would take their foes down and pummel them on the ground, typically choking them until they tapped. It was amazing. I imported these videos directly from UFC creator Rorion Gracie and advertised them in magazines. I had spoken directly to Rorion, who offered me a wholesale discount. Again, this time, I placed double-page spread ads in two magazines to attract martial arts enthusiasts to join.

Members received heavily discounted instructional videos and had to commit to purchasing at least one video every three months as a member. The American martial arts magazines were littered with ads for instructional videos. Panther Productions, based in southern California, was the leading producer. Unique Videos was the other company that was making strides. I dealt with them and several others. I was still a teenager and was now doing business with America, a country I had my eyes set on ever since I was a young boy.

Suddenly, there was a problem. Red lights flashing. Yes, this would be my first run-in with the Americans. There was a mail-order company based in Birmingham that imported videos from Panther. Because of the huge discounted prices my company was offering, the owner had complained to Panther and other suppliers that there was alleged piracy going on. He thought, *How can these be sold for such low prices?* Next thing you know, I receive a letter from the production company (you communicated via mail, fax, or phone before the invention of e-mail). The producers then stopped supplying me, which left me stunned. I protested and proceeded to explain that this was an introductory offer and the idea was to make money on future orders when members were committed to purchasing further videos. First, they informed me that I had to go through their already established U.K. distributor, but then the matter was resolved, and they continued to supply me. The producers realized that it was all a mistake, convinced that I hadn't done anything illegal because there was no evidence. I was relieved.

So, I had purchased a writing course, took a government-backed business course, was on the brink of joining the British army, and worked as a laborer in several jobs, culminating in running a national martial arts mail-order business for a year. The situation, though, remained precarious. Money was scarce, and times were hard. Financial difficulties would be something that would plague me for a long time throughout the years. But I always reverted back to my passion, which was martial arts, to get through life, consoling myself that there was a light at the end of the tunnel as I forged ahead.

೧‑

No matter how much I forged ahead, I had my critics and people who dragged me down. Growing up in my Asian community didn't help matters. Hell, no! I had expectations and a standard to adhere to; otherwise, people would have disdain for me. I also faced social pressures that impinged on my daily life. Once, I was with a group of friends having a meal at a restaurant, and the subject of judging others came up. One friend said that people judge others based on how they dress. I have to say, although that is true, I feel that people first and foremost judge you based on what job you do—what profession you are in. Second, it's a combination of what kind of vehicle you drive and the friends and people you associate with, followed by what hobbies you take part in, that determine what kind of a person you are to others. And third is how you dress.

When I left school, I became a victim of prejudice. It wasn't unusual that when we had visitors at our house, more often than not I would get the standard, "What do you do?" from these friends of the family. A lot of the times I would be stuck for words. These men were not going to comprehend and appreciate my martial arts venture. They were expecting me to say that I was a solicitor, an accountant, or a doctor—these were the three kings—or a taxi driver or takeout worker. This is all that registered on their radar.

The elder generation from the South Indian continent came to the West in the 1960s and were relegated to the mill. They had no choice but to endure hard labor working in a factory. Most weren't educated, and the lack of language and technical skills was an obstacle for them. They encouraged us, the new generation, to endeavor to get a good education and build a better future. They always stressed that we had the opportunities and the language to develop skills that would land us good jobs and career prospects. This is something I came to comprehend later in life.

But at the same time, the attitude of looking down on and judging someone based on their profession is something I have always vehemently opposed. In Pakistan, there is a caste system where people are judged on their profession. A barber or a shoemaker, for example, will be looked down on. Then you have landlords and the higher echelons of society. Unfortunately, where I'm from, generally, respect was earned this way, through your profession. I am, of course, an advocate of equal opportunity, meaning that if someone who has the skill to do a job, then he or she should be given a chance regardless of caste. I respect people regardless of whether they're laborers or doctors. One's character is much more important than position or materialistic wealth.

I'm all for people being achievers and making something of themselves, and it's something that I've aspired to do and have been doing all my life. But parallel to this, I believe in a humble attitude. Treating everyone with the same dignity that all humans deserve regardless of their status is a principle I abide by. As Muhammad Ali once said, "I don't trust anyone who's nice to me but rude to the waiter. Because they would treat me the same way if I were in that position."

Despite feeling despondent, I refused to throw in the towel. Suddenly, an idea circled in my head that would take me to a place far away. I was ready to embark on a journey that would change my life forever. Yes, it was time to earnestly pursue the American Dream.

4

The American Dream

America is a country that has captured my interest for as long I can remember. Like most other people in the United Kingdom (and around the world for that matter), my early exposure to the land of opportunity was, to a large degree, via the screen: Hollywood movies and TV. As a young boy, I used to religiously watch *The A-Team*, and the image of the downtown skyscrapers in Los Angeles from the opening credits was forever embedded in my head. It wasn't long before I realized that Los Angeles was the Mecca of martial arts and bodybuilding. It was also where Bruce Lee had resided. Naturally, this further piqued my interest in the sunny state of California.

The second-largest city in America, Los Angeles is a sprawling southern California city famed as the global center of film and the entertainment industry. Every neighborhood in this vibrant, multicultural metropolis sets a different scene. With 75 miles of coastline, the city is the home to people from 140 counties speaking 224 different languages. That's a hell of a lot of languages being spoken in one city, with more than half the population made up of Latinos.

I had heard, too, about the notorious Los Angeles gang culture, which includes gangs of almost every ethnicity, leading Los Angeles to being nicknamed "The Gang Capital of America." According to the Los Angeles Police Department, there are 450 gangs with an estimated 45,000 members in Los Angeles and 1,300 gangs and an estimated 120,000 gang members in the whole of Los Angeles County. I learned that people were reluctant to pursue a career in the police force there because it's just too damn dangerous. The whole of Los Angeles has fewer than 10,000 police officers serving a population of under 4 million, while gang membership has continued to rise over the years even in times when crime has decreased. Whenever I think about gangs, it always brings back memories of Hollywood action films in which they frequently make an appearance as fodder for the heroes to defeat.

Growing up, I had always fantasized about visiting the City of Angels one day. Being an ardent follower of Bruce Lee, back then my ultimate dream was to have direct lineage to the master. And this ambition motivated me more and more as I got closer to fulfilling it. Crucially, I wanted to be able to say that I had trained with one of Bruce Lee's original students, to train with the best and not settle for anything less. I had been inspired by a couple of prominent British martial artists who had made trips to Los Angeles in the early 1980s, training under well-known Bruce Lee disciples like Dan Inosanto, so I got in touch with two who had experienced training across the pond. One revealed to me that he had worked as a bricklayer, which meant six months of hard work to save up money to finance the trip. The other individual whom I had the opportunity to talk with was one of the first-ever students who had made the over-the-pond journey in the early 1980s. Again, he told me that he had done meager labor jobs to save up money. We had a chat, and he was more than happy to give me his advice.

I felt a bubble of excitement rising in my stomach as I conversed with him over the phone. It felt, at the time, like talking to a famous person who had performed the pilgrimage, one that I wanted to embark on myself. I truly believed this could be the best thing that would happen to me in my life, as my desire to pursue California was fueled by these men who had walked the same path. To say I was feeling elated just to have the opportunity to talk with this man, who I felt had a direct lineage to Bruce Lee, is an understatement.

So, in June 1996, just as I exited my teenage years, I packed my bag and jetted off to Los Angeles in search of the American Dream. At last, I would be meeting and training with a disciple of Bruce Lee. A fantasy that had been beyond my grasp was now actually manifesting into reality. Not in a million years did I envision this would come true. I thought to myself, *How on earth am I going to be allowed to jet off to America?* It was a daunting prospect, but I plucked up the courage to ask my parents, and the trip was sanctioned to my great surprise.

With nothing but a small bag, a couple of credit cards, cash, and an obsessive drive on my side, I arrived at Los Angeles International on my new American adventure. From the moment I stepped onto the tarmac, everything seemed bigger. The cops were taller and well built, the cars were longer, the roads were wider, and the sun was brighter. *This is what I'm talking about*, I thought to myself as I started to get goose bumps despite the bright sunshine.

Now, we all have a perception of things and certain expectations when we see things from afar, when things are out of our reach. I was no different in this regard. I had watched the movies like everyone else. This was where it all happened. This was the place where Hollywood actors, fighters, bodybuilders, and music stars all lived in one magical spot. This was the place to be, the place to venture if you wanted to make it big time. Indeed, this was where thousands of people came to pursue their dreams, even if many came only to find themselves unemployed and disillusioned. There is so much competition. Everyone wants a piece of the action and a slice of the cash cake. As I know now, it's where dreams come true but, equally, where dreams are shattered.

I hailed a cab to drive me to South Los Angeles, and it dropped me off outside the famous academy. I had read about my to-be instructor and Bruce's protégé and the academy that perpetuated the teachings of their late master after the untimely death that had sent shock waves around the world. A couple of months prior to my departure, I had phoned the instructor to inform him that I was coming and asked if I could become a member of his prestigious class. To my delight, he said I was welcome. To further galvanize me, I had recently seen this instructor in a Bruce Lee documentary in 1993 being interviewed. All in all, I felt this trip would bring me closer to the late master in association and spirit. Yes, I longed to be accepted as a pupil of one of Bruce Lee's students.

As I stepped onto the premises and into the reception area with my battered black handbag in my hand, I was greeted by the instructor. When he saw me with a black Bruce Lee T-shirt, I immediately sensed alarm bells going off. My psychological human behavior radar instantly kicked in as my intuition took the front seat. The expression on his face said, *Oh, not another Bruce Lee fanatic!*

꒰꒱

During Bruce's lifetime, he had a closed-door policy at his small but prestigious private gym in the Chinatown district of Los Angeles. I had the pleasure of visiting his old school, located on 626 College Street, a couple of times when I visited Los Angeles again. This is where he had taught his carefully screened hand-selected devoted students, and my instructor had been one of them. The closed-door training sessions would become much talked about after his demise. Those who were part of the close-knit select group were fortunate enough to train with Bruce at his house, too. Visiting this rather obscure-looking place in Chinatown was like a pilgrimage. The one part of the traditional Bruce Lee pilgrimage I never took part in was visiting the late master's grave for the sole reason that to do so would have gone against my religious beliefs.

Bruce told his students that to keep something prestigious, you have to refrain from making it available to the masses. As a result, his gym was far from a commercial school. Moreover, Bruce broke tradition—no uniforms, ranks, and traditional rituals. He was an innovator and borrowed from everyone and integrated training concepts intended to elevate and unleash his students' potential far beyond what other schools thought possible at the time. His coaching method, which I found appealing, more or less closely resembled that of a boxing coach—today an approach typical among MMA coaches. He was an advocate of one-on-one and small-group tuition, with none of the endless punching drills conducted in lines that characterized many traditional martial arts academies. This was another thing that attracted me to his art. I had never been a sheep, and I wasn't planning on becoming one.

Still, division seems almost inevitable in any group, and a division existed between two groups in the jeet kune do world. One was stuck in the past, latching on to the art's founder's every word and technique as gospel truth and refusing to evolve. The other group seemed to be the majority, by and large, because Bruce's protégé, Dan Inosanto, had promoted this, and the group used what was referred to as the "concepts" method. This group evolved, integrating elements from different arts into Bruce's original. Dan firmly believed that Bruce would have evolved to incorporate new techniques into his art if he had lived longer. In addition, he had made a promise to his master not to teach his art commercially, giving him less incentive to push a "pure" form of jeet kune do. The classes at the academy at which I was training focused primarily on this "concepts" method, embracing a philosophy that emphasized finding your own path.

Now, of course, politics filter into everything, from religion to martial arts. And politics pertaining to Bruce's art have been present since the day he died: the regular debates being around who was right in their approach and who was allowed to teach and who was not. For all the argument, I think years later most people realized evolution is inevitable and indeed almost an absolute necessity to survive in a modern combat environment, even if a few refused to embrace new concepts.

Either way, if you were one of the very fortunate foreign or out-of-town students to make it into one of the academies, your hopes were shattered if you were expecting to learn the complete original framework art that Bruce taught. Another foreign student, who had also religiously made the trip from Europe to southern California in search of Bruce Lee enlightenment, agreed that the tuition we received when we walked into the academy wasn't exactly what he was expecting. It dawned on us that the art being taught was far removed from what Bruce was doing in his lifetime—although at times, certain original material would be shared by the instructor.

I remember having a conversation with an older man who was checking out the academy because he wanted to enroll his son. He was telling me how he was impressed with Bruce's philosophy, and was of the impression that this subject would be touched on in classes. I thought, *He's going to be disappointed because this isn't the place you're going to find philosophy classes, far from it.*

Still, several of Bruce's original students did continue their teacher's tradition by teaching privately and in small groups at their homes or in a private setting. Today, the commercial route is taken by most instructors as they fit into the modern-day commercial-driven world. That's not to say it's wrong.

I trained at the academy for three months taking the jeet kune do classes. I was very happy to be in Los Angeles. The day I discovered that Bruce had developed his own brand of martial art, I had developed tunnel vision. Why would I want to train in Thai boxing or karate when the man I admired the most trained in and developed his own personal brand of martial art? Like many other crazy enthusiasts who idolized the great master, I would try to follow his concepts and train at home and with other like-minded martial arts enthusiasts in what was more of a private setting. I was a fervent follower of the originator's method and thought it was the gospel truth. But many years later as I matured, I would learn the truth of what Bruce himself had said: a kick was a kick, a punch was a punch, and a lock was a lock, no matter who taught you or where it came from. It was great to have a famous and well-known instructor (or at least one who knew what he was doing), but I realized you could learn and achieve a level of excellence in your own country in a gym nobody had heard of and from an instructor nobody cared for if learning an art and how to fight was your goal.

If you train in the martial arts long enough and seriously enough, the mystique starts to fade, to be replaced by practicality.

So, when I realized that in order to survive in today's environment adaptability was paramount, my mentality changed. I eventually embraced grappling—the term MMA hadn't coined yet. I arrived at a conclusion: as long as you can box and wrestle and were prepared to use a few sneaky kung fu street tactics, such as strikes to vital spots (which would be a groin kick, eye gouging, or biting), and had the mentality to do it all under pressure, you can laugh your way to survival. That's all you need if you are genuinely looking for self-defense and a realistic fighting art.

Furthermore, the texture of the art that I had been attracted to and so desperately sought had been somewhat eroded with the advent of the UFC. Many philosophies and principles of Bruce's art are still valid and I still believe are embedded in me. But you can't fool yourself, or at least you should try to break away from bullshit, as I said, even if there are those who are ardent followers who continue to be lost. At the end of the day, all arts have something to offer, and all have weaknesses. You have to ask yourself, *What is it that you're looking to achieve?* Some people pursue the arts for self-defense, fitness, and to compete, while others merely want to learn an art. The choice is yours. So, I eradicated my closed-minded mentality as my goal gravitated toward studying for the right reasons. Training at the American academy opened my eyes.

Over the years, I have always trained on and off. Bruce believed tournament fighting isn't an all-out fight, so he was against competing. But as the sport of MMA—and my exposure to grappling—spread, my attitude toward this changed. At some point, one should even pursue grappling tournaments to see what it feels like to dip your feet into the waters of competition and to use your skills against a fully resisting opponent. Setting challenges and goals should be a never-ending process.

Anyway, as a 20-year-old, I was training and soaking up the sun in my favorite city. One afternoon, there was a meeting with a number of Bruce's original students and Bruce's widow, Linda Lee, at the academy. These were members of a prestigious board. Somehow, the news of this meeting reached my ears. At the time, I was residing in the apartment around the corner. Now that this rare opportunity had presented itself, I had to drop by to get a glimpse of which famous martial arts personalities were in attendance in the vain hope that I may be able to meet Bruce's wife and the rest. I walked into the reception area acting innocent but then left after a quick chat with the academy desk staff. Later that evening when I came to the academy to train, I told my instructor I had come in earlier when the meeting was going on. "You should've come inside," he said to me. "I would've introduced you to Linda." I told him I didn't want to intrude. I couldn't believe it: Bruce's wife was there, and I was in the same building. I had been on the brink of meeting his wife, but my courage had failed me.

$\curlyeqprec$

My stay wasn't going to be complete without a visit to the Inosanto Academy, which was in Marina Del Rey, headed by Dan Inosanto, famed for being Bruce Lee's training partner and number-one student. The Inosanto Academy had been connected in the past with the academy I was training at. Both were the most prestigious places in the world, offering instruction in Bruce's art. In fact, when I landed in Los Angeles, I first dropped by at this academy. I asked Dan's wife, "Do you have a weight training room at the gym?" She said, "No, you can lift students up in the air instead." I burst out laughing. The fact they didn't have a weight training facility was the initial reason I decided not to train there. I was that obsessed with building muscle in my youth. However, I ended up training in Dan's class on several occasions on my future visits to Los Angeles.

When I walked into the Inosanto Academy, my attention was captured by the signed framed photos of famous martial artists, fighters, and personalities from the action movie industry that adorned the walls. The Inosanto Academy is frequented by many Hollywood actors and stuntmen who come to train there. Bruce's original wooden dummy and heavy bag (which weighed 300 pounds) were displayed at this academy. A couple of years earlier, the gigantic red bag had been at the academy I was training at, but then Dan took it. It was amazing to actually touch the training devices that Bruce had trained with. It was like being in a museum checking out these artifacts, which were a part of history. The academy I trained at also had one of Bruce's original grip exerciser machines. I would often use this to build my forearm and grip when I trained with the weights. Bruce had used this same device to strengthen his arms.

I had met Dan before, in London in 1993 when I was 17. It was like meeting a celebrity. This talented master not only was Bruce's protégé but also appeared in Bruce's final film, *Game of Death*, in which he fights Bruce in a classic duel that includes an epic battle of nunchaku against nunchaku. After meeting him, I met Ted Wong the same year. Ted was one of Bruce's closest friends and personal students and workout partners. What really amazed me was how Ted had never disclosed to his work colleagues for 20 years that he was one of Bruce's best friends. I found that extraordinary.

Thousands of like-minded enthusiasts around the globe are exposed to Bruce's art, and some could only fantasize about making the pilgrimage to train with the original source. Others find gyms with second-generation lineage to the master. But the crazy, obsessed ones, a category I certainly fit into back then, make the trip abroad in the hope of getting closer to the late master.

⌀

I found the people in Los Angeles very friendly. I realized there were more Hispanic Mexicans in this exotic city than there were Caucasians. That was something of a surprise. In fact, I blended in with the Hispanics well because being an Asian, it wasn't difficult for people to mistake me for one of their own. To further illustrate this point, one day a kid on a bike stopped by and started speaking Spanish to me. I told him I wasn't Hispanic. It was the dark hair.

It slowly dawned on me that many Americans are focused on making as much money as possible. It's all about the dollar. Where I come from, although money is important, we have a somewhat different attitude. I have done business in the past and worked just like anyone else, but my mentality has always been slightly offtrack, so to speak. We all want more money and to be in a position to be able to afford things, but having money at all costs is just something that doesn't resonate with me.

Other than the fact that Los Angeles is the Mecca of martial arts and bodybuilding, I was inevitably attracted to all things Hollywood. Many people are programmed in a way that attracts them to fame and fortune, and I was no different. The palm trees that I had seen on TV and the skyscrapers of downtown Los Angeles brought back memories of my childhood. I remember seeing the Hollywood sign for the first time when a group of us were being driven to Hollywood and Beverly Hills. It was an exhilarating experience. We passed pop sensation Janet Jackson's house in Beverly Hills when there was a party going on. Outside was a black limousine and a chauffeur, and a burly bodyguard stood as the music blared inside the mansion. Madonna's pink mansion lay above a hill in West Hollywood on Sunset Boulevard, the famous road that I'd heard about countless times, which stretches from Figueroa Street in downtown Los Angeles to the Pacific Coast

Highway at the Pacific Ocean. This 22-mile Sunset Strip portion of the highway in West Hollywood has been famous for its nightlife. In the sunset, it was awe-inspiring.

It's surprising, but Hollywood really is often the way it's portrayed in films that you think must be exaggerated. You have a young woman with headphones jogging, a movie executive pulling up in a Mercedes on the phone making a multi-million-dollar deal, a soft-top Jeep stopping at the red lights with a guy in a tank top with music blasting away, and a posh middle-aged woman in an expensive designer hat walking her cute little designer dog against a Beverly Hills backdrop.

Not everything was golden, however. The sunny weather is one of California's attractions, but the heat always drained my energy. Los Angeles compared to New York is very serene and laid back. And as you take a stroll in Hollywood, you often get a rather pessimistic vibe of this moviemaking capital of the world. Some areas of Hollywood were run down and infested with prostitutes and homeless people in the streets, something that is invisible to many outsiders who have never visited the place. Ironically, hardly any prominent actors live in Hollywood itself; they live in the classy Beverly Hills and more to the north in neighborhoods such as Bel Air and Brentwood—except for Quentin Tarantino, who lives in Hollywood Hills last time I heard. He's probably one of the only top Tinseltown personalities living there.

Big cities such as Los Angeles are crime infested, and becoming a potential crime victim was often in the back of my head whenever I was on my walks. The probability of getting shot never quite left my mind. As I was walking one night not far from my apartment block, two African American guys got into a fight on the driveway of a gas station, the first street fight I had witnessed there. I didn't intervene, not sure who was right or wrong or whether one might be carrying a weapon. Another situation I witnessed was in Hollywood when I was having a meal on Hollywood Boulevard, which I used to frequent on a daily basis when I stayed there, talking to a Moroccan guy who worked there and the two elderly Chinese owners. A Caucasian guy and his partner got into an argument with the Moroccan worker. I was having my burger, and my instincts told me that something was going to happen. The Caucasian guy launched into a verbal tirade aimed at the staff member, coming across as very aggressive. I felt he was being a bully and a loudmouth, but I didn't know what it was all about, and so again, I didn't intervene. Finally, the guy and his partner walked out, and the situation was defused. I never really became a victim of crime or vulnerable to any incident, considering I was floating around in a city that was the gang capital of the world and where gun crime was rife. I actually found almost everyone friendly.

Meanwhile, I did end up seeing stars. One came as I was taking a stroll in Santa Monica. *There's a familiar face*, I thought to myself. This blonde guy was being interviewed by a TV crew. It was none other than Hollywood actor Gary Busey! I had seen him in *Point Break*, but I could never forget him fighting Mel Gibson in *Lethal Weapon*, where Mel employs Gracie Jiu-Jitsu skills that Rorion and Royce Gracie had taught him for the movie. For a moment, I thought of going over but felt reluctant. Gary, I was unaware at the time, was a friend of the Gracies. Rorion and Royce were responsible for choreographing the fight scene in *Lethal Weapon*. They would be on set and would drop the mats and roll around with Mel, and later I would notice Gary in the first UFC videotapes when they hit the market a year later after the first UFC debuted. If I'd known about the connection at the time, I might have talked to him: more the pity.

5

Enter the Gracies

Although I typically trained at the jeet kune do academy in Los Angeles, I was aware that the famous Gracie Academy was located only five minutes away from the academy I was training at. So I decided to enroll there, too. This was purely because of UFC champion Royce Gracie, the skinny, lanky jiu-jitsu master who won three of the first four UFCs. Students flocked to the academy soon after Royce was catapulted to fame after being crowned the first-ever UFC champion a couple of years earlier, revolutionizing the way we perceived fighting. The Gracie approach to combat accentuated the need for ground fighting, with most of their techniques revolving around ground grappling. Their realistic approach and extremely effective method struck a chord with the martial arts community, much of which saw, for the first time, just how likely it was that a no-holds-barred fight would go to the ground. And, yes, they had made me a believer, which was an accomplishment in itself since I was an ardent jeet kune do lover who at one time refused to even entertain the thought of practicing any other style.

I had heard of Royce in 1990 and a couple of years later, in 1993, when I had come across an article in a new magazine, *Today Martial Arts*. It was a report on the first-ever UFC event, stating that the winner of the tournament was a Brazilian Gracie Jiu-Jitsu exponent by the name of Royce Gracie. By the way, this new magazine was the worst magazine of its kind to ever hit the newsstands. How they thought they would survive is beyond belief. I wouldn't have read it for free, never mind parting with my hard-earned cash—at the time.

The reason the Gracie family invoked my interest was because they were different and real. They had started what was known as the Gracie Challenge, an open bare-knuckle invitation to all challengers who wanted to take them on that became the precursor to the UFC. Rorion, who was the elder brother, had first visited America in the 1970s, but by then, back in Brazil, the Gracie name was already huge. Their father, Helio Gracie, of diminutive stature, had made a reputation for taking on all comers and had fought in two high-profile grappling matches against a pair of Japan's best judoka. Now the elder son had bigger plans beyond the confines of his homeland.

Royce once explained to me what the Gracie Challenge was all about and cleared up a misconception. People misunderstand the idea of the Gracie Challenge. The major objective of this controversial challenge has always been to find out how effective the style of Gracie Jiu-Jitsu is—it's a practical avenue to prove the effectiveness of ground fighting. The Gracies wanted to propagate a message relating to the superiority of their art and open people's eyes and let them discern for themselves. "Then they can say, 'Hey, this jiu-jitsu is a great style and can complement any other style,'" Royce explained to me. "So, when we were challenging people, a lot of people thought we were challenging other martial artists to put them down. No!" According to Royce, the Gracies had no intention of showing a lack of respect to other styles and martial artists. Rather, the objective was to address the importance and effectiveness of this once-unknown martial arts system and to use it as a platform to ascertain if they could make it work in a more reality-based fight.

"When we taught our students, we would tell them that Gracie Jiu-Jitsu was the best, as it addresses ground fighting and grappling," the three-time UFC champion told me. Sometimes, he said, a martial arts student would walk in and argue with the Gracies, the classic being along the lines of "I have an instructor of mine who teaches karate and he says Gracie Jiu-Jitsu grappling is nothing!" The valiant Gracies would encourage the individual to bring his instructor or friend over to the garage, and they'd send the challenger home "baptized." "That's a challenge right there! It's about putting your money where your mouth is," Royce told me. Soon, the challenger would concede to the superiority of this technical-based style, typically after he was grappled to the ground, which would neutralize his striking tools and leave him floundering and with no idea what to do. The Gracies weren't all that concerned if you weighed 300 pounds, looked like the Hulk, were built like a truck, had world title belts, or were a raw street fighter with a notorious reputation. If you wanted to test yourself in a real street fight environment, you were more than welcome to step onto the mat or, at times, a hard wooden floor or the street with these crazy men.

As I said, the Gracies had become notorious in Brazil and were treated with great reverence long before they made it in the United States. Rorion once said that they didn't have to wait in lines, as they were a household name, but when he moved to America, he had to start all over again. In the beginning, he did menial jobs to survive while teaching his beloved art, cleaning homes, and flipping burgers, while the brothers were teaching their brand of jiu-jitsu in their garage out of their home. But as the word spread, it got to a stage where the garage would no longer accommodate the number of students who wanted to train. There was a waiting list of 150 students, according to Royce. They were conducting private classes three days a week—Tuesday, Thursday, and Saturday—and Rorion would work on movies as an extra on Fridays. In the garage days, the Gracies attracted some well-known martial arts personalities who had taken an interest in learning from them. Some of the more prominent personalities who sought out private tuition included John Saxon, Jim Kelly, and Bob Wall, better known as costars of the epic Bruce Lee smash hit *Enter the Dragon*, and Chuck Norris, world champion martial artist, film star, and costar of Bruce Lee's *Way of the Dragon*. The Brazilian brothers had something unique to offer the American martial arts fraternity, who slowly came to understand that they were missing an element, a part of the jigsaw that would complement their own art. It wasn't uncommon to see well-known elite martial artists and professional baseball and football players on the mat, all being manhandled by the Brazilian beasts.

Rorion eventually became influenced by American marketing strategies, and Gracie Jiu-Jitsu became a commodity, something that would appeal to people who weren't just interested in becoming better no-holds-barred fighters. One of the factors in the sales pitch of his "product" was the effectiveness of his brand of fighting. The Gracies were astute enough to know that once America was introduced to Gracie Jiu-Jitsu, the entire world would recognize it. American culture, music, and movies had all been embraced by the world. Once something hits big in the land of opportunity and has the American seal of approval, it gets accepted by the world. It's that simple.

᠙

Rorion was a man on a mission. His goal was to spread his father's teachings and ultimately have Gracie Jiu-Jitsu embraced by not only the combat sports fraternity but also a wider audience. In an effort to achieve this, Rorion joined forces with an advertising executive by the name of Art Davie, who had a beer client he was trying to get to sponsor kickboxing shows. Art had read about this fantastic family of fighters in the September 1989 issue of *Playboy* magazine, and the bespectacled, frail-looking, yet enthusiastic businessman wasted no time calling them up to arrange a meeting. Subsequently, Art became a student of Rorion and witnessed several of the challenge matches that took place in the garage and later at the Gracie Academy. So he knew what these men were all about. Meanwhile, film director John Millius was taking lessons from Rorion, who also had been exposed to the exploits of these notorious men and witnessed their brutal and bloody challenge matches. The three men—Rorion, Art, and John—joined forces to develop the idea of having a no-holds-barred tournament, giving martial arts fighters from different styles an opportunity to showcase their skills. The ultimate concept was to ascertain what the best and most effective fighting style was. Finally, after hundreds of challenge matches in the garage and the academy in front of dozens of students who loved the exciting action of a real fight, they were ready to take the idea to another level. And the UFC was born.

The creation of the UFC would be a turning point in the history of martial arts, giving the Gracies a major platform to perpetuate their message to a wider audience. "When Rorion explained to the guys the concept, a lot of people were like, 'Hold on, we are not allowed to fight on the street because we get arrested, and you're planning on putting this on national TV?,'" said Royce. "'Are you out of your mind?! It's going to be like human cockfighting! You can't fight on the street.'" Sure enough, when Rorion started working on getting the brutal fights televised, plenty of obstacles lay ahead—getting the money, finding the fighters, and finding broadcasters willing to put the show on. Not surprisingly, one of the main hurdles was to find a place that they could do this type of a tournament where it would be legally allowed. Colorado, it emerged, was the only place without a boxing commission. And so that was the only legal place to have the tournament.

Originally, the first UFC was intended to be a 16-man tournament, but it was changed to an eight-man single elimination tournament after some deliberation. The title "Ultimate Fighting Championship" stuck after several other names were considered. Rorion at one time suggested "War of the Worlds," but that soon went out of the window.

Art Davie, who came in as a partner, became the matchmaker responsible for putting together the fights and hiring the fighters. He was kind of the "legs" of the show, Royce told me. But who would represent the Gracies in the Octagon? Those who were around Rorion advised him to pick Rickson, the third-oldest son of the family, because he was much more menacing, heavier, muscular, and stronger. He was the family champion and had fought countless times back in Brazil, at one time claiming to have amassed 400 fights with no losses.

However, Rorion had his own ideas, and he said, "If I pick Rickson and he wins, it's no big deal." It would be a like a tank running everybody over. Rorion believed his younger sibling Royce, an unimposing figure, was the perfect warrior in disguise who would do the family proud.

Art was stunned. To Art, Royce was the young brother who lived above Rorion's garage with a fishtank, didn't have a checking account, didn't have a credit card, and was just a big kid. "He's the one who babysits your kids," Art protested, failing to grasp the younger brother's significance. "Royce is a really good kid, but Royce!?" Art was far from impressed with his business partner's choice. "He would show up at the academy on Saturday afternoon, and Rorion would open the safe and take out three or four $20 bills, and he'd give Royce the money," he recounted in an interview more than two decades later. "And Royce would go down to Redondo Beach pier and hang out, surf a little bit, and flirt with the girls." He wasn't many people's idea of a fighter.

The reason behind Royce representing the Gracie family, though, was that he was a perfect example of what Gracie Jiu-Jitsu exemplifies—a smaller, not very strong person capable of overcoming much bigger, stronger adversaries. "I believe my brothers and cousins were capable, but I was chosen to take the mantle," Royce once told me. His younger brother Royler was too light—at the time, he weighed 155 pounds. On the other hand, his older brother Rickson was too heavy—he was 195 or 200 pounds, too heavy and strong to drive home the lesson. If you witness a 200-pound muscular guy beat up someone with the stature of Ken Shamrock, a 220-pound guy, it doesn't look that impressive. On the other hand, Royce, weighing 175 pounds with a skinny build, beating up someone weighing 220 pounds such as Ken, who is full of muscle with an impressive body frame? Now that is very compelling. The concept, beyond putting on a show, was to prove a point and impress people. Royce had been training and teaching with Rorion at the academy, so Rorion had total faith in his younger brother's ability despite the naysayers who felt it was potentially a suicide mission.

The first-ever UFC event debuted on November 12, 1993, in Denver, Colorado. Much of the American public was outraged and found it excessively brutal, but for others, it instantly struck a chord. I remember watching the first couple of UFCs and being knocked out by not just the brutality but also the realities of real fighting. It was messy and scrappy, with fighters losing teeth and (illegally) gouging eyes, tumbling to the floor, and engaging in grappling exchanges that they barely understood. Meanwhile, fight fans around the world were drawn to the sight of Royce, this rather frail-looking grappler who proceeded to wipe the floor with everyone they had put in front of him. His performance was nothing short of superb. This man didn't need to punch his adversaries into oblivion. Instead, he would gently make them submit with his trademark techniques and walk off calmly. He beat a boxer with barely a punch thrown, choked out Ken Shamrock with a gi technique, and then put a clinic on the brutal savate expert Gerard Gordeau, who had earlier eye-gouged another competitor so excessively that the man lost his vision in one eye. A legend was born. Royce Gracie was my new hero.

⌒⌒

It was only a year after watching Royce in the UFC via VHS tape that I was training at the Gracie Academy. To my delight, Royce would come in and teach the intermediate classes, greeting me with a "good morning" when he walked in. I was just a young 135-pound guy who had just exited his teenage years months earlier in a foreign land. Royce was one of the most famous and feared fighters on the planet. But a man of his caliber and position made me feel special.

Back in those days, Royce had a serious demeanor. I can't blame him because at that time, he had earned the moniker of "Baddest Man on the Planet" and had to have his guard up—he was the man to beat. Can you imagine having that weight on your shoulders? He couldn't have people taking liberties. If you laid your eyes on him in the street and didn't know who he was, you'd think this man probably never stepped into a gym in his life. But believe me, you wouldn't want to make the mistake of messing with this man.

In class, it was mesmerizing witnessing an average-looking guy teaching students who were bigger, meaner, and stronger-looking how to fight. Some were from law enforcement agencies such as the Los Angeles Police Department and the FBI, but he would handle them all.

I was a novice grappler at the time. For me, the academy was an experience, and it was all I could do to hang in there, getting beat by a lot of experienced students. I was quite aggressive, but it was time to get technical. To build up a base, Royce even suggested I take some additional beginner classes, but I was there to train with him, so I wasn't going to deviate from my original plan, anything that would put a dent in my ego. To me, this was the best fighter, the guy who had the capacity to put you to sleep within seconds with his trademark chokehold. And I was in his presence not merely as a fan but as a student.

Even though he had a serious demeanor with regular people, Royce always cracked jokes and had a laugh with us in class, so the atmosphere was relaxed. Once in class, I was having a problem choking one of the senior students named Corey. I was then shown the right way to do it. I proceeded to choke him, and he had to go get some water as he continued coughing. From the corner of my eye, I could see Royce joking with another student, Lewis, and several other pupils. "Now he has to go get some water, he's been choked," he said as he laughed with a group of students. Not only did you learn discipline, technique, and how to fight in a sparring situation, but you also learned to get along with people from all walks of life. The academy had developed a reputation around America, and so it attracted students and visitors not only from California but from other states as well.

I always took the morning classes, usually at 10:00, which by my standards was an achievement in itself because it was too early for me and my body to be awake after my evening lessons at the jeet kune do academy. The Gracie Academy was a modern training facility with rooms on the ground floor and a massive hall upstairs. And there were tons of offices, giving you the impression it was a big professional company with people working in different departments, which it was in its own way. Rorion had mastered the American business strategy and made the most of it.

After Royce emerged victorious in the first UFC, he exclaimed, "It will open everybody's eyes—especially the weaker guys—that you don't have to be a monster to be a champ. You don't have to be the biggest guy or the one who hits the hardest." Oh, boy, did he open everyone's eyes and become a catalyst for change. I'm glad he proved that a smaller, less physically imposing fighter could beat a much bigger, stronger, and heavier giant. This man gave hope to the smaller guys, just as Bruce Lee had done. Never did I know that one day I'd be meeting the man himself—and training with him—and that years later a friendship would ensue.

I compared my stay in Los Angeles to the experience of a university student. I had left my country and embarked on a voyage to study martial arts at two world-famous academies, my own form of university. Back in the 1960s and 1970s, just before and after the kung fu boom, some westerners had made trips to the Orient, notably Japan and China, to experience the arts from their birthplace, training with the great masters and then returning to their respective countries with newfound knowledge and wisdom. This was the case for me as well. After three months, it was time to go home. I had overstayed a week, which would have dire consequences when I returned two years later. But I had achieved what I longed for. I could tick this off because this was the one thing I really wanted to achieve in life. Little did I suspect that this was just the beginning.

6

Returning to Los Angeles

Back home several months after my trip, I got a job in a gas station and, at almost the same time, set up a martial arts business—a publishing label specializing in martial arts publications for a niche market—from my bedroom. I was only 21 years old. And as I further established the business venture, I continued to hold my day job for a good while. It was a life of constant grind. Waking up at 5 a.m. on cold, freezing mornings to drive to my job, I would reassure myself it was only a matter of time before I made a success of myself in the martial arts business world in one capacity or another, that the early morning torture would fade away into oblivion, that the harsh morning wake-up calls were merely temporary.

I quickly attracted some prominent martial arts authorities from the United States and eventually moved into an office. Fortunately, I had made several connections and a couple of friends in America—all of them consummate professionals involved with martial arts and MMA and a few connected to the motion picture industry in Hollywood. I recall having a meeting in New York with a company I was doing business with. When Gail, one of the directors, first laid eyes on me as I walked into her office, she was surprised. "I thought you'd be a lot older," she said, letting out a smile. Being in the trade I was, she suspected I would be in my fifties. I was merely 24 years old at the time. I laughed out loud and told her that I started early.

When I returned to Los Angeles on what would be my third or fourth trip, I received a call from my friend Ron Balicki. He had fought professionally in shoot fighting—a style similar to MMA that incorporates wrestling and striking but very limited groundwork, as practiced by the UFC's Ken Shamrock. Ron and his wife, Diana Lee Inosanto, picked me up from my apartment in Santa Monica for an evening meal. Diana, a very amicable person, is part of Bruce Lee history. Her father is, of course, Dan Inosanto, who named his daughter Lee in honor of his friend. Ever since I've known Diana and Ron, they have treated me like a family member, a real honor.

On this occasion, they pointed out there was a nice restaurant not far from where I was staying, but first we drove down to their house, which was near the beach in Hermosa Beach. Sometimes, Ron's phone wouldn't go through whenever I called from abroad because the signal is very bad near the coast, but it was worth it for them to live in a beautiful place right on the beach. By the time we arrived, it was late evening and was getting somewhat dark. Ron ushered me upstairs and showed me his extensive library. I was impressed with his vast collection, which included videos, all relating to the martial arts. We talked and relaxed while Diana got ready. Then we drove to the restaurant to start our evening out. Other than Ron and Diana, there was Joey (a teenager back then, now an MMA fighter who was like an adopted son to Ron), a martial artist and actor who appeared in a Hulk Hogan movie, and Diana's first son, Sebastian, from her previous marriage.

When it comes to food, I wasn't the most informed person. Furthermore, because of my Muslim heritage, I have to restrict myself to eating only what we call "halal" food. Once when I dined with Ron and Diana, I wasn't sure if the food was halal. After giving it a great deal of thought, I got the attention of one of the waiters. "Is this halal?" I asked politely. He said it wasn't, which caught me by surprise. I froze for a second. So I spent the whole evening pretending to eat my food. I told my friends that I wasn't hungry as I watched them tuck into their delicious dishes as we conversed about martial arts, movies, and Bruce Lee.

Luckily, there were some halal dishes at this Thai place that we were at. I think this was the first time I had actually been to this type of a restaurant. I learned that there were certain similarities to the Asian food that I was familiar with. So it wasn't a complete shocker.

Diana was the best friend of Bruce Lee's son Brandon when they were kids. Bruce's daughter Shannon was also friends with Diana, but Brandon was closer to her age, and so they shared more of a bond. She would be playing with Brandon, and their dads would be training and discussing martial arts. "As a child, I used to play with Brandon," I remember Diana telling me. "We both used to have arguments and disputes about playing with toys. It was kind of funny to see Uncle Bruce intervene. He would kind of have to sort things out between Brandon and me." It was fascinating to listen to her reminisce about growing up with Bruce Lee and his kids. Had Brandon lived, I can say with great conviction that I would have got to meet him since he was very close to Diana. Unfortunately, he died in 1993 on the set of a movie at the tender age of 28. It was tragic. It became apparent to me that whenever Diana would talk about Brandon or his dad, more often than not, there was this sad emotion that radiated. Having lost not one but two of the closest people to her family left an indelible mark on her. In fact, she admitted that she still cries a little bit when someone brings up Brandon's name. The bond was so strong with the Lees and Inosantos that you'd think they were blood related.

Having myself grown up in a normal family, I always wondered what it's like to grow up with famous parents, and so I asked Diana how other kids treated her when they found out that she was close to the famous Bruce Lee. "I actually didn't want to tell people because I thought they might think I was lying," she told me, laughing. "Or, sometimes I'd get challenged. The school bully would want to challenge me and say, 'Hey, what can you do?'" As she got older, she told me, it got easier, but as a kid, it was a huge amount of pressure.

Bruce had promised Diana's dad that no matter what, for the rest of her life, she could take lessons with him, that he'd be her teacher. Surprisingly, though, Diana didn't seriously pursue the arts until much later in life. Her father started teaching her some martial arts after Bruce had passed away to help her defend herself against bullies, but she didn't embark on the martial arts journey in earnest until much later. A talented individual, she wanted to make her own choices and pursue her passion in ways that went beyond the confines of being known for being the goddaughter of one of the most iconic figures of the century. She eventually pursued Hollywood—first with stunt work and acting and later taking the leap into directing. Her brother Lance, a musician, kept a low profile, but Diana was working on movies and TV shows, doubling on *Buffy theVampire Slayer*, *Face Off*, *Hulk*, *Blade*, and *Barb Wire*. Ron was also working as a stuntman while at the same time teaching martial arts seminars around the world. He told me that in addition to working on major Hollywood movies, he had also done extra work and low-budget films, with credits including *Escape from LA*, *The Rock*, *Glimmer Man*, and *Barbwire*. The Inosantoses' talking about their backgrounds really opened up a whole new world for me, a world that I would eventually dip into myself.

Diana and Ron are very much family oriented, which is something I have great admiration for. Ron grew up in the windy city of Chicago, a place well known for its famed gangsters and high crime rate. He had been a police officer, a career Diana had considered when she was younger, but he talked her out of it. I was also shocked to learn that Ron's best friend back in Chicago was Pakistani. This took me by surprise because I didn't know there were enough Pakistanis there for him to have met one! Where I come from, there is a huge Asian Muslim community, but in America, the Asians immigrated much later. By now, the community has grown, and a new generation has sprung up. Having known and been friends since 2001—so 20 years—it's always great to see them. It was a great evening.

Not long after that meeting, I got to work with another close friend of Bruce Lee. My focus now was to work with, in one capacity or another, as many of the prominent individuals who were associated with the late martial arts master as I could, but it was never easy. Bruce taught very few students and did so only in a private setting. Among the gentlemen who were fortunate enough to be part of an elite group was the late Larry Hartsell, a leading authority on Bruce Lee's art of jeet kune do. He trained with Bruce at the Los Angeles Chinatown closed-door gym from 1967 to 1969 after serving in Vietnam. A personal student of the great master, Larry would later gravitate toward the grappling aspects of combat, and in the jeet kune do world, he was referred to as the "JKD Street Fighter." In the 1980s, the grappling supremo also worked as a bouncer in the kind of bars that would have made *Roadhouse* look tame. And Larry even offered his services as a bodyguard to Mr. T and the notorious magazine publisher Larry Flynt.

Although I had heard of Larry in 1990, the first time I met him was in 1995, when I was still a teenager. I had heard him say that his students could say they trained with an original student of Bruce Lee, gain a certification, and be a member of his association—something that really inspired me with my interest in lineage. His hybrid street-fighting style, encompassing boxing and grappling, which leaned toward practical techniques, was also right up my alley. If you can learn to strike and grapple full contact, I thought, what more do you need? Six years later, I was in business with Larry.

Whenever I was in Los Angeles, I occasionally went to his house to train privately with him in his garage. I became a private student for a little while, training one-on-one. Larry lived in the affluent seaside community Marina Del Rey, a part of West Los Angeles, the world's largest man-made small-craft harbor with 19 marinas with capacity for more than 5,000 boats. When Ron first moved to Los Angeles, he stayed with Larry and told me that Larry kept a gun at home. Apparently, he enjoyed his beer and would often get out of control and start shooting at the ceiling in the house. He was a wild man, but he was always very polite and embodied the humble approach. You couldn't find anyone nicer than this guy, who, by the way, had the capacity to break your limbs in a split second.

Larry's home garage gym was spacious enough to house a standing punching bag, striking pads, weights bench, exercise rowing machine, free weights and various hitting devices, and mats to work on grappling, his specialty. Once when we were training together, he whacked me on my chin. catching me with an uppercut by mistake. Boy, I felt it. For a second. I thought I had been stung by a bee really hard. Then he got me with a Thai-style round kick outside of my left thigh and gave me a dead leg, which left me literally unable to walk for a while. Take into account that this wasn't even sparring but a controlled demo and that this was a 60-year-old man. The man was hard. He could give men half his age a rough experience.

One day, I asked him if I could grapple with one of his other students, who was also there conducting a lesson. Larry said that this guy was an instructor under him and that he'd crush me because the guy was bigger than me, but when we got down to business, I managed to give the guy a hard time. Renowned for being an experienced grappling authority, I thought Larry might have been more optimistic about my chances since grappling's not always about size, something that earlier UFCs proved. I found it out of character of a man of his caliber and understanding, but maybe he simply wasn't thinking straight.

Although later we parted ways purely due to a business misunderstanding, Larry was a great guy. Our falling out came over an overpayment. Larry had been sent some boxes of his martial arts–related product by my company that he had the company produce. He wasn't invoiced but was told in advance that instead, the payment would be deducted from his next payment period. It should have been a simple matter but spiraled out of control, and I never grasped the opportunity to have my say. I was very saddened by the deterioration of the relationship between Larry and myself. I later learned that back in the day, he had a business relationship with a video producer that also went down the drain because of another misunderstanding. So, others had experienced the same issues that I was being subjected to, but it didn't help my cause. I sincerely believe our relationship would have never come to an end if a third party hadn't been involved in Larry's business affairs. Larry passed away in 2007 from liver cancer.

∽

Larry was not the only revered martial arts personality I fell out with in the early years of my business. The company I owned had signed up a prominent, retired fighting legend we will refer to as "Mr. Z," who was set to pen his autobiography. This particular individual had worked with another American martial arts specialist publisher previously, and unbeknownst to me, there had been some issues. Eventually, I'd have to contend with unnecessary problems, ego, misunderstanding, control, and hard-to-work-with individuals.

What was all the fuss about? Mr. Z fell out over concerns surrounding creative and production issues. There was a disagreement over what image to use on the cover. My company had already brought to this notorious fighting legend's attention the image that was sourced, which he had actually cordially okayed. And after the proofreading process, his rep had sent the manuscript to my company as the deadline was approaching. Subsequently, the production process went ahead. As it happens, Mr. Z and his rep not only had a problem with the image but also claimed they were still in the process of finalizing the proofreading.

Not wanting to get into a legal battle, my company presented the man with another opportunity. So the image in question was changed immediately, and the original manuscript replaced with the newly delivered version from Mr. Z after the first print run arrived. But after a new print run, he still wasn't happy. In spite of conferring with him—it was an image he said was okay and one he had provided for the inside too—he then went back on his word, coming up with additional complaints. My company had incurred significant costs to please this individual, but he was now pursuing legal action. To aggravate matters further, I was dumbfounded when he said, "Well, it's done now. I'll take the money." This is the same guy who was suing my company and had earlier told me that it wasn't about money to him at all but about getting things done his way or no way. When I later offered him what amounted to $8,000 based on what he was entitled to at that point, he refused to accept this. He said this would mean I can say I've paid him now. In retrospect, I'm glad he didn't accept because he would've continued to make defamatory remarks. Moreover, I actually ended up giving away that money to someone else—it was a small investment, but because the other person was struggling, I just wrote it off completely with no hesitation.

Interestingly, I spoke to several other professionals who had worked with this longtime retired fighter, and they all revealed he was very hard to work with. By then, though, it was too late. One of his close friends, a famous martial artist who appeared in a couple of high-profile martial arts movies, had even disclosed to me in front of a witness that he would never do business with Mr. Z. Furthermore, Mr. Z had accused numerous associates and collaborators of either short-changing him or producing material he claimed he never sanctioned. This put the whole thing into perspective in terms of his track record. If God had sent an angel to warn me what was in store, not in a million years would my company have worked with this man. I honestly believe that had it not been for third-party tampering, things wouldn't have spiraled out of control.

Eventually, I came to the realization that what I had experienced was nothing out of the ordinary. If you are in the entertainment or sports business, it's inevitable you will sooner or later fall out with a few people. Look at the rapacious boxing promoters, music and film agents, and stars—there are plethora of cases involving legal battles. It's a dirty business—sometimes creative differences are the cause, but more often, it's about money. I didn't need to be so hard on myself, which I was in the beginning and for a long time. There's a saying— "never judge someone by the opinions of others"—but, unfortunately, people will. It's amazing how someone's influence has an immediate blind impact on others. They start seeing the accused person through a tinted lens. His word seemed to have more weight than mine. And my company's name and reputation was tarnished and my character defamed, leading to pressure that took a toll on me. He had tarnished several people's names, and most people seem to "buy" his story based on supposition because of his notorious position and fame. The version in circulation was that my company had stolen from him, that he hadn't been paid a dime. Perhaps I should have pursued to sue for libel, but I let it go. In any event, what I did learn is to exercise prudence for the future and the grim realities of working in the sports and entertainment business.

So in America, I had made some good friends. Equally, I had made a couple of enemies, which left me with a somewhat bitter taste. Sometime later, a more affable UFC champion, Randy Couture, would have his *New York Times* best-selling autobiography published in the United Kingdom through the company I owned—and he followed up with a second book, inking both a North American and a U.K. deal. Nevertheless, another door already opened amid all the disarray. And I was going to get my foot in.

7

Enter the Journalist

Before the widespread adoption of the internet, magazines and newspapers were, of course, your best source of information for news and sport. And in the martial arts press, the now defunct *Martial Arts Illustrated*, which was published for three decades, was, in the United Kingdom, the best-selling and number-one martial arts magazine despite sometimes ferocious competition. Directly in competition was the now defunct *Combat*, which had been going since 1974. The latter was printed on paper that felt like toilet paper, and for me, that was more or less what much of the content was suited to. *Martial Arts Illustrated*, I felt, was the more serious magazine, focused on giving coverage to more freestyle, semi–contact-style fighting—later adding MMA coverage—as well as staying true to and promoting the traditional arts and also martial arts cinema.

I had met the editor, Bob Sykes, back in early 1997 when I visited him for the first time at his offices in my first unsuccessful attempt to carve out a writing career following my first trip to America. When I first visited the magazine offices in Huddersfield, West Yorkshire, I had a rather difficult time finding the premises, which were located in a rather obscure building in the town's center. To get to the offices, you had to go upstairs and through some corridors and doors. It was hidden away like it was a CIA or MI5 building that no one could figure out or penetrate. There wasn't even a sign on the door to identify the business, but eventually, I found it, and there inside was a different story.

As I walked into the office, one thing that immediately caught my attention was all the magazine issue covers adorning the walls. Bruce

Lee, Jean-Claude Van Damme, Chuck Norris, Steven Seagal, and Jackie Chan graced the covers of my favorite monthly magazine, large as life.

Bob made me very welcome. I found him to be a really down-to-earth and humble individual. These days, Bob looks like a prisoner of war, as dramatic weight and muscle loss, gray hair, and a couple of hip surgeries have had a profound impact on his deteriorating body. But in those days, he looked healthy and physically fit and solid.

Five years later, I reconnected with Bob, and he offered me a regular slot in the magazine, kick-starting my writing career. Several years prior, in 1998, I had submitted two articles on Bruce Lee to *Black Belt* magazine in America, for which I received checks in dollars through the mail, which was amazing to me as a 22-year-old. But this was my first big break, when my journey as a journalist began. I was an official member of the combat sports press, and I felt a sense of validation. I would finally be writing about the subject that I had the most passion for. I thought it couldn't get any better.

I was wrong.

This was merely the beginning, a platform and a stepping-stone that would later lead to even bigger and better things. I started out by conducting interviews, which eventually became my forte. Fans are interested in finding out what famous fighters and athletes have to say. I know this because I am a fan and enthusiast myself. So, in the beginning, my primary focus was conducting interviews with prominent fighters and figures in the world of martial arts, and I did my best to get as much out of them as I could. Working with the monthly magazine gave me an opportunity to hone my craft, meeting and interviewing dozens of people, including many who trained with and were close friends and associates of Bruce Lee. My official position as a columnist afforded me a platform to connect with these individuals who were part of the legend's history, firsthand witnesses to the Bruce Lee phenomenon.

Most editors have substantial experience as journalists and a good grasp of the magazine and their industry. To be an editor of a specialist publication, you need a huge amount of knowledge and experience in that subject area. And on more than one occasion, I told Bob that he was the best martial arts magazine editor in the world—and I meant it.

Editors can be difficult people to work with. They have their own vision, and a lot of times, a writer receives rejections. Bob, however, would always accommodate me and my ideas. It was as if he felt he had a moral duty toward his writers and the people featured in his magazine. Yes, Bob was sometimes too affable and allowed many martial arts experts and businessmen to promote their own products, but everyone who met him developed an affinity toward him. He knew everyone in the martial arts fraternity and inspired reverence from these authorities on the deadliest arts known to man. Part of his appeal was his nonpolitical approach. He refused to get involved in the petty squabbles that often become a hindrance in martial arts circles. Despite his position—a position that most individuals in the trade could only aspire to land—Bob was gifted with a quality that most lacked: he seemed to genuinely want to help people. And the role he played gave him enormous power and pride.

In the literary world, making it is not easy. People are always happy to call themselves "writers," but being a "published writer" is just a whole new ball game. It's same with a fighter—a person who merely trains isn't a true fighter unless he actually competes or fights. I have always, without a shadow of doubt, acknowledged Bob and his magazine for giving me that big break. All I wanted was to prove myself worthy of the opportunity.

Bob and I had an amicable working relationship from the moment I joined the magazine. In fact, he became one of my best friends from the world of combat sports, a friendship that to this day has endured. Sure, he pisses me off sometimes—all editors do from time to time—but I'm sure I piss him off more than he does me.

I always felt Bob had the best job in the world as a matter of fact. Popping into the office about three times a week, spending about 30 minutes there on each visit, picking up his papers, shoving them in a bag (often a black bin bag), and spending the rest of his time working from home was his weekly routine. Bob is an old-fashioned guy. He didn't believe in briefcases or even own one.

Sometimes I'd visit Bob at his house, which was about 15 minutes from Huddersfield on the outskirts of a small village called Linthwaite. Huddersfield gave me a taste of West Yorkshire, countryside living, a region full of amiable people. I would always look forward to the drive down, which took 35 minutes and then another 10 minutes of off-highway driving to get into the sleepy countryside town. More often than not, I would spend more time at Bob's house than in the office. The place Bob lived in looked like a bungalow from the outside, but it was a good place and very comfortable. As we sipped tea in his living room—Bob, unfortunately, did not make good tea—we would converse, and he'd start going off on somebody he'd just had dealings with. That was his style, but whether it was me, fellow columnist Andy Staton, or some other martial arts personality, it was all done in good humor.

Actually, sometimes Bob took things too lightly. Sometimes you'd be faced with a dilemma and unable to gauge whether he was serious or pulling your leg. And when he pulled your leg, he had the capacity to tear it off if you drifted into believing what he spewed out.

"I should marry Shannon Lee, Bruce Lee's daughter, and carry on the family tree," he used to joke with me. I feel he would've made a good comedian. In his less humorous moments, he eventually started to complain to me about martial artists using him, trying to squeeze favors out of him. Although he was always willing to accommodate, he got to a stage when he was stressed out and felt used. At one point, he told me he'd simply had enough of doing his job—after all, he'd been at it for 25 years. I joked with him, saying I was going to steal his job, a job I'd have loved to have had at the time despite having some reservations.

When I wasn't making my memorable visits to see Bob, I spent an inordinate amount of time talking with him on the phone. It wasn't long before I filtered into the habit of calling him at 10 p.m., which he didn't mind. I always worked antisocial hours. The only time he would find me infuriating was when I rang him when he was in the middle of watching his favorite TV show, *Deal or No Deal*, in the evening. He would rant and rave, saying I was disturbing him.

At that time, besides the martial arts specialist press, no other media were seriously offering coverage to the UFC. Those who were astute enough to see the benefits of cross-training continued to appreciate the rise of MMA, but in sharp contrast to these more open-minded exponents, the ardent traditionalists often felt it was a bad look for the martial arts to promote such a bloody spectacle. Take into account, too, that the advent of the UFC exposed some traditionalists as far as the effectiveness of their own approaches went. Many of the traditional arts became the target of derision as the more practical styles prevailed, with fans wondering why they were so unsuccessful inside the cage. Bob, for his part, didn't quite warm up to MMA as much as he, I feel, should have. And he actually made this known to me. Maybe he felt it was too violent or lacked traditional arts within its framework. I think it was this combination. Still, his own distaste didn't stop him from promoting MMA in the magazine and giving the public what they wanted. It was a natural evolution.

Aside from his prestigious position in one of the most well-known magazines, what set Bob apart from other martial arts and sports editors is that he was an active competitor, meaning that he had a broader outlook and understanding of the arts than most of the other armchair authorities in his field. In fact, he had given world champion Bill Wallace a good go in an exhibition fight in 1987—two years before the magazine first hit the shelves. Wallace, who would be a co-commentator on the first-ever UFC and had trained Elvis Presley's daughter and even battled Jackie Chan in *The Protector*, was no joke. He was among the best world champion fighters and could really fight. Bob didn't rest on his laurels after his retirement from competition, either. He would often invite top martial arts exponents to train with him before a photo shoot and interview. Not many magazine editors do that.

☙

As time went by, I started working for more magazines published by the *Martial Arts Illustrated* stable. They had several magazines, including *Impact: The Global Action Entertainment Magazine*, *Horse Riding*, *Combat & Survival*, *Equestrian*, and, later, *MMA Uncaged*. *Impact* ran for 15 years, of which I was a regular contributor for three. *MMA Uncaged* used me as a columnist/contributing writer for five years.

The martial arts press really surfaced back in the early 1970s. During the kung fu boom of the 1970s, publisher and entrepreneur Felix Dennis launched a poster magazine aptly named *Kung Fu Monthly*. Although I wasn't around at the time of the boom, I later got my hands on some of these classic out-of-print magazines. Back then, Bruce Lee had exploded onto our screens, and people in the West went kung fu crazy. Felix jumped on the bandwagon, and in addition to the magazine, he produced some booklets on the kung fu star. Felix and his business partner were small-time publishers who had become bankrupt, but as Bruce Lee emerged, he reignited a flame, saving them from debt.

"Our salvation came in the form of a Chinese martial arts athlete called Bruce Lee," Felix recounted in his own autobiography. "*Kung Fu Monthly* was born in 1974, and within six months there was £60,000 in the bank. We were rich beyond our wildest dreams. Every day sacks full of postal orders from Bruce Lee fans would arrive in locked post office bags, deposited in our Goodge Street hallway by a postman who refused to lug them up the rickety stairs." The enormous success of the eight-page poster publication led to licensing foreign editions. At its height, *Kung Fu Monthly* was being published in 14 countries and 11 languages.

I tried tracking down Felix at one point for an interview to get him to relive the Bruce Lee boom with me. Instead, I got to speak to a member of the staff, Bruce Sawford, who had been the editor of *Kung Fu Monthly*. He told me that Felix had made a lot of his money from the computer magazines. This is the same publisher who publishes *Men's Fitness* and the defunct *MAXIM* magazine. But *Kung Fu Monthly* was one of the first martial arts magazines, and it had nothing but "King of Kung Fu" plastered all over it. What really struck me was the history of it all.

There was a photo frame shop near where I lived and I often popped in there. While talking to the owner one day, I came to learn that he was a martial arts enthusiast and had collected the *Kung Fu Monthly* copies back in the day. He had a photocopier in the shop and was kind enough to photocopy his precious collection for me. No way in hell was he going to give me his original collection—it was his treasure trove, and he was refusing to let his "babies" go. He was a smart man because today a single copy can fetch hundreds of dollars.

⌒

Although my main love was Bruce Lee, like many people growing up in the 1980s, I had spent part of my childhood also watching Jean-Claude Van Damme, the "Muscles from Brussels," perform helicopter kicks on the screen. I'd even attempted them myself a couple of times, but one of my friends could replicate Van Damme's kick perfectly. So, in 2005, when I found out that Bob was going to be hanging out with the Hollywood martial arts star, I wasted no time calling him up.

Known for his mood swings and out-of-character attitude, Van Damme has had more than his fair share of drama off-screen. At least once, the actor's grandiose attitude got him into a physical altercation. A known martial artist and bodyguard to the stars, Chuck Zito, knocked out the action movie star in a New York nightclub with just one punch. He had lived the celebrity lifestyle, with all the drinking and drugs and everything else that often come with the package. On one occasion, he walked out of a TV interview in Australia after complaining that the questions he was being asked were boring. "It's difficult for me to answer those questions," he complained, "so I start to sweat and I don't feel good because they are boring."

Bob's friend Jon Jepson, a martial arts instructor and businessman, had managed to secure a tour with his childhood idol. It was quite the trip. Jon, Bob, I, the editor of a rival martial arts magazine (who was a friend of Jepson), and several others jumped into a fleet of BMWs with Van Damme and his then partner and some bodyguards for the drive between Derby, Burton-on-Trent, and London. Bob spent the bulk of the time in back of the X5 telling me Van Damme wasn't a nice person and the rest of the time on his phone texting a lady friend and making derogatory comments about the fallen star. Bob had, in his previous encounters with the star, fallen victim to the karate champ's attitude. To say that Van Damme had an ego the size of an elephant would be keeping it light. Bob was always a cheerleader for the underdog and detested show-offs, which meant that he had no time for Van Damme. Now I'd be able to witness his behavior for myself.

Sure enough, Van Damme was a demanding diva from the start. When we were all at the hotel relaxing in the lobby, Bob realized the actor was treating Jon like shit. There had been a problem with transportation somewhere beforehand, and Van Damme was giving the promoter problems. Van Damme was no longer in the top ranks of Hollywood by this point; he was a fallen star but seemed to still act like he was an A-lister. Treating people with dignity should be part of every true martial artist's character, but apparently Van Damme never got the memo.

In this world, if you want to be liked by others, it's a good practice to actually treat them well. It doesn't cost money. Bob embodied this behavior and tried his best to keep our spirits up, but it was an effort from the start.

When I told Bob that we should pose for a photo with Van Damme, he told me not to bother. Like I said, he had dealt with him several times in the past and knew exactly what he was all about when it came to treating others. Besides, Bob was never starstruck. As a loyal friend, I gave up on my quest to pose with Van Damme. However, Bob had brought along a young man, Nikol Gojka, whom he had adopted from eastern Europe and who was a big Van Damme fan. So he wanted to make sure the kid got to meet his hero. The kid did and was over the moon. Mission accomplished!

On the tour, the Muscles from Brussels was embraced by screaming fans who were treated to inspirational speeches and a little demo that I found rather mundane. In London, it was a black-tie dinner in conjunction with a karate tournament. For a couple of days of work, the actor bagged a substantial sum of money.

The martial arts action star was lucky enough not to get a pasting by someone while on the tour. But he came close years earlier when one of Bob's friends attacked Van Damme. The first time Bob encountered the Belgium-born star was back in the early 1990s when he did a photo shoot to coincide with the release of one of his movies. One of the most bizarre incidents took place in London when Bob, his brother Tony, martial arts journalist Bey Logan, and friend Nirman Sahota Singh went down to London to meet Van Damme, who was doing a press junket. The meeting and a photo shoot had been prearranged.

When Van Damme walked into the room with his entourage, Bob and his crew proceeded to greet him and exchanged a few friendly words. But Nirman had other devious plans up his sleeve. This, he felt, was a rare opportunity for him to make a name for himself. As he moved toward Van Damme to greet him, he charged at him like a lunatic, making a high-pitched noise. Nirman couldn't speak properly because he was dumb and deaf, but he was certainly quite aggressive in his attack. With his spontaneous reflexes, Van Damme, dressed smartly in a nice suit and despite being mystified, threw his side kick-out to intercept the oncoming assault. He flicked the kick-out real fast and held it out, stopping his attacker in his tracks while barely touching him. He was quite vulnerable to attack because he didn't have bodyguards, but he certainly held his own.

"Everyone was shocked," Bob recounted. "Nirman didn't think Van Damme was that good, but on that day, he showed how good he was with that lightning-fast kick, and he held it out." Nirman's temperature dropped on the spot, and everybody else just clapped. "We were all shocked at what Van Damme actually was—the real deal," Bob told me. "You thought he was just a movie star, but you could tell he could move." Truth be told, Bob admits he hadn't been convinced about the martial arts actor's credentials prior to this incident. Bob and his brother, who was also a martial arts champion, weren't into the action showbiz razzmatazz, and martial arts movies were never really their cup of tea. When one of Bob's closest friends and martial arts champion Buster Reeves, originally from Huddersfield, invited him to his wedding in America, Bob declined. Among the guests, there were going to be some heavyweights from the Hollywood crowd, but it didn't mean anything to Bob. Buster was a big Hollywood stuntman rubbing shoulders with the likes of Brad Pitt and Tom Cruise, but Bob couldn't have cared less.

Van Damme shook the incident off. But unbeknownst to him, he was in for a second surprise—round 2. Nirman wasn't quite just yet satisfied and yearned for his two minutes of fame. After the professional photo shoot was over, Van Damme agreed to have a picture taken with his attacker at the end. To aggravate matters further, the Huddersfield madman flicked out a sneaky spinning back kick, thrown in for good measure, which just missed the star's head. Again, Van Damme just laughed it off. Nirman's foot had just skimmed past his head. "I think what Nirman tried to do was he was trying to hit Van Damme in the head," Bob recalled, "but he just moved out of the way with good reflexes." He had his two chances now. It's an experience Nirman could take away with him and cherish for the rest of his life and boast about over a beer in his local drinking establishment even though he couldn't land a blow on the action star.

Nirman was a street fighter who apparently used to get into three fights a night. That's a hell of a number of fights in a day. Making it into the local newspaper was a regular occurrence. Only a few years before his death, he made it into the newspaper for running around in the street with a samurai sword like a lunatic. The story made front-page news. I guess he got what he craved—fame and attention. I was falling over laughing when Bob was telling me this story. *This man is a lunatic*, I thought. "He was mental and a dangerous man," Bob said. "Van Damme sorted him out. Nirman was lucky to survive. If Van Damme had hit him with that kick, well, he's got super control."

On the way back home, there were further tensions, as Bob and the crew were quite mean to their fame-seeking friend. "We ripped up his train ticket on the way home," Bob told me. "He was fighting all of us. So we did that. And then he started banging on the side of the train so they had to stop the train. The staff told us off." I could listen to Bob's adventures in the martial arts all day long. Having experienced so much and dealt with so many people, he could really tell a story. There was never a dull moment with Bob the Ninja.

8

UFC Assignment

Now that I had settled into my role with the magazine after the better part of two years, it was finally time to experience a little of the jet-set lifestyle. In 2004, I flew to Los Angeles—my fifth trip to the City of Angels but one of my first in my capacity as a columnist. This time, I wasn't going to just meet up with Royce Gracie again—the purpose of the trip was to interview him. The last time I had seen him was in 1996 when I was training with him at the world-famous Gracie Academy. This time, I was staying in Santa Monica, the beachfront area in western Los Angeles.

Later that evening, I received a call from the man himself, in great spirits, and the next afternoon, I made my way to his now ex-wife Marianne's office in the Hermosa Beach area. There, a tall bald man wearing dark blue jeans and a blue T-shirt walked up armed with a radiating smile and shook my hand. I got the impression he was half asleep. Given the nonstop nature of his travel schedule, I assumed he was jetlagged. After all, he spent six months a year flying all around the world on seminar tours spreading Gracie Jiu-Jitsu. Still, jetlagged or not, it was great to see him again. As we settled in for a chat, what immediately captivated my attention was the fact that he was much friendlier and more relaxed than the Royce Gracie I had known eight years prior. He had been living life to the fullest and exuded confidence and positive energy. I never sensed the ego that some famous personalities possess—to be honest, you rarely see it from real fighters—but now, with the pressure of his fighting career gone, Royce was happy and in great humor.

We sat down for a long chat. I had endless questions to throw at him. Perhaps the one I was most curious about was, "What goes through your mind when you face a 250-pound muscular guy who's ready to tear you apart?"

"The mind is blank," he told me after thinking a little. "I think he's more concerned about it than I am. He's the one looking across the ring and seeing someone much stronger, much faster than him. He's the one who sees a monster."

Wow, I thought, *he is super confident*. Royce is far from intimidating. His fluid, nonaggressive style and calm demeanor is something that always puts a smile on my face, but it all comes from a guy who can walk the walk. I think this is one of the reasons why many find him intriguing—he is a normal-looking guy who can rip a monster's head off with ease. In the Octagon, he always looked at home, calm even amid the storm. If you look at the earlier UFCs, he's utterly focused but completely determined.

Still, now that grappling was more widely understood, did he believe that a weight advantage plays a pivotal role in the art of grappling? "My next opponent is 490 pounds," he laughed, "That's a lot of stones." If both fighters know the same technique and have same level of technical skill, he explained, then whoever is faster and heavier can contribute to the outcome. It had been almost nine years since he had exited the UFC, and now he was fighting in Japan, set to face the giant sumo fighter Akebono. Much as I revered his technique, I just couldn't get my head around how he was going to submit this giant. It just wasn't plausible. From our conversation, it seemed that I feared for Royce's safety more than he did.

Another thing I had always been curious about was if Royce had ever encountered any real-life incidents in the street outside the professional arena or at the academy. "Have you ever come close to a fight because someone recognized you from the UFC or wanted to make a name?" I asked him. Again, he responded with brimming confidence, "No, never! People read on my forehead 'Don't fuck with me,'" he said, laughing. Royce's siblings and cousins have been part of countless street fights—Rickson, Relson, and Renzo are the tough nuts of the Gracie clan, but Royce is more of a gentleman. The Gracie family embody the warrior spirit of being willing to fight anyone, and their philosophy of life has inspired me profoundly.

Why did Royce exit the UFC? This was much simpler. Royce exited the world's most prodigious battleground in 1995 after they started to implement rules. He also admitted that MMA had evolved and that everybody was cross-training, wrestlers were knocking people out, and kickboxers were choking people out. "I think the competition has got much better," said Royce. "The guys are better prepared and more versatile now, even if I cannot say they've got bigger."

Royce was in the middle of a training camp, so I was keen to ask him about his typical training schedule, and I was impressed when he shared it. His day started at 5 a.m. He left the house at 5:30 and did his first training from 6:00 until 7:30. Fight strategies would be drilled with three training partners, grappling for five-minute rounds with a two-minute rest between each round. After this grueling session, he would go home, have breakfast, sleep, and rest for an hour. Then at around 11:00, he hit the weights for an hour or an hour and a half under the watchful eye of his conditioning coach, James Strom—former strength coach for the tennis superstar Serena Williams and the Los Angeles Rams of the National Football League. Then it is lunch, rest, and, at 6 p.m., stand-up training, again, for an hour or an hour and a half. A couple of times a week, he'd run and ride the bicycle. "I take a lot of ice baths to put the body together, too," he laughed.

Despite all the fame and fortune Royce had garnered, he didn't really seem to have a chip on his shoulder. He certainly didn't act like a tough guy throwing his weight around. Whether he was engaging with a famous fighter or a celebrity, sharing a platform professionally or on a social level, or meeting fans, I never really witnessed anything that gave you the impression that he was above people. Being able to mix with people, devoid of ego, is something that really elevates the respect that I have for Royce (and any other champion for that matter). In fact, he actually once said to me, "I know where I come from. I don't let it get to my head." Take into account that he came from a badass family that was famed in Brazil, where their father was treated like a sports hero and his siblings were revered also. Some people perceive Royce and the Gracies as being arrogant, but outside the fight environment, they are great human beings. It was a great feeling reconnecting with the legend and was the initiation of what would be a fruitful friendship.

᷍

Being an enthusiastic student, whenever I flew to Los Angeles, I would arrange to train personally one-on-one with Royce whenever possible. Back then, he taught out of a friend's modest martial arts gym called Nando's Hapkido, which is in Redondo Beach. Eventually, he moved his base and was teaching private lessons at Evaldo's Brazilian Jiu-Jitsu

Academy in Long Beach. From my first experience at the Gracie Academy onward, I've learned that Royce is not only a great fighter and extremely confident warrior but also a great teacher. He has the ability to disseminate information that is easy to absorb and follow, and he always emphasized the importance of rudimentary techniques.

The next year, in 2005, I met up with him again. Royce often picked me up from my hotel or apartment, as I didn't drive in Los Angeles, and would drop me off after the training sessions. *How many world-famous fighters and champions would do that?* I thought at the time. Once when I was taking a private lesson, a skinny, 22-year-old named Xavier, who was his brother Robin's neighbor in Spain, had come over to train. This lanky guy was far from being physically imposing. Furthermore, he was not physically strong in the pure sense of the word. As Royce said, "He can't do two push-ups." I was on the mat, and this guy gave me a real hard time on the ground. His skill and technique had been honed to perfection. He'd been diligently mastering the art and training for years. I had already learned not to judge anyone when I had trained at the original Gracie Academy, let alone in the fight game, but this guy was good. He knew how to distribute his weight and use leverage. Royce always taught that smaller and weaker students can build a strategy and a game around the assets they have, and this young man epitomized the beauty of Gracie Jiu-Jitsu. It was inspiring and humbling.

With Royce, I always had fun rolling around and a good laugh. I would refrain from going hard, although even if I did, I'd be destroyed by the champ. Men of his caliber had the capacity to control you like a little baby and literally wipe the floor with you. He could obviously submit me within seconds if he chose to, but never did he take advantage or go hard to impress me. Back at the academy when I first trained with him, he was assertive, almost aggressive, when you didn't perform the technique the correct way after he repeatedly explained and demonstrated it. But that was good because to instill discipline in the students, that assertive approach was almost imperative. At times, I remember, it felt like being told off by my parents.

On another occasion when I was training with Royce, there were about half a dozen firefighters in attendance on an official training program financed by a government department. Almost all of them were bigger and heavier than the Brazilian master. Again, just as I had experienced when I first trained with him at the academy years earlier, it was quite surreal whenever I saw people like that and a rather diminutive-looking Royce teaching these monsters. Royce's brother

Relson—veteran of 60 street fights—couldn't have put it better when he once said, "The big strong guy goes to class. And he keeps getting tapped by the skinny, technical guy. It begins to change him. It makes him humble. That's what jiu-jitsu does to you. It makes you humble."

On this day, I, Xavier, and Royce finished our training session, walked over to the beach, and did a short run. We also did a photo shoot on the beach for the magazine where I assisted. The Californian sunshine was in full glow, and the next stop was at Royce's physician. We jumped into his Jeep and drove down to his physician's office. "Man, your body is like Bruce Lee's," he commented as we made our way to the upper-level floor in the lift. That was a compliment I almost blushed at, particularly coming from the legend.

Although I was brought up in the United Kingdom, I've always had a mixed accent—a British Pakistani one. When I was a young kid, I couldn't say the number "three." I had a problem pronouncing it, so I would avoid saying it out loud in school so as not to embarrass myself. I was always and still am very conscious about my accent. I can filter in and out of it consciously or subconsciously, and more often than not, I have to consciously make that transition mid-conversation. I've often encountered people with an Asian background who didn't know me, and whenever I opened my mouth, they got the impression that I was an immigrant. When I say that, I mean from Pakistan. A few even went as far as accusing me of looking for a British passport. Oh, yeah, I was off a banana boat, according to one person. One day Royce told me that he had a similar problem as far as not losing his accent. "Look at mine, man," he said. Royce never lost his accent even though he had been in America since 1984, just like Arnold Schwarzenegger never lost his. Watching *Sesame Street* on TV to get a better grasp on English was an avenue Royce took in his early years in America. He also picked up English from his nephews—Rorion's kids. Again, this humble man was ready to learn from anyone who had something to teach him.

<2~

I've never really believed in first impressions. You can't always judge a person from your first impression—that's my belief. My education in the martial arts helped me embrace the "never judge a person based on their outer personality" philosophy because it's the easiest way to set yourself up for a shock. Big muscles or a skinny guy, the way he talks and carries himself won't allow you to discern a fighter's true ability. From my participation on a physical level as well as a writer, I've been around some of the most dangerous men in the fight world who you wouldn't even think were fighters. One of Bruce Lee's personal students, one of the most amiable people but a tough street fighter, the late Larry Hartsell, was often underrated. He's a perfect example. He was an affable figure and epitomized the gentlemanly, soft-spoken individual. Bruce Lee's original students were unimposing—they hardly looked like fighters. But most of them, I believe, had the capacity to decapitate mere mortals with their lethal techniques as far as street-fight encounters are concerned.

Having studied the lives of some of the toughest men and fighters in the world, I came to the realization that, by and large, they are very nice people. I had learned a lot in life from so many of these physical specimens whose vocation involves blood, brutality, and violence. Way back when I was training at the Gracie Academy in Los Angeles as a youngster with Royce, I learned something salient—a lesson that would be embedded in my head for the rest of my life. At the Academy, there was a bespectacled older-looking gentleman, a pleasant person who hardly looked like a fighter—far from formidable. But, boy, he could wipe the floor with you with his ground grappling skills. His striking wasn't of a high standard (far from it), but he was an extremely efficient grappler who could eat you for breakfast. Then he'd have you for lunch and even dinner if you weren't careful. That's how dangerous and vicious he was. But he was always very polite.

What amazes me is that despite the fact Royce is a top professional fighter, he has this nonchalant demeanor. However, the confidence he possesses in his fighting and technical ability is on another level. His bearing and look don't give the impression of his being a fighter, let alone the best fighter, but this slender-built man is as savage as they come. Don't let his friendly approach fool you. This man is one of the deadliest men you'll ever lay your eyes on. Your big mouth and muscles aren't going to get you anywhere or intimidate him. Royce's physical capability and mental strength are matched by very few. I soon learned he is one of those people who refuses to be beaten; to beat him, you have to kill him.

He once told me something that I found extremely thought provoking based on a conversation that he had had with his older brother Rorion. He said to me, "One time my brother said to me, 'In a perfect world, you wouldn't be a fighter.' And I looked at him thinking, *After all I've done in the fight world!*" Royce went home contemplating and after a week phoned his sibling back. "You're right, in a perfect world, I wouldn't be a fighter," Royce admitted to Rorion. "I never had a fight in the street. I'm not a mean person. All my fights are won in kind of a nice way where I'm not pounding my opponent's face inside out. I don't have to. So, yes, in a perfect world, I wouldn't be a fighter, but the world isn't perfect. However, if I want to be a fighter, I might as well be the best."

There's a saying that coins always make sounds, but paper money is mostly silent. Royce Gracie is the living embodiment of this philosophy. This man doesn't need to act tough or talk trash.

I believe there are two types of fighters. There's the big, rough-looking, mean, 250-pound fighter who looks like a ferocious beast. In contrast to this, there's the Royce Gracie type—calm demeanor, smaller, and unimposing, which can easily be misleading to the eye and hard to antagonize. Even fighters of repute such as Randy Couture would fit into this latter category, though you'd certainly never mistake Randy for weak if you saw him in shorts!

Some of the greatest fighters don't look tough or give you the impression that they are tough. But deep down, they are hard as an ox. Moreover, I learned that some of these men are of a shy disposition, lacking certain social skills and confidence. But confidence comes in different shapes and forms. When you're in their arena, you could bet your bottom dollar that these men could play with you like a baby. Being a combat sports journalist afforded me the opportunities to meet, interview, observe, interact, and even train to a certain extent with a multitude of elite exponents and champions, giving me the inside track on their behavior and tendencies. I soon learned that professional athletes revered on world, national, regional, and even local stages have a common denominator—respect and humbleness is ingrained in them by the training they undergo. I learned that when your value increases, you keep yourself silent and humble. These great champions do just that. They have the capacity to really incapacitate a mere mortal but are good role models, as martial arts teach you ethics and respect.

I learned that the worst fear in the world is to be afraid of the opinion of others. The idea is not to let the behaviors of others destroy your inner peace. When an athlete or fighter reaches a professional level or is content and of a high caliber at an amateur level, he doesn't need validation from the outside world. That's perhaps the greatest lesson I learned from Royce Gracie.

9

More Real Than the UFC

Just before the advent of the UFC exploding onto the global stage, martial arts in Britain were going through a transitional phase—a revolution was taking place. The individual responsible for this was a doorman and martial arts exponent named Geoff Thompson, born and bred in Coventry, England. Coming from a traditional martial arts background, the once-bullied teenager went on to study an array of fighting disciplines: Greco wrestling, freestyle wrestling, Thai boxing, judo, boxing, traditional karate, and several other martial arts systems. Eventually, he came to advocate what he referred to as the "real approach." He isn't the biggest guy and doesn't even really come across as intimidating—until, of course, he switches on the red destruction button of his and you see a whole new Geoff, ready to pulverize. In a quest to vanquish his own fears, he worked on the roughest doors in the country for 10 long years—an odd approach to most but one that certainly worked for him.

"I had a debilitating fear of violent confrontation," Geoff said, "so I became a doorman to confront my fears." Thrown into the frontline of street violence, he soon realized that what worked in the confines of the dojo environment didn't necessarily work outside on the street. Consequently, he started to address real street scenario drills in his dojo. The purpose of everything he taught was to survive a real encounter, eradicating the bullshit and embracing the raw street approach and mentality. To many traditionalists' horror, Geoff advocated shouting and swearing in his epic training sessions as he proceeded to add an element of realism that was all too absent in the confines of the dojo. He played out realistic scenarios with his students to get them to acclimatize to the street environment so that they wouldn't be overcome by adrenaline the first time someone got in their face. Only by stepping out of the comfort zone could one really get a "feel" for what real fighting encompassed, Geoff would explain. After all, even the UFC had rules.

Everyone feels fear. Geoff, in particular, embraced it. He became known for broaching the subject of fear as much as he did for his brutal fighting tactics. Indeed, fear was at the forefront of his teachings, unlike most instructors who spent time in merely the physical component or spiritual aspects of the arts. I found it compelling that the psychological aspects of violence, which play an integral role in confrontations, were the focus point of this doorman who had experienced the harsh realities of confrontations in what he referred to as the "pavement arena."

A big part of Geoff's teaching is that we can eliminate (or at least minimize) the fear within us when we know ourselves better. As the great Sun Tzu said, "When you know yourself and your opponent, you will win every time. When you know yourself but not your opponent, you will win one and lose one. However, when you do not know yourself or your opponent, you will be imperilled every time." You cannot elude fear altogether. For an athlete and exponent of combat arts, fear is infectious. Thus, the key is to understand, master, and control it. Embracing and understanding psychology pertaining to raw street savage encounters is essential. I soon came to the realization that when it comes to fight psychology, I don't think you can be more of an expert than Geoff is. He is a fight professor. Moreover, for me, he was one of the first people to really admit it was okay to have fear. And when I say this, I mean in all situations of life. "It is easier to deny fear than admit it," Geoff once said. "One of our greatest fears is to admit when we're afraid." When he documented his own life experiences and fights, instead of just talking about how he beat people up, he took a more honest avenue, confessing the fear he frequently experienced. Studying his work, it dawned on me not only that it was perfectly fine to embrace fear but also that it was okay to divulge to others that you had fear, that you were scared at one time or another, and that you sometimes wanted to run from whatever situation was presented to you, not just in a combat environment but also in life in general. This was an eye-opener to say the least. I had grown up with people around me who, by and large, concealed their fears. The bravado and "I am perfect" attitude were all too common. Fearing to fight, fear of losing, fear of embarrassment, fear of being subjected to verbal attacks, or any situation for that matter was perceived as a huge dent in one's ego and pride.

Of course, Geoff also had plenty to teach about fighting. Violence was at the center of Geoff's life, as he fought his way through hundreds of street encounters, not losing once. Domestically, if you were seriously involved in the martial arts field and hadn't heard of Geoff Thompson, you were living on another planet. What I found equally gripping was his life story. How do you relate a doorman and street fighter with more than 300 fights on his résumé to the literary world? First, as I mentioned earlier, never judge anyone from their look because appearances can be deceptive. I discovered that behind Geoff's brawn was an amazing intellect. Here was a martial artist and doorman who ultimately wanted to become a writer ever since he was young. Yes, maybe this is hard to comprehend for some, and indeed he was surrounded by naysayers who screamed, "People like us don't write!" Eventually, though, Geoff found his way, writing about his own tragic and painful experiences. Having started his journey working with specialist martial arts press and authoring books (writing more than 26 martial arts books) the doorman turned author transitioned into writing for more mainstream outlets, culminating in articles being published in the *Times* newspaper. His transition into mainstream territory further resulted in churning out self-help tomes. As of today, he has written more than 40 books. His crowning achievement was his autobiography, *Watch My Back*, which became a *Sunday Times* bestseller and really made him a household name. This fight psychologist even churned out scripts for short films, grabbing a BAFTA along the way. Now, you are talking my language. I could resonate with this man in more than one way. Geoff spent many years writing columns for martial arts magazines, and we had several mutual friends, including my editor friend Bob Sykes and Peter Consterdine, cofounder of Geoff's combat association.

But it was never a smooth ride. When Geoff attracted the attention of the martial arts fraternity and, not surprisingly, the media as well, they made him out to be a controversial character, as he provoked widespread outrage. Like anything else, you will always have the critics. Some people voiced their opinions, griping he was advocating brutal violence. These people were missing the point, though. Geoff never enjoyed violence for the sake of it. The concept behind his teachings was to address the realities of street survival and the fear factor.

In spite of his harsh critics, he garnered a big following in the martial arts circles. *Black Belt* magazine in America voted him the

"Number-One Self-Defence Expert in the World," which is no small accolade. His influence was being felt across the pond as the UFC was being sold as a blood sport. In due course, he got invited to America to teach alongside some top masters. It was interesting to see a man of his caliber praising and being in awe of some of these American martial arts legends, such as the Machado brothers, who are cousins of the Gracie clan. It put everything into perspective for me in terms of the talent coming out of America.

Anyone looking for street-fighting self-defense has to look no further than Geoff Thompson. He is part of those higher echelons of the martial arts world who defied the odds and triumphed. Occasionally, I would talk to him and update him with some of my work, and he'd encourage me and appreciated it. Whenever I called him or left a message, he unfailingly returned my calls and gave me his time. Geoff's philosophy of fighting and life and literary works heavily impacted my own life and how certain things unfolded for me. Just like him, I left school with no qualifications. I, too, wanted to become a professional writer and author. I read voraciously just as he did on subjects of diverse taste. Geoff's story is an inspirational story of a boy who had a crappy job and scribbled on pieces of paper in the factory restroom in desperation to write. *Watch My Back* became one of the books that influenced me and so many people.

⌒

As I was making waves behind the scenes in combat sports, I would encounter a man who is a giant among men. He resided not far from Geoff, and he was involved in bodybuilding, another sport that, more often than not, was tarred with controversy but also with martial arts and MMA.

10

The Giants

For as long as I can remember, there has been a kinship between the martial arts and bodybuilding. Some alpha-male individuals take up a fighting art to prove their manliness, others are inclined toward pursuing the iron-pumping game, and more than a few do both in their quest to become the deadliest fighters they possibly can. In the early days of the UFC (and even before), many martial artists trained only with their own bodyweight or didn't do supplementary resistance training at all. But now, you'd be hard pressed to find a professional or amateur MMA fighter who doesn't implement some sort of weight training into his regime—it is part and parcel of a fighter's routine.

Two Canadian brothers, the late Joe and Ben Weider, are perhaps the most responsible for the current popularity of the once-mocked sport of bodybuilding. Joe, in particular, is widely acknowledged as being the founding father of this once misunderstood sport. Ever since I came across the name Weider when I was 13, I came to admire the brothers and what they stood for. Scouring through the muscle magazines, I came to realize that a whole industry was built around the Weider name.

The Weider brothers were born in a tough section of Montreal to Jewish parents who had emigrated from Poland. They had an impoverished childhood, and growing up in the 1930s, these 90-pound Jewish weaklings were regularly picked on by neighborhood hooligans. The slightly built, skinny Weider boys could hardly make it home from school without being beaten up or having insults thrown at them. Consequently, Joe tried to join a wrestling team but was rejected by the coach because the coach feared he was so small that he'd get hurt grappling. Joe, however, wasn't going to give up or even slow down. After picking up a copy of *Strength* magazine at a local newsstand, which would have set him back only a penny at the time, he started lifting weights to build up his body and feel strong. Being so poor that he couldn't afford real weights, he made a barbell out of an axle and a set of car wheels and trained with them relentlessly in his garage.

This young ambitious teenager merely managed a grade school education because his parents didn't have the money to send him to high school, but it didn't matter to Joe. He had bigger dreams and a vision that involved conquering the world and spreading the joy of physical strength to the corners of the globe. He became a magazine publisher at the age of 17, starting his empire from his kitchen in 1940 with a periodical called *Your Physique*, continuing his own love affair with the sport as he religiously lifted weights, built his body, and entered early physique competitions. By the age of 18, this teenager, who had been the victim of local bullies most of his childhood, became the strongest kid in the neighborhood, a feat that led to his victory in Quebec's best-known weightlifting competition. The road to success wasn't without struggle and adversity for Joe, but this only inspired me more as I read about him. Joe's journey resonated with me: here was a man who developed an obsession for a physical pursuit and excelled in promoting something he loved.

"Two things never entered my mind: that I was going to make money; it was never Joe's goal or my goal," Ben said, in an interview before his death. "What we did was because we loved what we were doing, and we wanted to do it the best way. The other thing that never entered my mind was it wouldn't work—it has to work." This reminded me of Rorion Gracie, who, like the Weiders, had a vision to bring his own brand of fighting to America and once said to me that money was just a consequence of his work. He always maintains that his main objective is to promote his art and message. I believe that the majority of people endeavor to create a balance so that both art and monetary elements play an integral role in their professional pursuits and success.

Regardless, the bodybuilding brothers made their mark. Inspired by the chiseled physiques of actors on the screen, the public grew to embrace bodybuilding, just as Hollywood stars did the same. Action stars such as Sylvester Stallone graced the cover of *Muscle & Fitness*, and Arnold Schwarzenegger's best friend and Mr. Olympia winner, Franco Columbu, was assigned to train the star for his second outing as John Rambo. Judging by Rambo's physique, Franco did a commendable job. Stallone looked ripped and huge, but I was still most envious of Bruce Lee, who had embraced the benefits of bodybuilding and working out with weights, leading the way for future action actors to follow. Bruce not only looked great but also had a physique that was functional enough to make it completely believable when he dispatched a whole herd of men with his fists and feet on the big screen. A resident of Los Angeles, Bruce himself made trips to Joe's muscle store in Santa Monica to purchase protein powders. As pumping iron became a cool thing to do, music rap stars pumping iron and displaying their chiseled frames in music videos inspired the young generation. These role models for the young generation were associated with bodybuilding, as were athletes from a wide spectrum of sports.

Building muscles and fitness can closely be associated with almost all sports that require the body to perform under exhaustion. As I mentioned earlier, the modern-day gladiators, MMA athletes, implement weight training, as do fighters competing in any combat sport. Building quality muscle mass that will increase your power in striking and grappling techniques and overall precision that will aid technique, stamina, and endurance makes the body fitter and helps performance. There had long been the negative belief that big muscles would impede a fighter's movement and speed. This myth has to be put into perspective. Athletes have their goals in mind when working out with weights, not building massive muscles.

Pop your head into any well-equipped MMA gym, and you will see state-of-the-art equipment, including kettle bells, medicine balls, all sorts of benches and weights and weight resistance machines, heavy ropes, gigantic tires for flipping, and big hammers to develop body power. Experts agree that athletes around the globe benefit from using weights. And although there will always be controversy surrounding bodybuilding, there is no doubt that the benefits that can be derived from training with weights are huge.

༚

Although my primary focus was covering fight sports, bodybuilding was another area I felt I could venture into. Because there has long been a kinship between the two endeavors, I could relate to it quite easily. Whatever area I branched out in, I set my bar high. I started to contribute to *Muscle & Fitness* occasionally while maintaining my position at the martial arts periodical.

I had heard of the bodybuilder named Dorian Yates way back in 1990. So, what made this champion different from the other elite iron-pumping physique champions? Essentially, the sport of bodybuilding was American. If someone told you that they were going to rule the bodybuilding contests but lived outside of America, you'd laugh at the thought. Dorian was British. He lived in a city called Birmingham, which most Americans had never heard of. The Mr. Olympia title had always been won by the Americans; America is where the champions trained or came from, and the rest were relegated to the "also ran" category.

But "The British Bulldog," as he came to be known, broke the myth, proving what one can achieve if he puts his mind to it. This giant became a pioneer, a leader, and the best bodybuilder in the world and achieved the coveted title of "one of the all-time greats." I knew Dorian was a martial arts and Bruce Lee fan. So that's one thing we had in common. He had trained in karate as a young teenager before making the conscious decision to pursue the iron-pumping sport.

I had always been curious as to which professional bodybuilders Bruce actually did meet and interact with in his lifetime. Bear in mind that Bruce wasn't globally famous yet in the 1960s. One iron-pumping legend he did meet was Bill Pearl, who gave him his training booklets. They met at Venice Beach. Bill was equally impressed with the martial arts master, and Bruce admired him. "He was very muscular, he was extremely agile and a tremendous athlete, and I admire him," Bill told me when I had an opportunity to interview him in 2009. I pressed Bill further after he answered a few more questions I chucked at him relating to Bruce. Sensing I was stuck in a time frame, he suddenly said in a somewhat sarcastic tone, "He was God!" Needless to say, the Bruce questions came to halt as I steered myself back to the bodybuilding questions.

In 2004 or 2005, I officially arranged to meet the six-time Mr. Olympia winner in Birmingham at his world-famous Temple Gym, which was located in the heart of the city center, to sit down with him and interview him. I found the place without much trouble, although it was tucked away in a backstreet alley. When I arrived at this obscure location, I found that you had to go down the stairs into a basement cellar. It was far from a visually pleasing, modernized, well-equipped gym that people frequent. Instead, it looked more like a dark dungeon. As a matter of fact, it was nicknamed "The Dungeon." A year or so later when I was at IFBB star Shawn Ray's house in California to interview him, I asked him if he had been to Dorian's gym. "Is that what you call a gym?" he mocked. Dorian may have trained in a "shithole," as Shawn referred to it, but he proved you didn't need a fancy place and equipment to excel and become a champion. Sometimes training in such a gritty environment is actually beneficial. Training is rough, tough, and torturous, and the environment you train in should reflect this.

The reception area was actually in the gym training space—not partitioned. It wasn't the biggest gym. I waited for the man to arrive. Adorning the gritty walls, the personally signed photos of famous bodybuilders and fitness competitors captivated my attention, as did magazine covers adorned with Dorian's image. Dorian walked in some time later, holding a gym bag in one hand and shaking my hand with the other as we greeted each other. He was shorter than I thought he would be, but he was very wide. I could tell, despite being retired about nine years before, he still had good size on him. The beast looked every bit the bodybuilder I imagined he would. I asked him if I could have a peek at his physique. He rolled his top up so I could see his abs and part of his pecs. His physique had diminished quite considerably, he told me, but I told him he still looked good.

Dorian is a very humble person. He's more on the diffident side and reserved end of the spectrum. Some people, fueled by their own ignorance and stubborn machismo, may have had a totally different effect. But he was welcoming. What he achieved in his sport is matched by very few.

We sat down and talked. The conversation leaned toward bodybuilding, his love for the martial arts and Bruce Lee, and, of course, his involvement with a new sport that had changed people's perception of fighting—MMA. It was a great piece that showed martial arts had a crossover appeal. Being a fan of MMA, he trained in the sport for fitness purposes, he told me. He was making it clear to me that he was no expert. "I've always been interested in martial arts," Dorian explained. "I really couldn't pursue any other sport when I was bodybuilding because it's going to interfere in what I'm doing. If you want to be the best in any sport, you have to focus totally on that." He was cognizant that if you dedicated too much time to activities and training that are not the core part of your main sport, then this could hinder your growth and performance—getting sidetracked was inevitable. The interest in martial arts was always there for him; however, he had a choice to walk one path when he was a teenager. For him, bodybuilding was the road he took.

His involvement in MMA training further invoked my interest, so I probed him with relevant questions, curious what answers would be thrown back at me. He told me how he had met the UFC legend Ken Shamrock in California when he was out there in the mid-1990s. "I had a friend who was a bodybuilder," Dorian said. "I trained him. He did very well in competition, then went into the U.S. military, and he started doing MMA. He was training with Ken Shamrock at the Lion's Den. The UFC was starting in the mid-1990s. It just appealed to me." Ken had told Dorian that he had participated in some small bodybuilding shows when he was younger, but he couldn't handle the dieting side of it. Ken had a great physique for a fighter, a physique that resembled a bodybuilder's. Dorian appreciated the physical torture these MMA athletes went through to excel in a bloody and brutal endeavor that not even the most muscular men could handle. "The training and the dedication the guys put in, bodybuilding training is tough, and the diet and everything makes it even harder, but this is a totally different type of training, and I have a lot of respect for the guys because it's very tough," he admitted.

After we finished discussing Ken, I was curious to find out what his thoughts were on a skinny-looking fighter who had beaten the hell out of muscular and stronger giants. The man in question, of course, was Ken's nemesis and former three-time UFC champion, the one and only Royce Gracie. If I'm honest, I had no clue what answer I could expect from one of the best-built men the sport of bodybuilding had ever created. But I was dying to get this question out and adamant in getting an answer. Dorian said he was impressed by Royce very much. He said Royce showed that with technique, you can beat someone bigger. "Royce Gracie was one of the first guys in the original UFCs that I watched when I spent time in the States," Dorian said. "So I watched it when nobody over here really knew it. It was amazing to watch him beat guys double his size."

Talking of MMA fighters and bodybuilders, the biggest bodybuilder in the world, Rich Piana, once told a prankster who was trying to pick a fight with him on the street, "I'm not a fighter but someone who works out. A fighter is always going to be tougher than a bodybuilder." Piana, a gentle giant and a huge fan of the UFC and the slender-looking Royce Gracie, once told Royce, "I believe that the technique that you have, knowing the technique a certain way, I don't think it matters how strong I am, that if you have the right technique, then you're going to be able to get me in an arm-bar regardless." Royce explained that it was all about his opponent making a mistake, then he would capitalize on that. Furthermore, it's about using strategy in a fight, he explained to the humble bodybuilder.

Dorian's love for the martial arts has never faded. "I do martial arts no-holds-barred because I like a challenge," the six-time Mr. Olympia told me. "And I'm still doing the weights, but I've kind of changed that now from bodybuilding training to more functional stuff." Cardiovascular training was boring to Dorian, but he found MMA training interesting because you're learning something and at the same time pushing yourself and elevating your fitness levels. He advocated that training with weights was a great way to accelerate one's potential in whatever sport you participated in. If a fighter could put on 25 pounds of muscle, he would progress better and feel stronger, and in turn this would aid him in his martial arts discipline. He said he could take me and put on an extra 25 pounds or so and really enhance my martial arts progress.

"Now it's pretty much accepted that weight training can improve your performance in a whole variety of sports," the former Mr. Olympia winner continued. "I think people have seen what Evander Holyfield did, moving from cruiserweight to heavyweight, and he was trained by Lee Haney, who was Mr. Olympia. So the guy put on bodyweight in terms of muscle. He should have been much slower and less effective, but obviously he wasn't because he was knocking heavyweights out. Everybody is doing weights from tennis players, to distance runners, to athletes."

At the time, Dorian was working with some UFC fighters, advising them on the diet and weight training. Dorian was the first professional champion bodybuilder I interviewed, and I eventually filtered into contributing to fitness-related media not long after. I even ended up doing some business with Dorian for a while.

11

Hollywood, Here We Come!

Fellow magazine columnist, friend, and Bruce Lee historian Andy Staton and I would occasionally have long telephone conversations about Bruce Lee. One day when I called him, somehow the conversation leaned toward the documentary film he had worked on in 1993 aptly titled *Bruce Lee: Martial Arts Master*. Andy was the technical adviser and credited as an associate producer on the project, and in this call, I revealed to him that I'd like to produce another documentary on Bruce. To my great surprise, he said he wanted to as well. Now he had my undivided attention. Documentary production was foreign territory for me. I had no real idea of what exactly it entailed, but I was always keen to expand my skills and learn about an area that that would present potential opportunities for me to work on bigger projects.

Andy is one of those rare Bruce Lee authorities who never really put his financial interests on top of his list of priorities. If anything, he is more likely to ignore monetary considerations altogether, willing to get involved for purely promoting Bruce's legacy for the greater good. That's what I love about "Uncle" Andy, as I call him—he's doing it for the pure passion of it. For decades, this man has promoted the legend and his legacy. He's been there for years and is still going strong when most so-called authorities have lost interest. He ran a fan club, the Bruce and Brandon Lee Association, for more than 20 years before its membership waned to the point where he shut it down, and Bruce Lee fanatics apparently often inundated him with phone calls like he was a celebrity. If only we had more Andys in the world.

77

Andy has been a devoted follower of the renowned martial artist ever since he first encountered the majestic presence of the kung fu star in *Enter the Dragon*. I think, like myself, Andy had been possessed by the spirit of the Little Dragon. The cultish fandom surrounding the late master has never wholly diminished over the decades; it inspires an almost cult-like zeal among its most ardent fans. For a few years, my obsession led to an irrational fear that I would die at the age of 32—the age Bruce had died—and as soon as I hit 33, I was relieved. Nobody encouraged the same intensity of emotion as this charismatic fighter, whose action sequences rendered the sometimes-laughable dialogue in his Hong Kong–produced movies redundant. Andy, who felt the same way as I did, was the perfect collaborator, and now that we were both running on the same track, we agreed on potentially collaborating on a new film venture.

If there's one strength I have, it's my persistent approach. Once an idea makes its way into my head, no one's going to stop me from reaching my objective. It also doesn't require much for me to get motivated. I think I was born like this. I knew I was stepping into unusual territory with documentary production, but I wasn't afraid of challenging myself; creating challenges and embracing them is something that I've done all my life. If there were none coming my way, I'd create new ones and grab them with both hands. Now, with this new project to focus on, I felt the first twinges of the high I always got from stepping into the unknown.

Producing a documentary is much more complex than it appears to many outsiders. It means getting the right technical people involved and securing financial backing, requiring endless phone calls and patience. Most documentary producers come up with a proposal and approach TV channels in the vain hope of getting their project commissioned. That's the norm. But that route never appealed to me. I never even entertained the idea of pitching the idea in the faint hope of receiving financial backing. I was accustomed to being in control of everything I did, doing things my way, and I wasn't going to change for anyone. This was my "baby." I wanted to make this a reality and wasn't prepared to play the waiting game and hear from a TV channel only to be left disenchanted when the project stalled in someone's in-box. Ninety-seven percent of pitches are rejected, and that's an awful lot of disappointed people. I wasn't going to wait in line or invite defeat in the form of a potential rejection. I'd go it alone.

Besides, producing a documentary would put me on a whole new platform. Going back for a moment to Andy's film that he had been involved with, it was probably the best documentary film ever produced on Bruce Lee. I had been really impressed by it, and I thought it would be difficult to improve on as a straight documentary. For my newly conceived project, then, I envisioned a theme that would be slightly different. Author John Little's writings had inspired me ever since I picked up a copy of *Muscle & Fitness* magazine in 1993, in which there was a special pullout booklet written by Little that focused on Bruce's bodybuilding secrets. In the piece, he explained how bodybuilding luminaries, boxing champions, and athletes from different sports all admired Bruce Lee. The message the author was trying to convey was that Bruce was not merely the greatest martial artist of the century but also a king among athletes and an influential figure to the stars of the action movie genre and beyond. I was enamored by that concept. To me, this is what really set the martial arts exponent apart from his peers, and I wanted to explore the idea further.

So, this was my plan. In addition to presenting the life story of the legend, legendary figures from other sports, including MMA, and the action entertainment industry would pay homage to the King of Kung Fu. It would be a first, I thought. Although several well-known personalities had expressed their appreciation for the late martial artist openly, I had never really seen major sporting figures paying homage to the great man on camera. So, with this added element as a hook, I had a strong conviction that this film would do the great master justice and catapult his legacy to another level. I'd been inspired by his story, and now I had found an opportunity to inspire others in the same way. This was my opportunity to take up the mantle.

While I would usually be inclined to go solo, this was intended to be a joint venture with Andy. I was still planning to take control. However, if you know Andy, you'll know that he has a weakness, which is that, more often than not, it takes him umpteen years before he takes the first step on a project. Constantly pushing him to get things done can get taxing. Having said this, he did have another full-time job at an education institute that took up a lot of his time. Still, I knew I could not let the project drag on, especially when I was on a high and had such a strong concept, which I was concerned could be stolen. Having the idea transform itself into reality, I had to walk the path alone before it turned to dust. So, when he dallied on the project, Andy was out of the picture as fast as he had slipped into it.

Even when it's run on interviews, a project of this size requires a script. Why? Because using a script is a logical way to make a film. One of its chief aims is to communicate the concept of the film to everyone concerned and the way it will flow. I knew that if the story wasn't strong enough, then the project could be doomed before even setting sail.

So, scouting for someone to write the script was on the agenda, and I had just the right man for the job—or so I thought. The man I had in mind was one of Andy's former associates, a Bruce Lee historian. I was even willing to give this guy a further coproducer credit. I tried to get hold of him, but it backfired in a surreal way. This individual's partner ended up complaining to Andy about me, saying I was trying to get hold of her partner. I'm glad I never brought this guy on board; otherwise, the ship would have sunk before even setting sail. It would have led to total disaster. The Bruce Lee world was infested with egos, backbiting, and politics, something I was just starting to really understand.

Enter Hong Kong! At my wit's end, I called Bey Logan. He has been a big Bruce Lee appreciator for most of his life. He told me he'd do whatever he could to help. I also got *Impact* magazine Far Eastern editor Mike Leeder involved. I sat down and started to jot down notes, listing prominent personalities whom I hoped to interview. First, I dipped into my ever-expanding contact list with all the direct and agency contacts I'd acquired in America. It always pays to reach out and expand your circle. One lady who was a friend of a friend and is a close friend of Mike Tyson and Sugar Ray Leonard sorted out an interview for me with the latter. She also threw a few more A-list names into the mix, including Tyson, Jamie Foxx, and Snoop Dogg. Meanwhile, I found myself reaching out to some A-list celebrities across the Atlantic who had never been on camera praising the late martial arts master, which proved more difficult than I expected. I got in touch with Sylvester Stallone's public relations team, Rogers & Cowan, the heavyweight talent agency in Beverly Hills, only to be rejected. Muhammad Ali was also on my list. I had someone promise me they would arrange a chat but found out later there was no substance to it. Even the governor of California, Arnold Schwarzenegger, was approached via his representative, whom I contacted personally.

After doing some leg work, slotting in interviews with various people in Los Angeles for September 2006, we were ready to fly out to Hollywood. But a fresh knot of anxiety gripped me as I was hit by another major problem requiring my immediate attention. Even though I had a standard visa, I learned that a media visa was required for the kind of work I planned to do. Also, I had hired a cinematographer who would be flying out with us on our American adventure, but it was brought to our attention that his professional camera equipment would be liable for heavy tax and duty in America. I'm talking thousands of dollars. Running around like a headless chicken in the hope of solving this issue, I was hit by the realities of the intricacies involved in being a producer as further frustration set in.

First, applying for a media visa was imperative so that I wouldn't risk being immediately ejected from America before I could even get out of the airport. I wasted no time applying for one and went to the American embassy with the cinematographer accompanying me. After sitting around for most of the day bored senseless, he walked out with his stamped visa, but I was told my visa would come through the mail, pending further investigation. I waited, waited, and waited more but no visa. This was a problem. Flights had already been booked. Interviews were already arranged. We were ready to rock and roll. And now I couldn't get into the country.

Meanwhile, to get the ball rolling in the United Kingdom at least, I made a trip along with the cinematographer to Dorian Yates's gym in Birmingham to interview the bodybuilding star. Numerous IFBB champions are ardent admirers of the late master, who cultivated a phenomenal physique despite never entering a physique competition in his life. After the interview, I offered an advance payment in the form of a check to the cinematographer. After he left, he phoned me to ask if it was okay to pay him in cash instead. I had no problem doing that, I told him. I told him to rip up the check, and I sent him cash via registered mail the next day. Big mistake!

Perhaps predictably, this guy went astray and ran off with the money. From that point, he would not answer the phone or his e-mails. He had signed a contract, but now he was breaking this legally binding contract. After I inundated him with text messages, the next thing I knew was that I got a call from the police. The officer said that this man claimed I had been threatening him. I couldn't deny this because the officer had apparently seen the messages on the culprit's phone. Since the police were now involved, I decided to leave the matter there and walk away. This guy was a wolf in sheep's clothing—he was a professional cinematographer and had a good résumé, but he thought he could default on the contract and make a dash with the cash, leaving me in dire straits. His excuse was he'd spent a hefty chunk of time on research and making calls and had already earned his cash. I thought, £1,500 advance for all that? I had figured there was something fishy about this guy from the start. When I meet someone or deal with someone, sometimes I get a feeling about them, and I should trust my intuition. This time I learned the hard way and paid a hefty price for it. It was an expensive lesson.

Fortunately, there was another lesson I had learned much earlier in my career: always have a plan B in the bag; otherwise, you're in trouble. If you're a fighter, invariably there's a plan B strategy if plan A goes down the drain, and it's no different with business. So, for me, it was time to find a camera crew in Los Angeles. I was back to square one, and it was driving me crazy. After checking out professional cinematographers, eventually I found a guy I thought I could trust. We agreed on the price for his services and stipulated the terms so there would be no misunderstanding or loopholes. I was ready to go, as I no longer required a media visa because no camera equipment would be going with me. *I wasn't going to take my chances and be burned again*, I thought. How wrong I was. Three crew members and I jetted off to Los Angeles on a roller-coaster journey that would end in despair.

かー

By this point, I had been to Hollywood many times, so I was quite familiar with the place. We stayed there for two weeks in an apartment block on Sunset Boulevard in the heart of Tinseltown.

Problems started early. Both Robert Lee, Bruce Lee's brother, and Bruce's protégé, Dan Inosanto, were scheduled to be interviewed at the Inosanto Academy. But for some unforeseeable circumstances, including third-party tampering, this didn't materialize. Still, it wasn't all doom and gloom. I had managed to secure an interview with basketball legend Kareem Abdul-Jabbar, who also appeared in Bruce's half-finished martial arts epic *Game of Death*. This wasn't usually easy. Kareem is one of the greatest NBA players in history—some believe the greatest basketball player of all time—and was also NBA's all-time leading scorer, but he didn't give many interviews. Excited, our team drove down to a Long Beach studio that had professional lighting and backdrops and waited for Kareem to arrive. His manager, Debra, worked out of an office there, but after so many setbacks, I started to be convinced that he had second thoughts about doing the interview. A sense of panic started to set in as I sat there with all kinds of emotions running through me, even as one of my crew guys consoled me, assuring me that Kareem would turn up. His words calmed me, and I tried extremely hard to convince myself, even though in the back of my mind, the ever-present "enemy" kept telling me to prepare for the worst. I already had to contend with a plethora of problems and had no desire to add another one to the ever-growing list.

After a long wait, Debra walked over with a *Game of Death* laminated poster personally signed by the man himself. "This is for you. Kareem apologizes for coming late," she said apologetically. It wasn't long before a serious-looking seven-foot, three-inch giant in dark blue jeans and a light blue shirt sauntered toward us. We greeted each other and shook hands, then sat down, and I proceeded with the interview. Interviewing Kareem Abdul-Jabbar is one of the highlights of my career—an experience I'd never forget. I had always seen him as the man who was Bruce Lee's celebrity friend and costar rather than a basketball player. Their shared screen time in the movie's climatic fight resulted in one of the greatest fight scenes ever to be captured on camera, a little man against a giant. But Kareem is more than that and much more than any of his other minor roles. Kareem is one of America's sporting legends and was a fascinating interview subject.

To my great surprise, he revealed that Bruce had a copy of the Koran in his personal home library. Although I was cognizant that Bruce had amassed an extensive library, I was oblivious to the fact that he had a copy of this holy book. "I gave Bruce books to read on Islam, and Bruce knew Chinese Muslims," Kareem told me. "They have a lot of Wushu techniques that are unique to them and from the martial arts in Indonesia and Malaysia. He was aware of Islam, and he investigated different techniques from the Islamic part of China."

For Kareem's part, this African American athlete had converted to Islam in 1971 at the age of 24, just like his famous friend Muhammad Ali had seven years earlier. Kareem had been introduced to Islam in the 1960s when he was still a freshman at UCLA, by which time the basketball legend had already achieved a certain degree of national exposure and fame as an athlete. By the time I interviewed him, despite his elevated profile, he endeavored to keep his private life private. Apparently, his celebrity made him disconcerted and nervous, and this gentle giant felt timid in the public eye. During the course of his illustrious career, he developed a reputation of being introverted and sullen, and despite becoming the NBA's all-time leading scorer, he chose to shut out the world, including the fans, and focus on the game and sport he loved. He mostly refrained from speaking to the press, and I later learned that he froze out reporters who gave him a too enthusiastic handshake or even physically embraced him. Moreover, during many interviews, he refused to stop reading the newspaper, according to a source. I was oblivious to much of this when our interview started, but it wasn't long before I couldn't ignore my interviewee's unique worldview.

The Long Beach airport is under one of the strictest ordinances in America regarding noise and numbers of flights. Commercial flights are restricted, but there are many charters, private aviation flight schools, and law and enforcement flights and helicopters operating from it, making it one of the busiest airports in the world. So, we regularly got planes flying over the building, which means the noise of the aircraft would inevitably intrude into the interview, and every time we heard a plane, we had to stop the interview for a short period. This episode repeated itself several times, and my interviewee would give us an upsetting frown each time. It was embarrassing for me, and I was beginning to feel a little uneasy.

As the interview resumed after one of these stoppages, I brought up the subject of modern-day icons like Arnold Schwarzenegger and Sylvester Stallone and asked Kareem if we will ever see another Bruce Lee. "I don't think Arnold Schwarzenegger and Sylvester Stallone really distinguished themselves in the same way as Bruce; they've only distinguished themselves as actors," he replied. "Arnold was a bodybuilder, and he said he did it using steroids, and it's a thing which really doesn't get that much respect."

Another interesting fact that I learned conversing with Kareem is that he really looked up to the Gracies. "I think Bruce and the senior Mr. Gracie [Helio Gracie] in Brazil were way ahead of everybody in understanding that the martial arts have to be pragmatic and useful; you just can't stick to one style above everything else," he said. He went on to say that Bruce and Royce were unique and way ahead of their time and did it by forming their arts around the concept of MMA. "Bruce was very pragmatic. It's funny that Bruce was more of a boxer or striker and Gracie was a grappler—you have to combine those two things to be a successful martial artist today," Kareem said. The basketball star had been exposed to the martial arts way back in the 1960s and became a private student of Bruce. When the Gracies were making a name for themselves in the 1980s teaching out of their garage, they attracted the attention of quite a few professional sportsmen, which included NFL and NBA stars, and so Kareem kept a close eye on their activities, I assume.

Interviewing Kareem Abdul-Jabbar was an interesting experience. I learned a lot. As we wrapped up the interview, the manager asked her client if he could stay behind and sign some of the photos and memorabilia that fans had sent in. By this point, his manager knew that he would likely get stuck in traffic, as it was the peak of rush hour, which is horrendous in Los Angeles. Suddenly, that frown on his face was back. I was there watching the manager literally shaking in her boots like she was asking her dad if she could stay out late but couldn't spit the words out of her mouth. She was a nice, professional woman—she even told me that if I wanted a distribution deal in Japan for my documentary, she had contacts there and she'd help—but Kareem inspired respect in everyone. Years later, I came to learn that the basketball legend just has a, let's say, different type of personality—diffident and reticent—compared to most famous figures. One *New York Times* writer, Jay Caspian Kang, in a 2015 feature, labeled him "the least understood basketball player of all time."

−

I couldn't wait to tell my friend Diana Lee Inosanto that I had interviewed Bruce's one-time collaborator. I went to her house, and when I told her, she said it had been so long since she'd seen him, back in the days when he was training with her Uncle Bruce and her dad, and she said she had decided she was going to reconnect with the former Milwaukee Bucks and Los Angeles Lakers star.

As always, it was good to see Diana. I would endeavor to make time for her and her husband Ron whenever I visited Los Angeles and we would go to dinner. I had been to their previous residence, but they were now living in another part of Los Angeles, Thousand Oaks. They have a nice home but recently moved again.

Speaking of the house, one experience that I will cherish forever is the memory of when Ron slid in a *Game of Death* DVD, the scene where Bruce is fighting Diana's dad, Dan Inosanto, which, of course, turns out to be an epic battle. Alongside the Bruce–Kareem fight, this is one of the classic fight scenes in cinematic history, climaxing in a nunchaku-versus-nunchaku battle between two of the greatest martial artists on Earth. Suddenly, I had goose bumps sitting there—it was pure exhilaration to watch this scene alongside the daughter of the man appearing in it. Dan was somewhat responsible for teaching Bruce some nunchaku techniques (although Fumio Demura, who was the stunt double for Mr. Miyagi in *The Karate Kid* and whom I once interviewed, also shared his skills with Bruce), and here I was at my friend's house watching her dad fighting Bruce Lee on the screen. It's something that you never really think about happening when you're younger. I could see that Diana was somewhat emotional watching the action unfold, and she eventually went into the other room choked up with emotion. I could see how much she missed Uncle Bruce.

While there, we had to discuss a film project she was working on. Diana had made a transition into directing and producing, influenced by directors like Guy Ritchie and Ang Lee. She had already written, directed, coproduced, and costarred in a new martial arts drama movie, so I was at the house to discuss both my documentary and her film, an indie film. Being her directorial debut, it was a very important project for her. Diana's friend Louis Mandylor, known for *My Big Fat Greek Wedding* and the TV show *Martial Law*, and Keith David, who played the father in *There's Something about Mary*, also starred in the film. Although it was an action film, it also was a thought-provoking drama, and despite the fact that the film was a low-budget deal, Diana was really passionate about doing this movie.

At the time, they were scouting for investors to come aboard. Diana had clearly put all her effort and every ounce of her being into this project, as did Ron, who had lost weight with all the accumulated stress of making calls trying to get potential investors onboard. We talked about potential investors as we sat at the house. One or two people came to my mind, and I later asked a millionaire whom I had met and who was a big fan of Bruce Lee, martial arts, and MMA, but he flatly declined. As we talked, I started to think about my own aspirations toward making more documentary films, and later, it dawned on me that I could possibly pursue further projects of this nature, perhaps by making documentaries about MMA.

Not everything, however, was going according to plan. To my regret, I had introduced Diana to someone I had known for merely a year. This guy, who was present at the meeting along with several others, said that he wanted to invest, but he was simply tantalizing us with his bullshit. He also clandestinely persuaded me to get him and a couple of others involved in my own documentary project, and this was one of the biggest mistakes I made in my life. The guy turned out to be a user—all talk, a Walter Mitty–type character that dripped with deceit. I had been naive to fall for this person's talk, and I felt used when the truth emerged. I even gave him some of my contacts, which I usually clung onto for dear life.

I felt betrayed, embarrassed, and conned. I had been played. I had been had. This guy was interested in rubbing shoulders with prominent personalities whom I was connected with and was a compulsive liar. He had the ability to get you under his spell and then leave you to fall flat on your ass. After this mishap, I made a pledge to myself that

I'd keep my guard up and never fall victim to such a huckster again or expose anyone else to one. I felt protective of Diana and my other friends and a little dispirited. But you have to pick yourself up, dust yourself off, and learn from your mistakes and forge on.

So, undeterred, I continued with filming further interviews. Among the interviews in the can included Lenda Murray, the greatest female bodybuilder of all time, whom I interviewed at the world-famous Gold's Gym in Venice Beach. I also talked with another IFBB star, Shawn Ray, who was the epitome of a bodybuilding star—the cool, young, professional bodybuilder with shades and a Ferrari sports car to go with it—at his home, and Franco Columbu, Arnold Schwarzenegger's best friend and an amazing bodybuilder in his own right. I also managed to interview Royce and Rorion Gracie and several original students and friends of Bruce. The footage was in the can. But there was a lot of work left to do. And I wasn't going to rest until I pulled it off.

12

Home Sweet Home

After two weeks in Hollywood, I arrived back home in the United Kingdom with a bump. To be completely honest, for the next three weeks, I couldn't get out of bed. I plunged into depression, feeling completely despondent as my life hit rock bottom. The hurdles and obstacles I'd already encountered, the charlatans I'd dealt with, and the politics affecting the project had drained my energy until my morale was at an all-time low.

Adding to the complications was my cell phone bill. Being the often careless person that I am when it comes to making international calls, I continued to use my cell phone in America, and to my horror, I was hit with a bill of almost £2,500 when I returned. I couldn't believe it. All I had to do was change the sim card—but, no, not me. I had to learn the hard way. Again, there's a lesson from martial arts: sometimes a single, simple mistake can cost you an arm and a leg. Always keep your guard up.

Still, I was determined to push on. Documentaries on famous figures are something that I've always enjoyed watching. I think it's a wonderful medium to showcase someone's life. And so I felt I had to put my heart and soul into this project. I was on the brink of reaching new heights in my career. I really believed this film was going to elevate my career to a new level. Another lesson from martial arts: sometimes, it's when you're just about to find success that things feel hardest.

So, without any further delays, I jumped back on the project with new vigor, calling up more fighting champions and forging ahead.

The next stop was Ricky Hatton's gym in Hyde, Manchester. The pride of Britain, Ricky was one of the many famous world boxing champions who had been inspired by Bruce Lee. I had interviewed him once before. Considering Ricky was a big name and resonated with the American public as well as the British, I felt he would be a great addition to the film. What I never set out to do with the documentary was to throw in random interviews just because a face was instantly familiar with the public. I had set myself stringent criteria and vowed to conform to them.

I was heavily invested in this project financially but also emotionally. Andy Staton had let slip how *Bruce Lee: Martial Arts Master* had done financially around the world. I can't be specific, but we're talking several millions of pounds, including TV rights and DVD sales worldwide. As I worked on the project, I realized that this could be the big one but also my biggest reward as far as the monetary side is concerned. What other opportunity in my life could potentially make me millions of pounds? I never played the lottery, and I wasn't going to find a briefcase in the bushes with that sort of money inside, even if I daydreamed about that scenario sometimes. I have always put my passion at the forefront of any project, with financial gain following, but now I was balancing these two out in my head like a seesaw. Andy said he'd be happy with a million, not that his primary intention was to benefit financially. Hey, if I could make several million, then Andy was welcome to his 1 million. When he told me he had received £54.75 for his services for the documentary he had worked on, I was shocked and almost fell over laughing out loud. But he explained to me that he wasn't on the payroll and that amount was part of the expenses he was reimbursed for.

The company that had produced *Bruce Lee: Martial Arts Master* had sold the Southeast Asian rights to Golden Harvest, a company that had produced Bruce's movies in the 1970s. Andy told me he had to resort to unorthodox tactics, including getting an executive at Golden Harvest drunk to seal the deal. Since Golden Harvest owned the film footage I needed, I would need to come to an arrangement with them to avoid inflating budget costs. Obtaining film footage would be costly, eating into a large chunk of my budget, and so I was prepared to sign over Southeast Asian rights to save me a huge licensing bill. Eventually, I made contact with Golden Harvest and did everything I could to make the deal happen. After the initial communication, though, things took a turn for the worse. I wasn't receiving any replies. I thought there could be political reasons why the company wouldn't respond, but it didn't matter. I simply couldn't force them to respond. I called back as often as I could, but in the end, things just didn't pan out. I was pouring my own money into this grand project without any financial backing. With the film going nowhere, the project had to be shelved.

What happened? I think it must have been politics. At the time, I was suspicious—back then, being paranoid was one of my worst weaknesses—and eventually, I was at least partly vindicated. Three years later, I came across a production company that was, in conjunction with a production company owned by Bruce Lee's daughter, Shannon Lee, producing a documentary with a core theme similar to what I had conceived. To this day, I often wonder if my idea was borrowed and leaked out by someone I spoke to. I have my suspicions, but I will never really know unless the producers one day make a surprise revelation to me. I guess I'll have to live with it.

After learning about the Shannon Lee project, I proceeded to call the company in charge and speak to the managing director, hoping to console myself with the fact I could at least make a contribution. I wasted no time in revealing to the producer that I had some great interview footage and was prepared to hand it over on a platter. The producer was excited and said he'd be sharing the good news with Shannon, especially after I dropped the names of some elite athletes and A-listers into the mix. The producer also contemplated interviewing me for the film.

After that, I was fully on board with Waddell Media and supplied some great footage for their project. When I watched the completed *How Bruce Lee Changed the World*, I was ambivalent toward it. I had had my own vision all mapped out to perfection and wanted to contribute to the lore of Bruce Lee in my own way. But I was happy to have contributed to the official documentary.

∽

I had learned another lesson. You can give something your all, whether it's a sport, a martial art, or a project dear to your heart, and still find yourself prone to politics stopping you in your tracks. I was a little disheartened but determined to learn from the master how to do better. And so, many years later when I finally interviewed Shannon myself, I asked her about the hurdles her father encountered, including racism, and how he ultimately defied the odds to prevail. "Well, racism is an obstacle that continues even to this day . . . there's still a long way to go. I mean, Hollywood in general has not embraced diversity very strongly. There are lot of conversations being had, but here we are 47 years later, and not much has changed. When he first came to the United States and watched movies like *Breakfast at Tiffany's*, he was very dismayed by the portrayal of the Asian characters in Hollywood. A lot of the times they were portrayed by Caucasian actors. And when there were Asian actors portraying them, a lot of the times it was as a caricature—either a villain or servants. He just didn't see himself like that and how he felt he was represented in Hollywood. He wanted to edify the public. He felt these weren't authentic portrayals, so he made it a mission of his to have a reflection of at least who he was—an authentic Asian male—in Hollywood. He worked hard at that. Of course, that would require teaching somebody something that wasn't going to be embraced easily by others."

I also asked her opinion of Quentin Tarantino's derogatory depiction of her father in *Once upon a Time in Hollywood*. "Quite frankly, you know, my position nowadays with certain things is that I'm happy to have a conversation with Quentin Tarantino anytime if he would like to have one," she said. "I really don't feel the need to scold him or set him straight or any of that kind of stuff. First of all, what's done is done. Second of all, he had his reasons for doing it. I don't know what they are. I don't know why he felt the need to go the direction he did." She further added that, quite frankly, it doesn't matter, and she feels very confident in who her father is and who he was and is cognizant he wasn't a perfect human being.

"It's unfortunate that Tarantino wanted to take a chip out of my father's legacy, but I really see no reason to convince him of anything if he feels he needs to be convinced," she said. "It's not my job to convince people that Bruce Lee is awesome. My job is just to present a man, his message is his words of who he was, and let people make up their own mind. So, it's not one of these things, *If I were to get into a room with Quentin Tarantino, I'd set him straight!* If I were to get into a room with Quentin Tarantino for any reason, if that ever happens, I would just have a conversation you usually have. I'm not here to scold him. If he had asked my opinion before he made the movie, then I certainly would've shared it, but he didn't. If I could ask him a question, the question would be, 'Why?' Why did he choose to do what he did? I wouldn't say, 'How dare you!' or 'You need to be taught a lesson.' I think there's too much of that in society right now. If he would have shared with me the reasons why, that would have been great, but I imagine he has zero desire to speak to me."

‿

Although I found this inspiring to hear all those years later, at the time, my failure with the documentary had a very unhealthy impact on me mentally. I had become so emotionally attached to the original project that losing it caused me what felt like actual pain. But life goes on, and you've got to take it on the chin and forge on. It took me several years to come to terms with the project's failure, but I resolved to push ahead.

Still, life wasn't getting any easier. I was plagued with further problems at this most inopportune time. Adding to my misery, the cinematographer in America decided to give me problems. This guy had uploaded a couple of the interviews on YouTube, and when I came across them, I was absolutely furious. Despite my phoning and messaging him, demanding he take the footage down immediately, he ignored me.

My concern, of course, was that having these fabulous interviews on YouTube would undermine them and make them less valuable. The rights were owned by me, and I wasn't going to let anyone steal my material and dilute it—it had been exclusively produced for a single purpose. After countless messages and repeated calls (which weren't too nice, I must admit), I decided firmly on a course of action. It was time to contact Sugar Ray Leonard's public relations agent and Kareem Abdul-Jabbar's manager to inform them of what was happening. After threats of legal action against him, including getting the sport stars' managements involved, he finally threw in the towel. But it was a battle I shouldn't have had to fight.

I think the power of YouTube has changed how we perceive the world. Today, many people, including myself, often don't bother watching or renting a DVD since we can just watch clips and scenes on YouTube for free. How many times have you watched Bruce Lee fights or a UFC fight on the YouTube platform instead of sticking the whole film or event into a DVD player? It's much easier to bypass the storyline and get right into the action. Beyond a shadow of a doubt, modern-day technology has really changed how we can view media, but that isn't always positive.

One thing I learned while working on the documentary, as well as during the rest of my life, is that if you try to help certain people or get them involved in your pursuits, it will backfire. They will take advantage. It's happened to me not once but several times, and I will never walk that path again.

Nevertheless, it was time to move on. God had granted me with good health, and I was continuing with what I loved the most—working in combat sports with some fabulous personalities.

13

The Sport of MMA Hits the Mainstream

The UFC and the sport of MMA were on the verge of mushrooming into the mainstream when the first *The Ultimate Fighter* series drew millions of viewers in January 2005. Produced by Fox Sports and the UFC, the series played a pivotal role in exposing the UFC to a much wider audience and educating them. Its broadcast on Spike TV was constantly ranking number one. At last, martial arts were on the brink of commanding a reverence and a wider exposure than some of the other sports had enjoyed for decades. Now that the sport was attracting the attention of fans across the board, in spite of the fact that the media had publicized it as "human cockfighting," it couldn't be ignored any longer. Indeed, the surge in popularity can no doubt be attributed to the power of mainstream media after much adversity in the past. Finally, the press had to accept the increasingly shuddering impact of UFC as a spectacle and a sport. So, I knew a burst of interest and support for MMA was now prevalent. Arenas were selling out UFC shows, and UFC fighters were now stars in their own right and taken seriously.

I would often hear MMA being referred to as "the world's fastest growing sport." And, boy, it felt good to hear that over and over again. One night, I remember sitting in a friend's house and watching UFC on TV. I quickly learned that friends who were casual enthusiasts were now familiar with the fighters' names. They had grown up watching boxing but now enjoyed and gravitated toward UFC more than the sweet science. Inside, I felt a sense of joy that the UFC was being embraced not only by the martial arts fraternity but also beyond the confines of the martial arts public. Indeed, it was making its way into the consciousness of people who otherwise wouldn't have tuned in.

Back in the day, martial arts champions were famous within their own world, but with the UFC breaking barriers, this gave the arts and its combatants the exposure they had longed for since the kung fu boom of the 1970s. Suddenly, there was a kung fu craze in the West, which would fade as the decade came to an end.

The UFC was making waves in North America for sure. UFC coverage in America was way ahead in contrast to anywhere else. In America, the sport had exploded and really filtered into the consciousness of the public. UFC stars were now bona fide celebrities in North America. Major TV network deals were being inked. Pay-per-view records were being broken. By now, the UFC in North America was being broadcast on major channels and making stars out of Chuck Liddell, Randy Couture, GSP, and others. The marketing became a well-oiled machine, and the UFC publicity department ensured their fighters were seen. There were MMA TV chat shows, and fighters were going on talk shows. *The Tonight Show with Jay Leno* had fighters on promoting themselves and the UFC. If you got on *The Tonight Show* or *The Late Show with David Letterman*, you knew you had "arrived."

Anderson Silva once said to me, "Obviously MMA in the USA is more in the media spotlight right now, and even though we've been doing it for a long time in Brazil, where it's got its heritage and is a traditional sport, it's not so much in the headlines compared to America." He further added, "It can get even bigger, and that's what they're working hard at, and there are chances it will."

Yet there were still hurdles to overcome. Once, UFC welterweight champion Matt Serra was promoting the UFC with Dana White on Fox TV when one presenter began debating with him, arguing MMA is not good for kids. I asked Matt, "What are your views on this rather controversial subject?" He said, "Do I think little kids should fight in a cage? No! Do I think they should be studying martial arts or mixed martial arts? Yes!" He further added that it taught the kids self-defense. Matt said he disagreed with the now-defunct promoter Elite XC, which was trying to make a spectacle of the street fighter Kimbo Slice. He made it clear that he wasn't knocking him and understood that the bare-knuckle fighter wants to make money, and that was fine. But the promoters that were hyping up this internet sensation were what he had an objection to. "Now, as a result, you are going to get a bunch of moron kids with camcorders trying to be in the UFC by fighting each other in the backyard, that's not the proper way to do it," he said. "Anybody can fight anybody in the street; you should come up the right way, get involved in the sport, get involved in wrestling, jiu-jitsu, boxing, Thai boxing—get involved in those kind of matches." This is the approach the UFC fighter was advocating, a medium that allows you to hone your skills, and you will be ready to fight competitors and, in his own words, "not on the street looking to make a name that way." He added that when no-holds-barred first emerged, it wasn't a sport but rather "a freak show." Now the UFC was doing the right thing, and it was legal.

When stars from showbiz start turning up ringside, you know you've made it. I recall former UFC heavyweight champion Tim Sylvia, who had made his UFC debut at UFC 39, proudly saying to me, "If you look at all these celebrities and pro athletes, such as NFL football players, soccer players, they're all coming to watch us. They know we are the next generation and the next big thing." Tim was right. Press conferences were very professional, like boxing conferences. In some cases, weigh-ins would attract several thousand fans. It was crazy. The phenomenon had gripped the nation.

⌒

Clearly, MMA was being embraced by the wider press in North America, but what was happening across the pond? The UFC had produced champions in America, but Britain had now produced a bona fide star. The first time I saw and heard of Mike Bisping was when he fought in the UFC in April 2007 at the M.E.N Arena at UFC 70. A friend pointed out "The Count" to me, telling me this was the fighter who came to prominence in the reality TV show *The Ultimate Fighter: Season 3* earlier same year. Prior to his fame from the show, the British fighter had held a national kickboxing title and won virtually all his MMA fights. He had won any belt on offer domestically. Eventually, he contemplated fighting overseas for larger promotions, and he pursued the UFC. Later, when I first interviewed Mike, he told me that the UFC had had their eyes on him and told him that they would offer him a fight in the UFC. "But they said I'd be great for *The Ultimate Fighter*," he told me. "In the meantime, I spoke to the executives at Spike TV who were creating the show. I was pretty much chosen before I went to the auditions." Mike snagged a decent contract with the promotion. After his triumph in the Octagon in the TV show, he collapsed on the floor, and the ring doctor rushed to his rescue. Mike assured him that he was fine and that there was nothing wrong with him. "I'm just lying on the floor, it's a sheer relief," he told the concerned doctor.

When he made his U.K. debut for the promotion, no matter how much the MMA experts endeavored to educate the public, there were always the naysayers sticking out like sore thumbs. During the same interview I conducted with Mike, I asked him how he perceived his relationship with the mainstream media. "On the whole, now compared to a couple of years, the media have taken more interest in covering the sport, and more people are interested in the sport," he responded. "They ask intelligent questions about the sport, as opposed to the start, when they asked stupid questions like, 'Is it dangerous?' or 'Has anyone died yet?' Now the reporters know what they're talking about." There were the exceptions, though, who were still not convinced.

Leading up to the UFC 70, Mike had a radio interview with BBC Manchester. A lady broadcaster who sometimes presented the weather was going to be grilling the so-called barbarian. Mike arrived at the studio oblivious to what trap lay ahead. He sat there calmly as she talked on air to her audience. She introduced the UFC fighter. "Up next, if you've seen the film *Fight Club*, our next guest is Michael Bisping." Mike related this story to me, which didn't surprise me. "So then she turns to me and she says, 'Right, Michael, so you fight in the UFC?' And I said, 'Yes.' She says, 'Look at the size of you, how big are you? You must be at least 18 stones.'" Mike told me he was around 14 stones and that he isn't a small guy but not overly big, either. So, she got his weight wrong for starters. He continued, "And she says, 'You're 18 stones and covered in scars.' I said, 'I'm not covered in scars. I've got a few scars on my head. I banged my head as a kid, but I'm not covered in scars.'"

The conversation leaned toward all things controversial in what seemed like a partial debate as the BBC host continued her assault on the fighter. The constant onslaught of negativity poured out of the host's mouth. Mike continued, "She says, 'This sport is for barbarians, isn't it?' I said, 'No, it's not for thugs.' She says, 'It's barbarians!' I said, 'It's not a sport for barbarians.' She says, 'Well, you look like a barbarian.'" Mike had heard enough by now and counterattacked with his own verbal artillery, which he had so far held back. But it was time to bring out the canons now. "I said, 'Really?'" he continued. "'I'll keep my thoughts on what you look like to myself, shall I?'" She looked like mutton dressed as a lamb, Mike told me. "Then she started criticizing the sport, saying people can die." The UFC fighter asked the host if she had ever watched the sport. She hadn't, she conceded. He asked her how the hell she could sit there passing judgment and talking about the sport when she'd never seen it and what she was basing her facts on. "We got into an argument on air. Basically, she didn't have a leg to stand on. She wrapped the interview and ushered me out."

After the scathing response from the presenter, the UFC poster boy had to focus on his bout. He went on to dominate his Australian opponent, Elvis Sinosic, that day. Mike's combination strikes in the second round really offset Sinosic. I could see his opponent dripping with blood, which was visible all the way up to the upper-tier seats. The ferocity of the fight was just hard core, and brutality was being demonstrated at its best. Mike, without a doubt, dominated the fight in true fashion. He looked dangerous and like an aggressive fighter with a heart. I remember thinking just how tough the sport is and the dangerous position these warriors put themselves in. When it comes to watching fights at an arena, I'm the type who watches quietly observing when most people are raving and ranting and some overzealous fans acting like hooligans.

Something that really stood out that day was the reaction of the packed crowd of more than 15,000 screaming fans. Undeniably, this fighter had huge support and love from the fans. Marking his first UFC bout in his home country, this was a pivotal moment. The crowd had embraced him like he was an Olympic athlete representing their country. The vibe I got was that Mike was fighting not only for his own glory and survival but also for the whole nation. The crowd would erupt every time the British poster boy, the hometown favorite, landed a strike or took his opponent down as he proceeded to brutally punish his foe. The atmosphere became increasingly raucous and raw in the packed arena. At the same time, I realized he was humble whenever he was interviewed. He always thanked his fans for their support. I felt he believed he had a moral duty to express this. I can sense that his feelings were genuine and that he wasn't merely putting up a fake front.

Among the UFC stars fighting on this card were Andrei Arlovski, Mirko Filipovick, and Lyoto Machida. Among the personalities in attendance at ringside were Randy Couture, Dana White, and Hollywood action star Jean-Claude Van Damme. I looked down where Van Damme sat ringside. His shocked reaction was priceless as "his" fighter Mirko Filipovick got knocked out with a kick to the head by the Brazilian Gabriel Gonzaga. Van Damme had both his hands on his head in disbelief, as if he had just lost all his fortune or something in the biggest gambling deal of his life. He seemed to me to be in a world of his own. At one point, it looked like he wanted to say a few words in front of the camera, but no media went up to him.

According to a source, the UFC had shelled out a collective $843,000 to its warriors—Mike received only $24,000. He was a new and rising star. The lowest earning for a fighter was $3,000, the highest $350,000. Mirko was the highest-paid fighter that day. To give you an idea of how Mike's earnings changed just under nine years later when he fought Anderson Silva in February 2016 at UFC Fight Night 84, attendances were still strong, with more than 16,000 at the O2, and reportedly he banked almost half a million dollars. This was broken down as follows: sponsor Reebok paid him $20,000, and the UFC paid him $275,000 to show, $150,000 to win, and a $50,000 Fight of the Night bonus. So nine years later, he was making 20 times more money—not bad for a small-town boy who had slaved away in numerous labor jobs that he utterly abhorred.

This event was broadcast live on pay-per-view on Setanta Sports and televised in America on Spike TV, which reportedly drew 3.5 million viewers for the main event. According to a source, the UFC organization was targeting this event for its debut on America's giant HBO. Dana White, who has done a tremendous job in really pushing the sport forward, has a drive and passion and is committed to breaking records and boundaries. This visionary man's desire to constantly expand and dream to make UFC massive has no doubt been realized. Unquestionably, he has worked tirelessly to bring the sport, what critics had long derided as human cockfighting, into the mainstream.

With the UFC landing on British shores, subsequently the media were making strides, too, as it was a propitious moment to jump on board. Those members of the media with open minds were now persuaded into recognizing the more positive sides of the sport. Suddenly, magazines and websites that were exclusive to the sport started to spring up out of nowhere with overnight "experts." The MMA industry just took another turn. More and more major magazines—*FHM*, *Men's Fitness*, and *Men's Health*—featured articles and interviews with the star athletes. Eventually, stars graced the covers of *Sports Illustrated*. I had managed to get my foot in, too. In addition to my regular slot in the combat sports press, I started liaising with newspapers and major periodicals, even if it was as a source in the beginning.

Still, to my disappointment, the major TV channels in the United Kingdom refused to embrace the UFC, and the major newspapers, although most were on board, refrained from giving the sport much attention when it came to print press coverage. In the beginning, it was an arduous task for the MMA promoters to persuade the higher-echelon sportswriters to come on board. Relegating it to online coverage seemed to make these editors content. Some major papers were still reluctant to publicize a sport of brutality that raised the ire of many. The press knew they would be inundated with complaints from the "civilized" public, who thought there was no room for promoting extreme and brutal violence. Oh, boy, the public was in need of edification. Kids have often had role models who were bad guys, in particular, gangster rappers, and for years were told you had to be bad to get ahead. I think the UFC showed you can be a good guy and tough and learn discipline. Having said this, unfortunately, now it's pretty much every other fighter who seems to portray the bad-boy image in the prefight hype, something that I'm no fan of.

As I started connecting with newspaper sportswriters, I realized they had the power and the capacity to publicize anything. One of the first to jump on the bandwagon and galvanize support for the UFC was the *Daily Telegraph*. Gareth Davies, boxing writer and sportswriter, is a big sports fan himself and started his own MMA blog. He was one of the sports journalists from tabloids and broadsheets who had developed a hard-core interest in the bone-crushing sport of MMA. His enthusiasm radiated as he eagerly set out on a mission to help break misconceptions despite the fact he needed to increase his knowledge of the sport.

Kevin Francis was the sports and boxing correspondent for the *Daily Star*. This tabloid was now offering coverage to the UFC, and Kevin became the correspondent. A nice, older gentleman, he reminded me of Paul Heller, the producer of *Enter the Dragon*. The *Daily Star*'s readership was 18- to 35-year-olds, the perfect market for the UFC.

Another prominent sportswriter at the time, Mark Gilbert, at the *Sun* was instrumental in positive coverage. It wasn't long before the *Sun* also became known for its UFC coverage, which I must state was relegated to its website. They, too, refused to cover the sport in the print version of the paper in the early years. The reason for this was obvious: they would have been inundated with complaints, some inevitably taking to Twitter. In fact, Mark told me himself that he was responsible for holding them back. But now the *Sun* does promote the UFC in its sports pages. Heavyweight tabloids were taking note of the UFC and covering it on their websites, which was a landmark victory for the UFC.

I would often find myself on the phone to Mark in deep conversation about the UFC. The young writer told me that he would always tell his boss positive things and educate him about the sport. I, myself, contributed to the *Sun*'s UFC coverage at a minimal level at the time. I never was an "online" journalist; I preferred the medium of print, which I was enjoying.

We, the specialist martial arts and MMA magazine journalists at the time, had more knowledge, as some of us had some "mat time" and genuine interest in the fighting arts. We were able to appreciate MMA and fighters more, and technically, we had a background and experience in the arts. Most of the sports columnists and writers in the mainstream press had never been on the mat or had experience on a physical level. Despite this, they played an integral role in bringing the sport to the forefront and having it embraced by a wider audience. Without their attention and action, MMA may have fizzled out at some point or at least been relegated to the hard-core niche market. So, yes, these men and women are as important as anyone and must be credited and appreciated. Mainstream magic had arrived in North America, and the United Kingdom had got a taste of it even though still behind their cousins across the Atlantic. Yet I felt the United Kingdom was not doing enough in terms of coverage.

14

Ringside and
Brock "The Beast" Lesnar

Personally, I was disappointed and quite frankly disgusted that the two major channels in the United Kingdom, BBC and ITV, were reticent in covering the UFC. In the spring of 2008, BBC did broadcast a news story when Dave O'Donnell's Cage Rage promotion garnered publicity. I'm sure it was only because two women were fighting in a brutal, bloody cage in a modern civilized society, so it naturally added to the outrage and attention. And when there's public outrage in the country, the media waste no time in sniffing and adding fuel to it. One of the female fighters was from Ireland under the banner of SBG Ireland, Conor McGregor's gym—my friend Karl Tanswell's SBG gym branch being the country's head office and the world head office being in Portland, Oregon.

Talking of women in MMA, Rosi Sexton, one of Karl's former top fighters, has a PhD in theoretical computer science, a BSc in osteopathy, and an MSc in mathematical logic and graduated from the University of Manchester. She was the first female from Britain to fight in the UFC. She pioneered women's MMA, especially in Europe. This was before Ronda Rousey emerged. I bumped into Rosi occasionally and had interviewed her because we used to frequent the same gym. She is a very down-to-earth and quiet person, but if you got on the mat with her, this innocent-looking girl would eat you up and chew you out before you could utter a word. There was more chance of her being on top of you than vice versa. And she had the capacity to bruise your face up and ground and pound you into oblivion.

Cage Rage was one of the more prominent MMA promotions in the country. Promoter Dave is a colorful character. He looks like your stereotypical London gangster with a shaved shiny head, gold jewelry, and a cockney accent to go with it. He was always dressed in a smart suit. As a matter of fact, he could stunt double the infamous London gangster Dave Courtney. I've known Dave O'Donnell for many years now. Cage Rage promotion was built up by the cockney martial artist who worked hard to get to where he is today. Whenever I phoned him, he was always polite and we had a laugh. Whenever I could help him out with articles promoting his events, I would try my best. He would throw in complimentary tickets for me. I would always try to squeeze something out of him. Sometimes, though, I had to squeeze hard.

I, along with three friends, went to his show in Wembley when UFC pioneer Ken Shamrock was headlining. MMA fighters come from a diverse background. You had college and university graduates, even schoolteachers, such as Rich "Ace" Franklin—the former UFC middleweight champion who was the spitting image of Jim Carey. On the other end of the spectrum, you had those who had a rough upbringing—and Ken was one of those that had a hard childhood and had to move from home to home. He was adopted by Bob Shamrock. "I got into trouble when I was about 10 years old, and I got shipped off to different group and juvenile homes," Ken told me once in an interview. "I ended up in a place called the Shamrock Boys Home with Bob Shamrock after I had stayed at several different places. I was 13 and a half years old. This was a time when I started learning how to change my ways."

"When you were growing up, did you get into trouble a lot?" I asked.

"Well, I grew up in group homes, so you were always fighting— all the time," he replied. "And I would fight for my territory and my space." The adopted young boy had to fight for his own respect. The MMA legend continued, "So it's something I did at a really young age when I was 10 years old. I was fighting all the time. Fighting to me was just kind of who I was and what I was all about and where I grew up. I had to fight in order to keep anything I had and any respect I had. Then when I got into mixed martial arts and started fighting professionally, that was fun."

When news reached Royce Gracie about Ken fighting at Cage Rage, he asked me how much his former adversary was getting paid. I said that I'd do my investigation and find out for him. Allegedly, it was only £20,000. Royce was quite shocked. Here was a UFC legend who had made a name in the history books and was now accepting £20,000 to fight. It was quite sad.

Driving down south was always mundane and a trek. As we got into Wembley, we had to stop to ask for directions. After a few wrong turns, my friends and I finally made it to the arena. I think there must have been 10,000 screaming MMA fans in the arena that day. I felt elated watching the crazy crowd. You could see Ken still possessed a good physique, but his best days were behind him. I was mingling ringside as I bumped into some people I knew. I was right by the cage when Ken got knocked out by Robert Berry and went down on the canvas as his opponent proceeded to pummel him on the ground before the referee intervened, stopping the fight in the first round. A left jab followed up by a glancing right hand to Ken's cheekbone dropped the former UFC champion. Ken's opponent kept busy and looked much more relaxed than Ken. The latter, I remember, looked weak, and nerves were getting the better of him. He was being cautious, avoiding rushing in, but every time he'd get hit, he'd flinch. He looked a miniature of his original self—not what I had anticipated.

As Ken went down, oddly enough, it felt like I was on the receiving end, too. Furthermore, I could honestly feel the friends who were in the upper-tier seats being treated to the same experience. It was a sixth sense that I can't explain. So, imagine what it feels like to actually be in the cage environment when you're facing another man who is ready to knock your head off. Being on the receiving end of violence, brutality that comes with entering the cage, is something these fighters have to endure day in and day out in a training environment and in competition. A lot of preparation, skill, mental toughness, and guts are prerequisites for survival.

My immediate thoughts were that I kind of felt sorry for Ken. I felt bad that another human, a few feet away from me, was being brutally savaged. Not that I ever was a friend of Ken—I had only interviewed him once—but it was just spontaneous empathy.

For weeks, I had been communicating with a Cage Rage official to set up a camera interview for me with Ken for the documentary that I had been working on a year and a half earlier. He had assured me that he'd sort it out. But when I got to the arena, the co-broadcaster who was sitting with Malcolm Martin acted like he didn't know what I was talking about. I thought to myself, *Is this guy for real?* He said Ken was unlikely to do an interview now before his bout. This was understandable because the focus is on the fight, and in no way should other distractions affect you mentally—but after the fight, still no interview.

If I thought I was going to grab the interview, I was gravely mistaken. Nevertheless, it was a good night. This was no UFC, but it was apparent that people from all backgrounds were flocking to these events. So, the sport had hit the mark and was winning legions of fans.

࿒

I had plenty of top UFC fighters and champions whom I ended up speaking to and really learning about their backgrounds and how their minds worked. One particular fighter was Brock "The Beast" Lesnar, whom I spoke to about four months later in July. Just about a month earlier, he had tasted defeat at the hands of Frank Mir in what was Brock's UFC debut—it was his second MMA fight. His transition from professional wrestling into a whole new world inevitably garnered attention. The UFC felt having this very popular WWE wrestler boasting a global fan base fighting in the organization would definitely bring in a crossover appeal—WWE fans into the UFC. And their instinct was proven right. I wonder how the Russian Olympic wrestler Aleksandr Karelin would have fared in UFC. A beast weighing 290 pounds, the most feared wrestler of all time, acknowledged as the greatest wrestler of the twentieth century, the heavyweight was virtually unbeatable. He did fight once in shoot wrestling in the Japanese RINGS promotion against Akira Maeda and beat him.

Growing up on a farm in South Dakota, Brock had a lot of work to do but not enough money to pay the bills. He wanted to wrestle in the senior Olympics when he was young, but he never had any specific career goal when he grew up. He was certain he didn't want to be a farmer, though. Boxing had invoked the young man's interest, but the boxing gym was 50 miles from his house. He could never get there. Friends of his actually went to boxing, but he could never afford to and never had the time to get there because of his work commitments and the distance factor. "I had interest to get into MMA many years ago, back in 1997, but I didn't really know how to get into it," he told me. At the time, he was living in California in 1997 training for wrestling. "Probably there was only one place I knew that had a gym that specifically trained for MMA fighting near me." He wanted to fulfill his college wrestling and pro wrestling dream, so it prevented him from pursuing MMA. When he got out of amateur wrestling, MMA wasn't very big at the time, and Brock had a guaranteed contract with pro wrestling sitting on the table, so it was easy enough for him to make the decision.

I asked him what the feeling was like when he first fought in MMA. "It was an excellent feeling, it was very surreal," he said. "To me, it was a great feeling to get in the ring and be competing." Before fighting in MMA, he checked out Pat Miletich's gym and numerous facilities in Arizona and Indianapolis. Since he had been on the road for a long time when he was wrestling professionally, it was really important for him to be at home and train and do what he always wanted to do, and that was to fight. For him, he told me, to be able to come home every night and sleep in his own bed and train was a major factor in choosing a gym.

"What is the difference between the pro wrestling training you were accustomed to and the MMA training you do now?" I asked. "It's not even the same," Brock said. "It's like amateur wrestling training is different to pro wrestling. Pro wrestling is entertainment." He's right, there's a sharp distinction between the two. You have to be an athlete to be in the wrestling ring, no doubt about that, but MMA athletes train in an array of disciplines every day—striking, kicking, jiu-jitsu, elbows, and Muay Thai. At the time, he was training one or two times a day, five or six days a week. The whole key to training is you are then able to recover and get the maximum out of it and be ready for the next day's workout. "We train pretty hard. I have to listen to my body. I'm not a spring chicken either, and day by day, week by week, the more we do, the more I can absorb and try to prepare myself when a fight's coming up."

When he fought Frank Mir, Mir was an expert in Brazilian jiu-jitsu and a former UFC heavyweight champion with experience and submission skills on his side. It took Brock less than five seconds to take Frank down, countering his right low kick, and he proceeded to land multiple right punches from the half guard position, overpowering his opponent completely, only to have the referee break up the action. A point was taken off Brock, as he had hit his downed opponent in the back of the head. Given another chance on the feet, Frank repeated the same leg kick, and Brock countered with a good right hand, knocking him down again. Again, the giant exploded with multiple hammer fists to the face, but this time, Frank almost got him in the armlock, forcing Brock to pull away—giving Frank space to grab his right foot and secure a deep-knee bar foot lock on the giant who was forced to tap out in the very first round.

"I knew he would attempt to go for my legs, I got over excited," Brock told me in our interview. "I spent time learning how to defend and learning every discipline, so only lack of experience is the key word there for my loss. Someday I may have a rematch with Frank." This was prescient. At the time we talked, Brock was preparing for his next bout with Heath Herring, who would suffer a punishing defeat at the hands of the former WWE star. Next, knocking out Randy Couture—a fighter who'd also been champion at light heavyweight—at UFC 91 on November 15 2008, made Brock the UFC heavyweight champion. As for Frank, Brock would avenge his loss by beating his opponent via a technical knockout at UFC 100, which would leave him on a three-fight winning streak. Eventually, Brock lost his title and returned to the WWE, then briefly returned to the UFC again before apparently giving up the game for good. Still, he was one of the big pay-per-view draws in the UFC—and one I felt privileged to interview.

15

UFC 105 Encounters

After his devastating loss to Brock Lesnar, Randy Couture had suffered another beating at the hands of Antonio Nogueira less than 10 months later. Randy would go on to fight Brandon Vera at the M.E.N. Arena—officially named the busiest arena venue in the world for many years—in Manchester at UFC 105 on November 14, 2009. When the news of this fight reached me, my brain went into overdrive. It immediately dawned on me that this would be a perfect opportunity to schedule a meet-and-greet autograph signing with the five-time UFC champion. Randy and I already had a business relationship established. I quickly got in touch with the sports presenter Mike Hall at ITV in Granada Studios to inform him.

Things were off to an auspicious start. Now that the wheel of publicity had started to turn, I got my pals from Fighters Inc. involved. We secured a venue, the Hard Rock Cafe, in Manchester's Printworks, a stone's throw from the arena. Fighters Inc. was great to work with and had experience in combat sports event management. They had previously worked with the likes of Chuck Liddell and other major names, so I was quite content that they would do a good job and not undermine Randy, an imperative when you're dealing with A-listers in the game.

A day before the big bout, I and two friends, Andy Farrell and Azmat Ali, arranged to meet Randy at the Crown Plaza Hotel, where he, the UFC fighters, and staff were staying, just down the road from the Hard Rock Cafe. Not long before we arrived at the hotel lobby, Randy's opponent Brandon walked up to us. I introduced myself, and we had a quick chat. I asked him what he thought of his adversary.

"Randy's my hero," he said. I was expecting him to be negative because he was going to fight Randy the next day, but Brandon had the utmost respect for his foe. This was one thing most UFC fighters had in common—a deep admiration and reverence for Randy, who'd proved to be a class act and a great role model when the sport was still growing into the behemoth it is today. I sometimes felt he was like their elder brother or a father figure, someone they wouldn't even dream about insulting. It was easy to see the appeal, as Randy was, by nature, an extremely affable and humble fighter and individual. He was never the type of athlete who would talk trash about anyone, yet he still managed to sell out arenas. He was revered by his peers. I just prayed Randy would be choking Brandon out on the day of the fight, or I'd be choking up myself.

We soon spotted Randy in the hotel lobby. We all made our way up to his hotel room, leaving a few boxes of goodies there because Randy was going to sign some in advance. "I love your red shoes," Randy joked with Azmat, always personable. After some back-and-forth banter, we left Randy in peace to relax. After all, he had an important fight the next day, and I was counting on him to win.

As we walked out of the room and made our way to the lobby, we hit the hat trick of headliners, spotting Mike Bisping, who was going to be fighting Denis Kang on the same card. As soon as Mike saw us, he smiled and shouted, "This guy kicked my ass!" He was referring to Andy, whom Mike had fought before he became a UFC fighter and star. Apparently unconcerned about his fight the next day, Mike stood there telling us proudly how Andy had slammed him again and again in their encounter, which Andy won. That was a very humbling conversation. Mike didn't have to do that, but in front of us and his own team members, he did. Andy, I must add, had already told me of his encounter with "The Count," so I was already aware. But when Mike confirmed the beating he had received at the hands of my friend, I thought to myself, *I have a friend with great potential who could be a star in the UFC.*

Andy, a former professional rugby player and natural bodybuilding champion, a Brazilian jiu-jitsu and MMA champion, and a contestant on the show *Gladiators*, is one of the nicest people you will ever meet. He's a cool guy, the type of a guy you can have a good laugh with, but also blessed with a great bodybuilder's physique, a strong grip, and a handshake that could crush your hand. He is one solid guy. On the day of the signing meet-and-greet event I had given Andy the responsibility of protecting Randy. Believe me, you get some fans who react strangely when they meet a professional fighter. Some have un-usual requests—they want to get choked, leg kicked, or even punched in the face by the star. I sometimes wondered if one day a lunatic would take it further either verbally or physically.

While in Manchester, Randy worked out at my friend Karl Tanswell's SBG gym, which was the number-one MMA facility in Manchester—and had been the number-one MMA gym in the country several years earlier—at the time. On Saturday, the day of the fight, M.E.N Arena had a sold-out crowd of almost 17,000 fans. Astonish-ingly, this event broke merchandise records that had previously been set by Britain's number-one boy band, Take That. I remember that some Amir Khan fights were apparently attracting only 8,000 people, with one of his fights reportedly selling only 4,000 tickets, and he was the biggest name in British boxing. *This is insane*, I thought. *The UFC is not only outselling world champion boxers but setting merchandise records.* This further bolstered my confidence in Randy's appeal, the future of the sport, and my MMA business endeavors.

In the end, I decided not to go to the fight, leaving Andy to go with-out me. I was wracked by nerves—had Randy lost the fight, I would have likely plunged back into depression, and, besides, Andy Farrell would be updating me on Randy's performance and the outcome. Randy was 46 years old and still fighting in the toughest sport at the highest level against a much younger man who many thought could be the future of the division. In the event, Randy tried to execute his normal game plan. After closing the distance, he would resort to dirty boxing in the clinch position followed up by a takedown, then ground and pound. Against Brandon, he failed. His opponent defended most of Randy's takedown attempts, forcing them to battle on the feet for much of the bout.

In the end, Randy had a very tough fight with Brandon but man-aged to secure a win via decision. I was constantly on the phone to Andy for updates, and he assured me that Randy never seemed to be in trouble. Still, this fight caused quite a controversy; some thought Brandon had been robbed, and at least one member of the media called the decision "daylight robbery." It didn't matter to me. I was joyful because Randy was the one to have his hand raised. That was good enough for me; the opinions of others didn't register as long as the judges made the right call. After the fight, I couldn't give a damn about the performance. I was interested in the end result.

"I wouldn't have been terribly disappointed had the decision gone the other way," Randy told presenter Joe Rogan in the postfight interview in front of the packed crowd. "I was very impressed with Brandon." He went on to say that you just never know what the judges will decide and that this had been seen in the past. You just don't know what the judges are looking at and how they perceive the fight. "And that's what ultimately, in a close fight like this, determines the judge's decision," he told Joe.

Now, not many fighters would have said this—perhaps only Randy. To be honest, I'd rather he hadn't said it because it felt like admitting defeat and giving others artillery to use against him. But that was Randy—he spoke his mind.

Brandon, for his part, made it known that he was really pissed off. Wouldn't you be if you thought you were robbed? No one could blame him for vocalizing his concerns. He expressed his views, saying that the sport of MMA is, as he put it, "a bitch" because if you let it go to the judge's hands, then you're no longer in control of the outcome. He felt that he should have finished his opponent when he was presented with the opportunity but let the chance slip away. And yet, regardless of the controversial decision, he was still in awe after the loss. "I'm super happy I got to fight Randy Couture, my hero, my legend," the defeated fighter told the crowd. It was a great night.

2

The next morning, I and my team—really, a group of friends, Seyfi, Abdul, Tash, Andy, Ahsan, Randy, Azmat, Daz, and our Fighters Inc. friends (Paul Alderson and Joe Long)—arrived at the Hard Rock Cafe. Several of us were in Azmat's Range Rover with Randy driving down to the Printworks when suddenly a police car appeared out of nowhere and followed us, signaling for the driver to stop. As the two officers got out and made their way to the driver, to their astonishment, they realized Randy Couture sat in the passenger seat. The officers had stopped us because Azmat didn't have his seat belt on. Azmat tried turning things around by taking a humorous approach, saying to Randy, "Randy, please save me the fine and take a picture with them." That day, the officers were of an understanding nature and let my friend off, and Randy got out of the Range Rover to pose with the officers for pictures. As it happens, they were fans of MMA, and Randy had made their day.

During the question-and-answer session, one young guy from the audience shouted out something to Randy. I think he was saying Randy needed to speak up because he couldn't hear him because the mic had suddenly turned off, but his tone was a little on the sarcastic side. Randy, a soft-spoken gentleman, countered by saying that maybe the young man should come forward. As much of a dangerous fighter as he is, you can't picture "The Natural" getting mad or angry, screaming, or even raising his voice. A rather quiet gentleman, he is blessed with a rather mellow personality, which some may find ironic considering his brutal profession. Besides, he always did his talking in the Octagon. That's where it really counts.

After Randy answered questions about his life and fight career, he signed and paused for photos for more than 250 ecstatic fans. The atmosphere was electric. The looks and smiles on the fans' faces are something that I will cherish forever. The event was an advance reservation event only, so although we let a few extra fans in, we had to turn back others, leaving them disappointed. Obviously, the city was flooded with UFC fans from the fight night the night before, so it was inevitable fans found out where Randy was. I'd have liked to give more people the chance to meet their idol, but there simply wasn't time.

For my part, I was relieved that the ITV Granada News team had made the effort to show up. I wasn't sure if they were going to follow through, to be honest. As the autograph signing and meet and greet came to an end, we were ready to leave the venue because we had to be out by 1 p.m., but the TV crew stopped us in our tracks. I could see a sense of uncertainty in Randy's eyes. He was like a little boy being whisked here, there, and everywhere. It dawned on me how some of these stars are shuffled all over the place like rag dolls, without much say or certainty about their next engagements. I saw the human side of Randy, the side the public seems to overlook when it comes to meeting their favorite celebrity.

One of my friends who had a martial arts gym and used to write for the martial arts press was in attendance that day in the capacity of a fan. Like all the other UFC fans there, he and some of his students were looking forward to meeting Randy. When the signing was in full force, I had my team control the line because personalizing autographs and posing for selfies can be time consuming if it's not regulated. The event ran from 11 a.m. to 1 p.m., so we had two hours to get through everything on the schedule. After the 30-minute interview, we had to get every single person in the room to meet Randy, get their autograph, and give them the opportunity to snap a photo. So I had someone move the guys along as soon as Randy scribbled his name and they snapped a photo with the star.

My friend, even though he was there as a fan, politely complained to me about this process. He said he wanted to talk to the UFC champion for only a few minutes but was left disappointed because it didn't happen. Suddenly, Randy was a bad guy! Let me tell you the truth: Randy is anything but bad. Randy had the tendency to often scold me and his handlers if we set restrictions on the fans when he did fan meets. He was a fan favorite and always endeavored to please them. He cared immensely about the image he projected but also about his fans. Be that as it may, you had to look at it through a more practical lens. If every fan had three minutes with Randy that day, we'd have been there for 12 hours or more. Randy might have done it—he's that much of a nice guy.

Anyway, after a quick on-the-spot interview with the TV crew, we rushed Randy out. Azmat had arranged a black Hummer as part of the logistics and transportation. We jumped in there and made our way to Zooks restaurant, a fairly classy place just on the border of the city center opposite the old BBC building. Azmat had recommended this place, as he knew the owners, who, sure enough, really took care of us. Another friend who was supposed to come to the event suddenly called me when we were on our way to the restaurant. I just told him to join us at the restaurant. He had a lady friend with him, but that was no surprise because he was always surrounded by nice women.

At the restaurant, Randy revealed that he was on a special diet. He had got heavily into food and nutrition, and fish and vegetables were a major part of his eating, with red meat almost off the menu entirely. We all listened attentively. Despite being one of the older UFC fighters, he was known for his physical fitness and supreme conditioning that the younger fighters could only envy in a sport that's a test of almost every aspect of human fitness. I once asked him what kept him going in his forties, and he told me, "What keeps me going is, I'm very passionate about the sport; it's what I love to do, and as long as I'm still capable of doing it, I don't see why I should do anything else. And I'm getting paid for it . . . I'll keep training."

Randy was a scholar when it came to training. He told me, "I like to peak 10 weeks before a fight. I study tapes of my opponent and decide what his strengths and weaknesses are and try to watch out for them. We get a game plan together, a lot of striking, sprint work, conditioning, and also lots of plyometrics. This, topped with a couple of days a week of real hard sparring where my partners try to wear me down— this is done with multiple partners. Other times, sparring and striking in different situations and worst-case-scenario training, putting myself in the worst position an opponent can potentially put me in so that I have to find a way to survive, neutralize it, and try to win the fight. All in all, a well-rounded approach."

As the afternoon progressed, we talked about fighting and Randy's movie career, which was progressing nicely. We all listened to the two-weight-class UFC champion as he shared his wisdom with us mere mortals. "I ask myself, what is the worst thing that the opponent can do to me?" Randy said to us—which seems sensible until you realize he's in a sport where people lose teeth and break arms. It takes a lot for someone to summon the courage to even step into the UFC arena. The worst thing that could happen is that the opponent could maybe knock him out in a fight, he explained. The impression he gave us was that it was no big deal and that it wasn't going to be the end of the world for him if he lost a fight or got knocked out cold in the Octagon. He went into his fights armed with this mentality, which helped him control fear and keep relaxed instead of being too anxious. As he once put it, "A lot of the guys who don't have a strong set of striking skills can take advantage of other gifts they have, such as mental attributes and approach."

Business was good. After a few months, I decided to purchase a BMW X5 with cash—in my mind, I often credited Randy Couture for that car. It was nice to be rewarded, and I felt I had earned it, but I never let it go to my head. My philosophy had always been that there's always someone better than you. So I would never look down on anyone or let status and materialistic things go to my head. I can say with great conviction that almost everyone who knows me personally can vouch for this.

Talking of cars, one day a family member and I picked up a family friend I have known almost all my life. I can't exactly remember where we were going, whether it was a wedding or a funeral. As the family friend jumped into the car, he quipped, "You've not had a police raid yet, have you?," implying that I had sold drugs and was reaping the benefits now—why else would I be driving a car of this caliber?

Although it was meant in jest, it got to me. You know what the funny thing is? His son was an active drug dealer. Wait! It gets better! His son allegedly bought him a car with the drug money. I had seen his son with my own eyes at least twice selling drugs in the street.

Drugs are something I never touched or used. Selling them was out of the question. Near where I grew up, some young lads were doing drugs, some driving sports cars, and they had just left college. Wanting to make fast and easy money and live the life was apparently their only ambition. Dealing in drugs is a huge risk, and if you get caught, your life, in essence, is over. It's better to live modestly and have less money than get plunged into the drugs game. And I have been in the company of friends who have taken drugs, even hard-core ones such as cocaine, but I was never tempted for one minute. "You've been around celebrities, you must have taken some cocaine," a friend once said to me. I told him I never have. I've never been interested in drugs, certainly not just because some famous people take them.

Considering my background as a journalist in the fighting sports, I know a lot of the top professional fighters have never touched drugs. I'm not referring to steroids here—we know that steroids are used by some athletes, and this is a whole different and controversial subject. On the other hand, some fighters use both—capitalizing on both the performance enhancement of steroids and the buzz of class A drugs. Not all of them, though. I remember sitting in the home of one of the toughest and notorious fighters on one trip to Los Angeles, and I'll never forget what he told me. He said he'd never taken drugs and didn't drink but instead got the biggest buzz out of training and competing. There's a lesson there: in life, getting a buzz can come from many different things, so find something outside of drugs to give you that buzz. For some, it can be a hobby, whether it's a simple thing such as playing chess or a more adrenaline-pumping activity such as racing cars or having a bone-crushing wrestling session. People often think that getting into the cage is dangerous—but in my book, it's a far better way to get a buzz than drugs.

16

Boxing versus UFC

The Tyson–Gracie Challenge

By the late 2000s, the UFC's enormous success had emboldened a slew of rival MMA organizations to jump on the bandwagon. But its biggest competitor was—and still is—the sport of boxing. For years, the UFC played second fiddle to the sweet science, and for the fledgling sport to surpass the global popularity of this ancient sport seemed almost impossible. Well into the explosion of the UFC, boxing superstars like Mike Tyson, Sugar Ray Leonard, and Floyd Mayweather were more recognizable names outside of their respective sport than any UFC athlete. And most casual fans still regarded the boxing heavyweight champion as the Baddest Man on the Planet.

Could the UFC make the leap ahead? *What are the chances of a 70-year-old grandma knowing who Randy Couture is?* I thought to myself at one point. You have to remember, the promoters had initially sold UFC as a blood-and-guts spectacle before the new owners instituted more rules in the transition to making MMA a true sport. Not even a decade before, the sport had provoked widespread outrage, but now, with personable champions and a growing audience, things were changing. Boxing had a serious challenger to its crown, and the old-school promoters had no choice but to play down their foe.

The arguments they put forward will be familiar to any UFC fan. Boxing pundits and promoters argued that the brutal and minimally skilled fighters of MMA could not compare with the warriors of sweet science—that boxing was simply a more sophisticated sport. What they failed to comprehend or neglected to mention was the fact that UFC athletes, even then, were highly skilled in multiple disciplines. Some of this was simply willful ignorance—afraid of being overpowered by this exciting new sport, they were vocal and disparaging of everything MMA. To this end, a lot of them made sure their fighters did not promote, directly or indirectly, anything that related to the new sport.

Whenever hard-core and casual boxing fans dismissed UFC fighters as being unskilled fighters knocking each other out for beer-drinking fans, stereotypical thugs interested only in violence, it made my skin crawl. Some of these diehard boxing lovers had no clue whatsoever as to the caliber of skill UFC athletes possessed. Just like boxing, MMA demands years of study and dedication, but unlike the sweet science, the MMA fighter has far more to worry about than his opponent's fists. Some of the jeers at MMA, of course, come from a lack of understanding. The complexity of arts such as Brazilian jiu-jitsu—the technical brilliance and strategic elements—mirrors that of playing a game of chess, at top speed, where the other competitor isn't waiting for you to move. While even a novice spectator can quite easily follow what's going on in a boxing match, most have no real concept of what's going on when they watch two men rolling around on the ground. The fight for small positional advantages can be invisible, just as much of the more nuanced footwork in a high-level boxing bout is incomprehensible to the average fan. As commentary improved and knowledge grew, things changed, but it took a while.

Boxers, too, were quick to disparage this sport that allowed kicks, joint locks, and throws as well as punches. Floyd Mayweather, always outspoken, was happy to throw some low blows. "It takes true skills to be in the sport of boxing," he remarked to an interviewer on CBS Sports, "and MMA is for beer drinkers, boxing is for everybody. There are no white fighters in boxing that are dominating, so they had to go to something else and start something new." As a longtime UFC fan and writer, I found this hard to take. I felt this guy needed to do his homework, like so many other boxing fans. And while, yes, things have changed, many hard-core boxing fans still utterly abhor MMA today. Part of the boxing fraternity has been living in denial.

On the other end of the spectrum, it wasn't long before you had boxing champions pictured at ringside at UFC events in America and the United Kingdom, fully appreciating the Octagon gladiators. Despite the fact that part of the boxing fraternity had strong reservations about UFC being a threat to their financial interests and fan base, there was no getting away from the fact that this new phenomenon had landed and created a new type of fighter. The smartest pugilists now, by and large, recognized the hard work, fitness, and skill that went into the making of a MMA champion. These men trained harder than Olympic athletes, aiming to master not just one skill—that of wrestling, say, an Olympic sport in itself—but three or four as well. And in this spirit, the more open-minded ones started to not merely acknowledge but also applaud the new breed of athlete, whom they perceived as elite-tier sportsmen. These modern-day gladiators might be a potential threat to their pay packet, but anyone who understood the game had to respect them.

As the boxing-versus-MMA feud reached epic proportions, it was time to ask the king of boxing promoters to share his thoughts. I'm always prepared to ask anyone for an interview, but to say that I was surprised when the most famous boxing promoter, Don King, personally shared his views with me relating to the UFC may be an understatement. It had taken me literally 18 phone calls to arrange to speak to Don. He was always up to something, meeting presidents, world leaders and the higher echelons of society, and globe-trotting all over the world. King definitely is the king of the promoters, although Bob Arum might give him a run for his money. Moreover, Don had been the subject of controversy ever since his early years in the sport. He was an intriguing character whom I couldn't wait to talk to.

Sure enough, the conversation was an epic one. During a lengthy and thought-provoking conversation, we talked about Muhammad Ali, some of the current boxing champions, and this new threat to the sport of boxing—the UFC. I asked Don whether he thought UFC was a genuine competitor to the boxing game—a sport that had made this flamboyant promoter millions of dollars and afforded him a lifestyle that mere mortals can only dream of. "I like ultimate fighting, it's a raw thing like street fighting!" he told me, his voice hitting the half yell familiar from his other interviews. "Ultimate fighting is raw, that's why it's got a huge number of fans. I intend to able to promote that, too." He had his own take on the evolution of the sport, too. "It was a raw type of barbarism, now it's become a sophisticated type of barbarism that the public loves. I think it's sensational, and I have nothing but praise for those who have been successful and carved a niche out."

I was astonished at what Don was saying. I wasn't expecting it— far from it. In fact, ahead of the interview, I feared he might even decline to answer any UFC-related questions. After all, the promoters of boxing often evaded questions about their competition if they weren't already bashing the new sport openly.

After a little thought, though, it was easy to see why he was full of such elation. Being an astute businessman, he was more than willing to jump on the MMA bandwagon himself and probably saw it as a way to reach a younger fan base that didn't care for boxing. How could I have missed this? He told me with great conviction that both sports could survive and bring people together and that he was all about bringing people together. This is how to understand Don King or any true promoter: where there's money to be made, they'll show up. "I think now with the ultimate fighting, there are new kinds of fans," he continued, exuding the charm he's famous for. "Not as per-se boxing fans but as fans of a brutal combat sport with elbows, kicking, biting. I have no quarrel with ultimate fighting because it's a people's sport, and a lot of people and youngsters are coming to see it—it's exciting!" Like I said, many other boxing promoters were and still are vehemently against this new craze. But Don was seeing another golden opportunity, one that apparently had the potential to fatten his bank account.

Some people at the time were opining that boxing was dying and that the future looked bleak. The new generation (and some of the old generation who had grown up watching the sweet science) is now flocking to UFC events, which often offer more action—and more fighters to root for than the headliners on each card. I have always said that the popularity of boxing has been, to a large degree, due to the mainstream coverage it had received for many decades on TV. I had once put the question to UFC legend Randy Couture to get his personal opinion: Was boxing dying and the new generation turning to a new combat sport? Or could it be that MMA had caught up with the sweet science and that both sports could coexist? "I don't think boxing is dying," the five-time UFC champion told me. "I think the attitude is that it's more one-dimensional compared to MMA. And the UFC has done a great job pioneering that, and it's something the younger generation are into—extreme sports—they like it."

How did boxers feel about the skill levels in the two sports? I once asked Sugar Ray Leonard for his opinions on the Gracies—the fighting family responsible for creating this new craze in the fight world. After all, this was Sugar Ray Leonard, one of the all-time boxing greats whose opinions mattered more than any promoter's. I expected his opinions to be interesting, but still I was surprised when he told me that he was friends with Rickson Gracie, something I was oblivious to. The former boxing champion's path had also crossed with Royce Gracie on a flight to Los Angeles. "Royce's presence is so unassuming," the former five-weight-division champion exclaimed. "He's so approachable. Because he's a tall skinny guy, he doesn't look ferocious. And that's what I like because he could really take your head off," he said, then let out a laugh as he remembered the UFC fighter.

As I've mentioned, before the first UFC took place on November 12, 1993, when Royce beat three opponents in the same night to become the first-ever UFC champion, a lot of people had a misconception about fighting. The general vibe was that the heavyweight boxing champion was the toughest guy in the world. However, when the world witnessed a rather frail-looking man with technically superior submission skills prevail as he proceeded to tap out a field of brutes, that myth would find its way out of the window—a window that has been firmly shut since. But before that, the Gracies tried to show the superiority of their style in a rather more direct way.

"Iron" Mike Tyson became the youngest-ever heavyweight champion at the age of 20 and was widely considered an unstoppable force—at least to those who considered boxing the only true form of fighting. Envied, revered, and feared, Tyson is one of the most ferocious fighters the heavyweight division has ever seen. When he faced opponents in the ring, they were often beaten before the bout actually got under way because of his intimidation tactics. His savage, aggressive, and violent style and invincibility made him fearless. Furthermore, he had tested himself countless times in savage street encounters that often made the front pages of newspapers. Driven by an intense will, he was equipped with psychological armor, which is as important as your raw skill when you are caught up in a street scenario. He was the perfect physical specimen you'd like to watch fight, but you would most definitely want to avoid being on the receiving end of his brutal blows. And you definitely would want to avoid encountering him in a dark alley—or, at least, that was basically the public's perception of him.

The Gracie family, of course, didn't think this way. In fact, the notorious boxer was challenged by the Gracie brothers, in particular, Royce, back in the early 1990s. The UFC champion's perception was that Tyson was the best boxer in the world, but he refused to accept that Tyson was the best "fighter." The Gracies had a point. They had been beating all comers from various styles long before the Octagon was first engineered. And Royce wasn't going to rest until he did everything within his means to provoke the heavyweight champion into accepting a real fight in a no-holds-barred setting. To settle the matter once and for all, Royce formally challenged the most feared boxer of our time to a fight to the finish, and so did his elder brother, Rickson, widely regarded as the most technical Brazilian jiu-jitsu fighter in the world. "Will Mike Tyson have more courage than Joe Louis, who was content to rest on his laurels and declined to step into the no-holds-barred arena?" they asked, referring to the fact that their father, Helio Gracie, had challenged the "Brown Bomber" back in his prime.

As news of the Tyson–Gracie challenge spread like wildfire in the combat sports world, I often came across absurd comments in "readers' letters" sections in the martial arts press, most notably in America's *Black Belt* and *Inside Kung Fu* and the United Kingdom's *Martial Arts Illustrated* and *Combat*. The readers, who, in those days, had very little experience of grappling, especially the ground grappling that was the specialty of the Gracies, would happily voice their opinions on this hypothetical matchup, most believing that the blistering power and brute force the heavyweight was capable of producing was enough to demoralize just about anyone you put in front of him. *If Tyson caught Gracie with one punch, Gracie would be knocked out*, was the most common trope. Fair enough. But you have to put it into perspective. Royce's challenge to Tyson was a no-holds-barred fight, not a boxing or grappling match. As a matter of fact, during one of my many conversations that I had with Royce, he actually told me that if Tyson hit him once in the face, he'd wake up in the hospital a week later. Royce has never claimed to be punch-proof. But for Royce, any fight was a matter of who could implement their own strategy, and much of the Gracie style was developed to avoid even the chance of their opponent landing a lucky punch. What Royce lacked in brute force he clearly made up for in technical skill, as his opponents—including a professional boxer—quickly discovered. "There's only one way to find out," he told me as a smirk crept across his face, followed by loud laughter. Sadly for posterity, Tyson declined.

Still, while Tyson was at least respectful, the armchair tough guys were much less so. Again, their argument was that Tyson was so lethal that the Brazilian grappling master was doomed in the stand-up. He would, they opined, have no chance to use his skills. Being an ardent admirer of the Gracie clan, I always beg to differ. These so-called critics obviously hadn't experienced Gracie Jiu-Jitsu firsthand, this amazing art that had sent shock waves around the globe and changed many people's perceptions of fighting. Jiu-jitsu can seem simple to counter until you experience it—feeling the crushing top pressure of a master grappler and having your options removed inch by inch.

As much as the Gracies were revered by many, they were equally abhorred by others. Part of the reason was their love of challenge matches. In "Iron" Mike's case, one rejection wasn't enough for Royce. In 1997, the Tyson–Gracie challenge made the headlines again in a one-page ad in the American magazine *Men's Health* when the UFC champion once again challenged the former heavyweight boxer "officially." Anywhere, anytime, no rules! Years later, I asked Royce about the famous challenge and discovered that the heavyweight had been, at least in theory, willing to put up. "I heard that my brother tried to bring him in [to the UFC]," Royce proceeded to explain. "He had accepted, but people around him—the lawyers, managers, and the Commission—said no way because boxing had too much to lose. But he had accepted, and he wanted to do it. I talked to him before and he's like, 'I'd love to try this stuff out, man.' But people around him did not allow him to do it. If he lost a fight, if it happened, well, boxing was already in the decline in America, so it wouldn't be good for boxing."

What would have happened if the bout had materialized is one of the great "what if?" stories in MMA history. Perhaps Tyson would have landed a lucky punch and derailed the Gracie hype train, or perhaps Royce would have choked the Baddest Man on the Planet unconscious and sent Brazilian jiu-jitsu into the stratosphere. It would have never happened, though. Tyson wasn't going to put his hard-earned reputation on the line, nor were the money men in the boxing game in their infinite wisdom going to allow this fight to take place. The notorious boxer was making millions of dollars, so it wouldn't make sense for him from a financial perspective, bearing in mind that the UFC pay packets were meager in comparison to what the top boxers were raking in.

⌒

So what does the notorious boxer think of all this? Was he "bad" enough to beat Royce Gracie, the man who had never beaten anyone with his fists, in a no-holds-barred bloody fight to the finish? Tyson was asked by a UFC host on *UFC Tonight* to transport himself back and consider how he would have fared in a fight against then–UFC champion. "Well, in 1993, I was in prison, so there wouldn't have been a fight," was his response before the champ gave his interviewer a surprise. "There is no way I would have won."

One thing that surprises modern interviewers most about Tyson is his humbleness. This is a man who dismantled the heavyweight division of his era and made history. But he has great reverence for the greats of boxing before him and now UFC athletes, too. "Iron" Mike has since gone on record admitting his appreciation for the Gracies and just how mesmerized he was watching the UFC when it first debuted and his challenger ruled the Octagon. Ever since being introduced to the UFC, Tyson became completely hooked and continues to be captivated by the sport even now. The first time he watched the UFC, he says, was at his home with friends. His guests would normally be inebriated, and Tyson would put on the UFC tapes, which back then were available in VHS format. They'd watch the warriors of the Octagon every time they'd get the chance. The former heavyweight champion has followed the careers of the great fighters ever since that early era of Ken Shamrock, Royce Gracie, and Dan Severn. He follows the sport to this day, and he recently paid homage to the Gracies and his former challenger. "The Gracies are not as big as they should be, and they showed that size didn't matter," he said. "The fighting world has the utmost respect for the Gracie clan, there's no doubt about that."

These words had a knockout effect on me. I mean, here is the guy who was the most feared fighter in the world, as well as the most famous sportsman of the 1980s and 1990s, praising his old nemesis who back then was virtually an unknown beyond the confines of the martial arts world. It was a momentous victory for the martial arts, which had always taken a backseat in the minds of the majority of the public as far as combat sports are concerned. The reason that the Gracies are less known compared to today's modern MMA superstars who have captivated the attention of the fans is simply because when Royce was fighting in the Octagon, the sport had not yet filtered into the mainstream. However, few would argue that the Gracie name undoubtedly is the most prominent in the history of the MMA movement. The fact will remain: the most unlikely-looking fighter you'll ever lay your eyes on had changed the way the world perceived fighting when he tore through his opponents in the earlier UFCs, steamrolling much bigger adversaries. He proved himself, and his grappling style of Gracie Jiu-Jitsu prevailed, solidifying his legacy in the history books. Today, every single MMA competitor has to implement Brazilian jiu-jitsu training as part of his core training in order to survive in the Octagon.

Now that the UFC has gone mainstream and he lives in Las Vegas, Tyson can often be seen ringside enjoying the fights. Both Royce and Tyson were VIP ringside guests at UFC 160 in Las Vegas in May 2013. It seemed like they were having a wonderful time laughing and joking around with each other. I obviously had great insight about the tension between the two when the famous challenge was made. So, once again, when I spoke to Royce, I asked him how he perceived Tyson now, the man he had challenged back in the day to a no-holds-barred literal fight to the death. "I like Tyson. I'm a big fan of Mike Tyson," he told me in his usual calm manner. "We met a couple of times, and he's a very nice guy." Royce is a man of few words. And despite the fact some people may perceive him as cocky or even someone with an ego, he's respectful to other fighters, even though he is never hesitant to speak his mind, and he is respectful to those he encounters. In fact, he is one of the most laid-back fighters you'll ever come across. Both men have mutual respect for each other, that's for sure. Both epitomize true sportsmanship, and many fans could learn a lesson from them.

17

UFC, Royals, and Rich Arabs

One thing that had caught my attention about the UFC was that its star athletes often did autograph signings—something you didn't see happening in the boxing game much. For the UFC stars, allowing access to fans for meet and greets at expos and pre-UFC shows was prevalent, and these sessions would attract thousands of fans. To further strengthen the British fan base and ensure UFC's continued popularity, in October 2010, the organization announced its first expo in the United Kingdom. This coincided with UFC 120, which was to take place at the O2 Arena and which would go on to set a European attendance record of 17,133. The previous record was 16,693, set by UFC 105 when Randy Couture fought at the M.E.N. Arena in November the year before. I thought this would be another golden opportunity for Randy to do some promotion, as I knew there would be thousands of hard-core fans attending the expo at Earl's Court.

Expos in the United States had been very successful. The support the UFC received from all the fringe industries connected to the sport of MMA was impressive. This time, the UFC promised to have the largest assemblage of fighters to hit Europe as they ventured into the lucrative European market. The world's premier MMA organization always made a noise about setting records and bringing their loyal fans the best fighters to meet, so this time, Randy was going to be flown over by the UFC to be one of the star athletes in attendance. With more than 100 MMA-related vendors exhibiting, I contacted *Fighters Only* magazine, the world's leading MMA publication, and they agreed to have Randy at their stand on the first day of the expo. Randy would meet fans and sign autographs for two hours—10 a.m. to 12 noon. I would have loved it if we could have done signings throughout the day, but Randy had been allocated a limited amount of time because of his obligations and commitments to the organization that had flown him over.

Seyfi, Ahsan, and I drove down in the morning to Earl's Court to meet Randy. He arrived a little later outside the venue, where we were waiting for him. I was somewhat disappointed and surprised when Randy told us that he had taken the tube from his hotel. I felt the UFC officials should have been assigned to him escorting the champion from the hotel to the venue. But I believe the organization and Randy were on shaky terms by that point, which would explain it, even though I'm sure a few fans were probably surprised to see him riding the tube. As I've mentioned, Randy is one of the most humble stars you will ever meet, never the one looking for star treatment. Whenever we picked him up from the airport, he wouldn't let us carry his bags; he insisted on carrying his own luggage. This down-to-earth attitude made him a fan favorite, and despite his high profile, Randy never had a high opinion of himself. He was never condescending to anyone, no matter who they were.

Outside the venue, you could see a whole herd of UFC fans flocking toward the gates. It's not rocket science to spot a UFC fan. Young and old folk alike with MMA branded Tapout T-shirts, caps, and hoodies were flooding toward the venue, eager to meet their favorite fighters. If there is one single thing that I have learned about fans of UFC, it's the fact they come in all shapes and from diverse backgrounds. Even though the UFC core fan base is the 18–34 demographic—mostly male—which is the most coveted target audience in the world, the sport has been embraced by people from all walks of life: from young kids to housewives to older men, male and female. Sure, there was once an image of tattooed tough guys flocking to fights, but these days, the majority of its followers are armchair fans, with only an extremely small fraction going to the gym to train and experience the sport.

Speaking of fan statistics, it's interesting to note that in a 2010 survey (Simmons Research Database), the size of the UFC fan base in America was estimated at 31 million. The "avid" fan base was estimated at 35 percent of that overall number, or 11 million. In Canada, the sport had exploded. With a population of 34 million, it was estimated that a whopping 6 million are fans, or roughly 18 percent of the population, almost one in five people. The UFC's interest levels in Canada far exceed that of the United States in every demographic—perhaps partly thanks to the dominance of Canadian hero GSP in the sport's welterweight division. Closer to home in Britain, it was estimated that 8 percent are fans, which equates to 5 million. The number of estimated fans for the rest of the world was near the 20 million mark. So, the over-all global size of the fan base was estimated at 65 million a decade ago. Considering the sport of MMA hadn't been around for long compared to other sports—and Conor McGregor hadn't emerged—and major positive mainstream media coverage eluded the sport for a long time, this was huge. Today, more than 300 million are fans of the UFC.

Interestingly, according to Dana White, the split between male and female fans of UFC is 56/44. But I feel that although there is a fairly large female following, this figure is disputable. The sport is still considered by many to be a violent and brutal pastime, and plenty of people I know still think of its bouts as unskilled slugfests. But the growth rate has been tremendous nevertheless.

These statistics, by the way, relate to UFC—the number-one brand—not MMA on a whole. Why do you wear Nike trainers or a Hugo Boss suit or a T-shirt with Mike Tyson's mug on the front? A brand represents your product and quality. Your brand is derived from who you are, who you want to be, and who people perceive you to be. The added value intrinsic to brand equity frequently comes in the form of perceived quality or emotional attachment. A good example is Nike, which associates its products with star athletes hoping customers will transfer their emotional attachment from the athlete to the product. No surprise that the UFC is so protective of its imaging—it doesn't want to become tarnished by associations with less regulated organizations. The UFC went on to ink a $70 million six-year sponsorship deal with Reebok four years later. It was a megabrand affiliated with the UFC.

On this particular day, the UFC was going gangbusters. In two hours, Randy must have met 400-plus fans. I'm sure half of them didn't purchase what was being sold, although we had a strict rule that only those making a purchase were allowed to meet Randy. I did get into an argument with one fan who thought he could ignore the rules, but there were professional film crew and fans snapping pictures as they walked past, so I resisted my initial urge to escalate things. In any case, Randy looked like a major sports celebrity being flocked by fans.

Suddenly, a smartly dressed man in a dark navy suit approached me. "I work for the PA [personal assistant] of the Prince of Dubai, DJ," he said politely as he introduced himself. "Can DJ meet Randy, please?" This guy was the driver for the Prince of Dubai's personal assistant. He looked like an accountant. After a couple of seconds of thought—because the line was long—I said to him, "Yes, five minutes!"

DJ sauntered forward and introduced himself to me and Randy. "How long are you in the United Kingdom?" he enquired. "We would like to show you around London." Randy said that he wasn't going to be around long, but that DJ should give his number to me. Sure enough, the PA wrote his number down on a piece of paper and handed it over to me, emphasizing to me not once but twice that I should call him. I assured him that I would call him later in the evening.

After a short chat and snapping a photo with Randy, as DJ was leaving, he grabbed my right hand and placed a bunch of crisp, rolled-up £50 notes into my hand and closed my fist. "No, it's okay," I halfheartedly protested in a vain attempt to hide my embarrassment—though, to be honest, I appreciated the tip. *I was certainly going to make the call, even if it meant I had to crawl to a telephone*, I joked to myself. This type of tipping, I came to learn, is common in the parts of the world where these royals came from. They weren't short of cash and often threw it away like tissue paper—well, some of them. Later that day when I checked, I realized I had been tipped several hundred pounds. I've never been tipped before in my life as far as I can remember.

As soon as it hit noon, a female UFC rep came to our stand and told us that she had to whisk Randy away. He had to fulfill other UFC promotional obligations. We thought we were about to face an angry mob, as there were still around 150 people waiting in line to meet Randy, but what happened next caught me and members of my team by complete surprise. Simply put, Randy burst into the line, randomly signing whatever the fans shoved in his face, without any worries about public order. Now we had fans flocking around trying to get a piece of "The Natural," with some resorting to desperate measures because he had to leave. It was total chaos. One silly kid repeatedly threw his head next to Randy's in an annoying manner several times as his friend snapped a quick photo in desperation.

As we left the venue, waiting outside for our car to pick us up, we spotted a bespectacled young man struggling with about 20 UFC expo bags full of goodies. He was a member of DJ's entourage. Suddenly, DJ and his driver emerged from the venue and walked toward us. Once again, he greeted us, and once again, I promised I would call him later. I joked about the bags, and DJ told me there were another 20 on the way, which made me laugh out loud. Seyfi had borrowed DJ's pen earlier, DJ remembered, and Seyfi had to hand it back. I don't think Seyfi was happy about getting caught. He thought he'd banked a golden souvenir pen from a member of the Dubai royal staff.

Later that evening, I made that all-important call to DJ. I told him that next time Randy was visiting the shores, we would be in touch because Randy was on a tight schedule and leaving the country. Although the event was attended by a huge number fans and they were all willing to part with their cash, some industry insiders felt it was much smaller compared to the American UFC expos, and long-term opportunities for the business networking weren't particularly present. Still, we had a great time, and I felt the event was attended by thousands of fans. And, perhaps most important for me, I had got one foot in the door with Middle Eastern royalty.

2

I found it intriguing that the royal families of Dubai and Abu Dhabi had become ardent UFC fans. In fact, they are big fans of combat sports in general, alongside many other adrenaline-fueled sports—motor sports, soccer, diving, horseback riding, you name it. This high echelon of society is an adventurous breed with a passion for living life to the max and beyond. I guess if you've got billions of dollars stacked up in the banks, then all you want to do is live life to the extreme and enjoy and explore the world.

Enter Sheik Thanoon Bin Zayed of Abu Dhabi. While studying at the university in San Diego, California, he fell in love with Brazilian jiu-jitsu, an art that at the time was spreading across the United States, inspired by the Gracie craze. After watching the first UFC, he became inspired by the Gracie family and Royce in particular. He went on to train with Renzo Gracie in New York, eventually earning the coveted black belt. One story I've heard is that when the prince was taking a private lesson with Renzo, he had told his instructor that he had a flight to catch but continued to chat for a prolonged period. "Don't you have a flight to catch?" Renzo asked his private student. It was then that the Brazilian jiu-jitsu instructor learned that this student had his own jet, as the Sheikh revealed his true identity.

Renzo has personally told me since that the Sheikh is blessed with one of the most creative minds he's ever seen in his lifetime and that at the same time as he was teaching him Gracie Jiu-Jitsu, Renzo was learning about life from his student. Renzo, who has taught many UFC champions, told me he was very lucky to have been chosen to be the Prince's teacher and that several other members of the royal family also privately study Brazilian jiu-jitsu. And the Prince's love affair with the great grappling art was far from over. He went on to purchase 10 percent of available shares in the UFC, now likely worth more than a billion dollars.

As for Abu Dhabi itself, the royals have transformed the city from a desert town to a thriving business center. It has become a hub for sports, cricket, motor racing, combat sports, and even bodybuilding to an extent. Because of their profound passion and financial strength, the royals have had the opportunity to promote and accommodate MMA in their region to a greater extent than almost everywhere except for Las Vegas and Brazil. There is a training center, the Abu Dhabi Combat Club, which is a facility for MMA and grappling training that Sheik Tahnoon has built into perhaps the best place to learn MMA and Brazilian jiu-jitsu in the Arab world, giving its name to the world's most prestigious grappling competition. Sheik Tahnoon has been at the forefront of promoting the art in the region, and it always seemed inevitable that the UFC would sooner or later make its debut in Abu Dhabi. On April 10, 2010, UFC finally landed in this magical city with none other than Renzo Gracie headlining.

Renzo, who hadn't fought for almost three years at the time, was set to fight one of the all-time greats, Matt Hughes, at UFC 112. I had seen Matt fight two years earlier at an arena when he was knocked out by a flying knee to the face, but he was still a dangerous fighter. Matt had dominated the UFC welterweight division for a long time. He wasn't much of a striker, but he was a savage wrestler and solid ground-and-pounder who'd developed a dangerous submission game. I was looking forward to watching Renzo obliterate Matt. No way was I going to idolize a fighter who had beaten my idol, Royce Gracie. I was banking on Renzo to avenge his cousin.

Perhaps not surprisingly given its two legendary participants, the bout had been huge. It broke pay-per-view records with more than 620,000 buys and was the first to break the $20 million mark in gross pay-per-view sales. UFC 112 was the first UFC to be held outdoors in an open-air arena, and it was attended by more than 11,000 fans. Sadly, the fight didn't go the way I would have liked. After a striking contest that many felt was more like a sparring session, Matt prevailed, winning the bout via TKO.

Needless to say, I wasn't thrilled with the result, but when it comes to combat sports, often you have to accept a loss and come to terms with it and motivate yourself to come back stronger. Renzo, a veteran of countless street fights, is still one of the best Gracies in my opinion, aggressive with the heart of a lion. He's the type of a fighter who could beat anyone on any given day.

⌒

Having a passion for sports and enterprise, the Middle Eastern royals have invested in America and Europe over the years, from acquiring soccer clubs to purchasing shares in Planet Hollywood. More recently, they have played host to some high-profile international boxing events. Money is like paper from a writing pad to these royals. Having said that, I've always firmly believed that money can't buy you everything in life, and I stand by this. Yes, money can, of course, present you with rare opportunities that you might not otherwise have. But there will always be something that money can't buy you. If you have a billion dollars, for example, you won't be able to transform yourself into a great professional sportsman, nor will you be able to become a Conor McGregor or Mike Tyson—the kind of character who inspires devotion among millions. There are billionaires who would give an arm and a leg to be in the position of some of the most revered athletes or movie stars. In fact, the nephew of one of the richest men in the world is on a professional soccer team yet hasn't made a full appearance or a name for himself. He is worth $20 billion, making him the richest soccer player in the world, but no one has really heard of him. Money can certainly buy you great training, good food, and a well-equipped gym, but if money were the one and only secret antidote, then the toughest guys in the world or the most admired and loved personalities would be the ones with a billion dollars. Both fame and fortune may be extremely inciting, but fame exceeds fortune in many ways.

As a journalist and student, whenever I traveled to America and met or spoke to some of the world-renowned martial arts instructors and MMA champions, I learned that most all of them would treat me well. Although I was thrust into a fighting environment, there were ethics and respect shown no matter who you were, how much money you were worth, or what level you were at. If you look carefully at the professional fighters who eventually made a name for themselves and made a fortune, they've often been through bleak periods. While dedicating themselves to the sport of MMA in the hope of one day making it, they either had to have a day job or made meager money to support themselves—often dipping into their own pockets to pay for travel and accommodations. In the case of Ronda Rousey, she slept in her car for months to save rent.

The key, I believe, is financial security. Indeed, for some, that's not enough. I had struggles like many other people during my early years and continued to have ups and downs financially even when I was doing fairly well. I've often had times in my life where I couldn't pay bills, and I can say with deep sincerity I have experienced my fair share of struggles. Obstacles I struggled to surmount, the mental draining of the self, are all too familiar to me—there were several periods when I felt almost helpless. Although developing a working relationship with my royal contact and doing something MMA related was enticing, I went into the relationship knowing that I'd do just fine whether it worked out or not.

18

Mike, Managers, and Me

By the end of the 2000s, Mike Bisping had firmly established himself as the number-one UFC fighter from the United Kingdom, blazing a trail for other fighters from his country by first winning *The Ultimate Fighter* reality show and then taking on a legion of top-tier competition. He was a recognizable face in North America and a star there. He was also a divisive figure, and although many Americans warmed up to him, others despised him in equal measure. You either loved or hated Mike—there was no middle ground. My personal opinion is that I can't see a valid reason why you would loathe him. He puts on a persona to hype up his fights, but he's a hard worker and a great representative of the sport who's always been appreciative to fans. But you know what, that's life—you will get your haters even if you're Mother Teresa.

Mike has certainly enjoyed the success he gets from his exposure more than any UFC fighter from his country. As soon as he was catapulted to the top, he was at the forefront of the business, promoting the UFC as much as he could. His enduring popularity is a testament to the UFC's astute marketing skills but also his own. He's a great interviewee who speaks his mind and is always ready to talk to fans. This would, I felt, make it easier to "sell" him to the public because he had an established fan base, so I wasn't going to let a lucrative potential opportunity elude me. A collaboration on an MMA project would, I thought, result in great success. One day, I met up with Mike to discuss potentially working together. I drove down to his hometown of Clitheroe, a small town next to Blackburn, Lancashire.

I hit it off with Mike right from the start. Before he came to prominence in the UFC, he had fought in kickboxing, making a then-respectable £300 a fight, and he was a deejay prior to his professional fighting career. "When I was younger, I used to go to a lot of amateur tournaments and the kickboxing," he told me. "I used to get paid for fights, but it wasn't much." You couldn't really eke out a living and make it as a profession, he told me, even fighting once or twice a month. The young man had toyed around with the idea of going back to college in a quest to get a degree and better qualifications, which would increase his career prospects and provide a better income for his family. "Just generally better myself because I wasn't happy with the way I turned out," he explained.

Although Mike enjoyed school and did quite well in classes, the lackluster effort he put into his schooling was all too apparent when he got his grades. He could have, according to him, done a lot better had he focused and tried harder. Instead, he ended up working factory jobs, including one in a slaughterhouse, until his career took off. "The UFC has changed my life utterly and completely," Mike said. "The main thing in how it's changed my life is I was never happy doing the other jobs I did. I used to hate them, to be honest." I'm sure a lot of us can relate to this, as we've all, at some point in our lives, been in dead-end jobs. I certainly went through a few unpleasant jobs after I left school before my dream manifested into a sportswriting career, and that feeling of dejection and gloom was all too familiar as I listened to this UFC athlete reliving his days in hell. "Now I'm earning more money," he told me across the pub table, "but the main thing is I'm doing what I love. I'm very lucky."

No surprise that he was such an approachable guy. This professional fighter had walked the path that many of us had, lacking direction in life after leaving school and being unhappy in his job. He could relate to the fans and the average man on the street. Back when he signed up with the organization, the real money was in boxing, but by the time he retired, the money was better, and he's been able to save enough to live very comfortably—he's a multimillionaire. Mike's story is inspirational. He is the epitome of the rags-to-riches story.

As we sat there conferring, Mike told me he had a lot of interesting stories that he had never revealed in interviews. I would later learn that Mike was the ideal athlete to interview because he would always have something compelling to say. He would elaborate instead of giving you one-liners. He would put every fiber of his being into telling his anecdotes. Some fighters were so damn hard to interview that you would be hard pressed to squeeze much other than one-sentence answers out of them. Others, who have been around for decades and lived a fascinating life, often tell the same old stories, even when they have experienced so much that they should never run short of material. But Mike always had something to say, which always resulted in a riveting interview. As we sat there sipping our coffees in the pub, he insisted that I not take a photo. He said to me, "It's my local, they'll think, 'Look at him, he was in here taking photos.'" This made me laugh out loud. Mike is a humble guy and, as I understand, never really let fame go to his head. I often phoned him late in the evenings—it's a bad habit of mine—and, by and large, he was okay with that.

I always dealt with Mike directly, not through any management. At the time, he was managed by the Wolfslair team, located in Merseyside, which was then the most famous MMA gym in the country. Eventually, he located to sunny California, joining the same management as Conor McGregor. I think Mike made the right decision to move and be managed in America as his career blossomed, even if it was somewhat bad news for me. After several meetings and countless phone calls, the talks just drifted apart, and nothing came to fruition. He said he'd just changed management, and we concluded that maybe down the line, we could talk again. It's like they say in martial arts: fall down seven times, get up eight.

Eventually, Mike went on to bigger and better things. He had seen title shots elude him for a decade, but some years later, he finally got his, knocking out Luke Rockhold in the first round at UFC 199 in the Los Angeles Forum arena to become the UFC middleweight champion and the first UFC champion from the United Kingdom. After he was crowned champion, I called him in California to ask whether we could reopen the negotiations. He said he did want to do something but had his plate full and said that we could talk when things calmed down.

❧

Being the multitasking individual that I am, I was writing for magazines, researching and exploring the lives of some of the most iconic figures, and taking care of the combat sports company I was a director of as I attempted to explore these endless opportunities within MMA, and now I had a new idea. I wanted to manage a UFC fighter on the side.

MMA management companies were springing up all over America. Some lawyers started to manage UFC fighters as they oversaw their contracts, and it was a good sideline for these big cats, while others made it their sole profession. Suddenly, you had American sports agents who represented athletes in the NBA and NFL adding UFC athletes to their client list. Furthermore, some big-name UFC stars were being represented by some of the most prestigious talent agencies in Beverly Hills who helped these fighters break into Hollywood. Mike Bisping, Rampage Jackson, GSP, Ronda Rousey, and, of course, Randy Couture made inroads into the movie business, starring in films from *The Expendables* franchise to *The A-Team*. It was the next step toward global domination for a sport whose champions have true crossover appeal.

Since I had been part of the world of MMA for a good number of years, adding this new tier to my résumé felt like a good idea, but most important, from my point of view, it would be an intriguing venture, possibly resulting in another stream of income. Managers typically get 10 to 15 percent of a fighter's purse and other earnings, which can amount to a nice figure if you're able to land a client with the power to do well in the business.

Since I had been dealing with professional fighters from the combat sports world in the media for years, I could plausibly venture into another arena quite easily—or at least that was my thinking. Unfortunately, the top UFC star from the country, Mike Bisping, was already taken, and stealing someone's fighter would not be a good idea, especially when you have the sort of management he had to deal with. Still, there was another potential window that I could open. Andy Farrell, whom I mentioned earlier and who had encountered Mike before he had pursued a UFC career, was eager to fight a prominent name in the MMA world and asked me to arrange a fight for him.

The idea was that I would manage Andy through my company as a side venture, as I was busy with other commitments in the literary world. In an attempt to get the ball rolling, I phoned a major MMA promoter whom I often had a good laugh with as I tried to squeeze free tickets out of him, which worked most of the time. Andy had an MMA fighter in mind whom he wanted to lock horns with. I won't mention names, but this fighter had married a glamour-girl celebrity, making him a household name. "Everyone wants to fight that guy!" the larger-than-life promoter laughed. Nevertheless, we agreed that I'd send the information for my fighter, and we'd take it from there. I told Andy to get a show reel ready so I could send them to the promoter and, more important, to the UFC and hopefully sign him up with the most prestigious MMA organization in the wake of what I was sure would be an emphatic win.

Always in the habit of pushing anything I touched to the extreme, I kept on pushing Andy to focus on the UFC. That was my only goal. I never had interest in the sort of domestic shows where you'd get a couple of thousand people attending and the fighter would walk away with a few thousand pounds. I wasn't going to invest my time in managing someone who would fight at that level. I always wanted to pursue things on a bigger scale and set the bar high. I feel every budding professional MMA competitor should make it one of his primary goals to sign up with the world's number-one MMA promotion—the UFC.

Besides, I had complete confidence in my friend as far as talent was concerned. The fact that he'd triumphed over the best UFC fighter from Britain was a big confidence booster for me. I thought I could use it to attract the attention of the UFC matchmaker, who at the time was John Perretti. Andy was in his early forties then but had a great physique and was in phenomenal shape. If there were any obstacle for the UFC matchmakers, then it would have been Andy's age, but I felt we could overcome this hurdle because of his almost clean record. And he could prove he had what it took, just like the other fighters on the UFC's roster.

Unfortunately, our partnership never did bear fruit. Being a persistent and highly motivated individual who has a tendency to be on the ball, I constantly pushed my friend. But despite my repeated attempts to guide him, he never did what I told him in spite of showing great enthusiasm and promising me the world in our conversations. Eventually, that idea made its way down the drain, which meant I was never going to produce a UFC champion. I was convinced I could have made it happen if Andy and I had been on the same page.

Sometimes things don't work out, and you have to live with it. This was one of those things. Often, I get carried away when excitement takes over when more often than not it's a good idea to look at things through the lens of reality. In this case, I was oblivious to Andy's commitment. I felt my friend would do well in the UFC and probably become a household name and a star if he put in the work. I could visualize him being interviewed by the mainstream press and signing autographs at UFC events.

I think being a professional fighter—be it in boxing or UFC—is, arguably, one of the best jobs in the world for some. The acclaim, fame, fortune, power, and glory that go with it are just part of the appeal. You're also giving your all to something you're truly passionate about. That said, I truly believe that world champions are blessed individuals. Genetics play a pivotal role, and not everyone can make it to the top, however dedicated they may be. For those who have a profound fascination with professional fight sports but lack what it takes to make it to the top, there are always behind-the-scenes roles in a professional capacity, be it coaching, managing, promoting, or journalism. The latter is what I, of course, pursued. Having been an enthusiastic student of the game who never quite possessed the genetics and skill that are required to excel in the arena—not that I ever had the inclination to pursue the arena on a professional or even amateur level in the first place—I was able to excel in another role instead.

Back when I was considering management, UFC fighters were not making really big money compared to now, but for some, it was a lot considering where they came from. The bigger names and the bigger paydays came later. Revenues from sponsors also poured in as the sport was being recognized in wider circles. I still wanted to get involved. Back then, $150,000 was a decent payday for a headliner, with a few making $500,000 or more—not a bad amount to get 15 percent of.

Although Andy had left me disenchanted, I was still having a damn good time reveling in the media spotlight, keeping busy working on other projects. I was able to use my MMA coverage as a springboard to get more involved in the sport of boxing in terms of a sportswriter, and eventually it paid off in a huge way. The greatest sportsman in history, the man whom I would eventually come to idolize would let me into his life via those who were close to him.

19

Muhammad Ali Encounters

Boxing as a sport and an art was something that I never really explored on a serious level until much later in life than most people discover it. I was intrigued by the martial arts, and when the UFC surfaced, I immediately became an avid follower and advocate of that, too. But it wasn't until the time UFC was making waves that I found myself interviewing world boxing champions. I did this partly to tap into another area within the realm of sports—from martial arts to pugilism—and I considered it my "promotion" as a writer, the moment when I stepped into the higher echelons of the sports world. If you were to ask an average guy on the street, "Who is the world kickboxing champion?," no one will have a clue. In contrast to this, the chances that the same individual would be able to name the world heavyweight boxing champion are pretty damn high. Boxing back then was on another level—on all levels, from the money and fame it offered to sponsorships and major broadcasting deals. Certainly, MMA now has an equal footing, but back then, it was different.

After exploring and piecing together the life and legacy of the late, great Bruce Lee, I contemplated researching the life of another iconic sporting figure. Above all others, Muhammad Ali's image floated into my head. A biography of Ali would be the perfect next project. Ali has long been recognized as the world's most famous man—no one was bigger. One of the twentieth century's towering figures, he transcended sport and had a huge impact on pop culture. To be honest, Ali didn't captivate me as a young boy growing up, and he wasn't an idol of mine even when I transitioned into my adult years, but I still was aware of him. It wasn't until many years later when boxing fever hit me that I was able to discern what I had been missing.

Another reason to investigate Ali was his huge appeal—my days of trying to appeal to a niche audience were long gone. The Greatest had sustained his celebrity status as he achieved more outside of the sport than inside the ring, becoming a political activist and a symbol of hope to billions. The media's wrath toward him during his career turned to adulation long after he retired from fighting as they came to terms with his humanitarian work and his status as a symbol of reconciliation.

The one thing that set the three-time heavyweight champion apart from all other public figures was how he evoked a feeling of shared belief and emotion with people from all walks of life. He came to prominence at a time when the United States was in a state of political and racial upheaval and stood, as I would come to learn, at the intersection of the athletic and the political. His association with Malcolm X and the Black Muslims alongside his refusal to fight in the Vietnam War show his faith in his beliefs—one never repudiates one's deepest values.

Speaking of Malcolm X, about a year ago, I managed to get hold of John Ali's cell phone number. John, a Nation of Islam secretary back in the day, was allegedly responsible for orchestrating Malcolm X's murder. He went into hiding after the death of Nation of Islam leader Elijah Muhammad in 1975. He was allegedly an FBI agent—the FBI's top informant in the Nation of Islam in the 1960s—or operative of U.S. intelligence agencies. This reclusive figure emerged after more than four decades, and I wasn't going to let this opportunity elude me, so I called him on his cell phone. I wasn't sure he'd answer—but he did. I told him who I was and that I'd like to interview him. He told me to call him Tuesday. When I called him that Tuesday, he didn't answer the phone. I followed up another day, and this time around, I managed to get hold of him, but again, he asked me to call on Tuesday. This exact scenario repeated several times until about the fourth attempt, when I got hold of him and we got talking casually—not about Malcolm X, though. The man—now in his mid-nineties—was initially reluctant, but then he said he'd want payment if I wanted to interview him. Sadly, nothing came to fruition.

༄

My burgeoning interest in researching Ali led me to some very interesting people indeed. But where do you start with such a well-known figure? In my opinion, family members are always the best to start with. I was surprised to learn that most people don't even know Ali has a son (in fact, he has another adopted son, too). But it is nearly impossible to come across any interview or media coverage with Muhammad Ali Jr.—his biological son—although in recent years, he's made headlines for all the wrong reasons. That seemed like a good starting point. And though my position has presented me with opportunities to talk to an array of diverse people—boxing legends, UFC champions, bodybuilding champions, and Hollywood actors—whenever I get asked, "Who was the best person that you've interviewed?," without hesitation, I would say that Muhammad Ali Jr. is close to the top of the list.

What impressed me most about Ali Jr. was his humble nature. For almost all his life, he was rarely one to seek publicity despite being the son of one of the most famous humans in the world. Furthermore, I was really shocked to hear that he was unemployed and looking for employment. *What?* I thought. That's another story in itself. As my research unfolded, I came to learn that he had a job at the fairground. Years later after the passing of his father, he reportedly inherited some money, which he rightly deserved, but for much of his life, he was forced to work like everyone else. Despite his father's status, he hasn't had an easy ride at all, unlike many children of A-list celebrities.

When I phoned Ali Jr. to discuss his father, he kindly obliged. He was living in Chicago, the city where his mother Khalilah (born Belinda Boyd) is from and where Ali spent many years. Early in our conversation, he told me about the political stand his dad took by not going to war and standing up for his rights. He revealed to me that he was sheltered while growing up because of possible kidnapping attempts because of who his father was. He also hadn't spent as much time around his father as most sons spend around their dads, as his grandparents had brought up Ali's four children. "My father let me be my own man," this soft-spoken, mild-mannered man told me. "But I was actually sheltered my whole life because of who my father was. We had family threats on our lives. It really hindered me instead of helping me because I wasn't able to put myself out there." Compared to the rest of Ali's children, he had a different upbringing, out of the public spotlight. "It really put a dent on my whole life. But everything is okay, it's not a total loss," he assured me.

He stunned me, however, when he revealed that Bruce Lee had taught his mother. For a split second, I froze in mid-interview. This was news to me. I didn't know what to make of it, to be honest. As far as I knew, there had been virtually no direct contact between Bruce Lee and Muhammad Ali, but had I missed something? For a second, my mind started to wander toward picking up a lie detector machine, but I did find out later that his mother had learned karate, something cleared up many years later when I queried this with Ali Jr.'s sister Rasheda. She told me that it was actually Jim Kelly, the costar of Bruce Lee's *Enter the Dragon*, who taught their mother.

However, when I spoke to their mother, Khalilah, I was left stunned. Setting the record straight, she revealed to me, "I had a conversation with Bruce. He asked me, 'Can you give me some fight films on him?' He said he would like to study them. I said, 'Sure.' So I delivered some 16-millimeter films to Bruce and gave him these so he could study Ali's movement." It was a pleasant surprise for me to learn that she had actually met and trained with the late master.

"When I went to Washington, D.C., Bruce and I worked out a little bit together. He showed me some jeet kune do, and I admired him as well. I tried to keep it a secret from Ali because I didn't want him knowing karate (martial arts)." All this was great, and I had bagged a world exclusive; nevertheless, what I really wanted to find out more than anything else was, what did Ali share with his wife about Bruce Lee?

Khalilah continued, "Ali admired Bruce Lee. He admired him as a great professional. He thought he was really smooth, and he thought he was good looking. And he would refer Bruce Lee to himself like they both are good looking—that's why a lot of people are attracted to them because they're not only good performers but are good looking too. Good-looking people draw attention. He asked me, and I said, 'Yeah, he's very good looking.'"

Ali, of course, has more often than not been compared to the late martial arts icon. A question that countless drunks have argued in bars is who would win a fight between Ali and Lee. Ali's son had his own opinion. He said Bruce Lee was the Muhammad Ali of karate (martial arts) and let out a timid laugh. "I think it would've been a good fight between my father and Bruce Lee," he said.

That said, he seemed to have strong reservations regarding Mike Tyson's status as a boxer. "Now, my father and Mike Tyson? My father would've kicked his butt," he told me. "Everybody says 'Oh, Mike Tyson would've kicked your father's butt.' I say no way. Mike Tyson can't go the distance, he couldn't go 15 rounds. He's not a boxer; he's a street fighter." I was eagerly listening to him now, hanging on his every word. "Bruce Lee, on the other hand, that would've been a good fight. They were both young, they were both agile, and both took it to the limit with their training. They were both the best at what they did." Now, this man was talking sense.

I switched the conversation to religion, something that Ali held close to his heart after he converted to Islam, especially when he became a Sunni Muslim in 1975. "Your father went to hajj in Mecca and later became zealously committed to his religion." I asked Ali Jr., "Did he relate any stories to you about how he felt about the experience?"

"Oh, yeah, yeah." Ali Jr. replied. "He felt actually sorry for a lot of things he had said like, 'the white man's a devil.' He really felt bad about that because the fact is that when he went to hajj, he saw black Muslims, white Muslims, yellow Muslims—all different types of races, all Muslims."

"Did your father give you advice as you were growing up?" I asked him.

"Oh, yeah," he said. "One thing he said to me, which I remember, is, don't care what people call you. I don't care what people think of you; everybody is equal under the eyes of God."

It was becoming apparent that, however distant his upbringing, Ali taught his son humility and principles as any good father would.

"He said, 'I care about people being as human and not what color they are,'" Ali Jr. told me. "He said that you should look at people and respect them as human beings. Don't judge people, period. He said what you need to look for is the content of their character. If they've got a good character and they're not stuck up, if they're not racists, then they're good people. If they are, then just leave them alone. He said watch what you say and watch what you do and respect your elders." It was a delightful experience to have the son of The Greatest share these insights with me. We continued talking off the record for quite some time.

↺

One of my more controversial interviewees from the same period was Joe Lewis, a karate champion who trained with Bruce Lee. Joe has had his fair share of critics for criticizing his friend and training partner, but you can't deny that Joe walks the walk. "Bruce Lee wasn't a fighter," he explained to me in a two-hour-long conversation, the first time I interviewed him. This was far from the first time he'd made questionable statements. "People say, 'Oh, yes, he was. He was a fighter.' But we're not talking about street fighters. Street fighters have records down at the police departments. A real fighter has a record. He has wins, losses, knockouts, and draws. If you don't have a record, you're not a fighter. That's it—it's a simple definition."

Joe himself had experienced boxing training at the famous Main Street gym in Los Angeles. In fact, he had Bruce accompany him on numerous occasions there where Joe had the great fortune to train with Sugar Ray Robinson, a fighter Ali had once admired.

Joe also had a run-in with Ali in 1975. The editor of a prominent martial arts magazine phoned Joe, informing him that Ali was going to be doing a media tour in Los Angeles promoting his upcoming fight with wrestler Antonio Inoki, which would be the first major boxer-versus-wrestler bout in the United States. Joe showed up to see Ali, who was wearing a long-sleeved black shirt and black pants, with about 20 photographers from the press and the major TV networks present, peppering the heavyweight champion with questions. Joe found his way to the ring apron alongside Bob Wall, the world karate champion who had played a villain in *Enter the Dragon* and the editor who had invited them.

"I turn to Bob Wall and say, 'You know what, Ali is talking about how he can beat any martial artist, boxer, or wrestler.' I'm thinking, *You can beat any wrestler? What the hell are you talking about?*" I was laughing just imagining it. If there was one person who could tell a compelling story, it was Joe Lewis. He would shock you, entertain you, and have you laugh out loud. Joe explained to me that wrestlers (and grapplers for that matter) are the best fighters on the planet and that, with the advent of the UFC, this fact had finally been proven on the world stage. I had been oblivious to the fact he had a wrestling background before he pursued the martial arts to become the greatest karate fighter of all time, but he had, first and foremost, been a wrestler, he revealed.

"So I'm watching Ali thinking, *You can't beat no damn wrestler*," he told me. Joe had been in the ring with boxers, of course. They were like babies, he told me. If you shoot to the legs and take them down, they last maybe 30 seconds. So Joe wasn't exactly impressed by Ali's claim to be The Greatest.

At the event he attended, the famous professional wrestler "Classy" Freddie Blassie was in the ring with Ali, all part of the pantomime. Bob and the editor encouraged Joe to needle Ali about his grappling ability and see what would bounce back. One of the photographers in the ring walked over to where the three were standing to get a shot. Turning to the photographer, Joe said, "Ask Ali what he would do if a wrestler faked a jab at the head and ducked down underneath, took the legs, and took him down?" The photographer shouted out, "Here, you ask him! Ali! Ali! Come here! Come here!" Joe, he told me, was thinking to himself, *Oh, my God, I don't want to ask him. I'm embarrassed.*

Ali walked over until he was a few feet from Joe. "What do you do if a guy fakes a jab to the head and then dives at your legs?" Joe put the golden question directly to The Greatest.

"Come on in here, boy, and show me," Ali responded. "Nah, I don't want to," Joe conceded. But he wasn't going to slip out of it that easily—after all, he had Ali's attention now. Three people shoved Joe into the ring.

Joe was down to 180 pounds because he was getting into shape for a film—he was pursuing acting at the time. He wasn't in really great shape but was pretty strong and could deadlift 400 pounds. His personal best at one time was 550 pounds, he told me. So lifting somebody Ali's size up was pretty much a walk in the park for him—if he could get his hands on them.

Ali got ready in a boxing stance with his hands up, shuffling from side to side, always the showman and never reluctant to spar with anyone at any given opportunity. "I could feel the energy of everyone in the room," Joe explained to me as I hung on every word. "'Come on, come on, show us!' the raucous crowd was shouting."

Joe, maintaining his distance, proceeded with a shoulder fake to Ali's head in an attempt to draw a reaction. Ali responded by trying to catch the jab with both hands. Joe, in a flash, ducked down and shot for the legs for a double-leg tackle. As soon as Joe wrapped his arms around Ali's legs, he paused because he was hesitant to actually follow through by taking the Champ down to the ground. However, a burst of laughter from the ecstatic crowd followed. There were 100 people in attendance besides the photographers and the press.

"I'll tell you what he did," Joe said to me. "He lay on my back as I was underneath holding his legs, and he made that face where he opened his mouth real wide. As soon as he laughed, it pissed me off. So I picked him up, spun him upside down, and dumped him." Joe refrained from applying a submission, instead just pinning Ali. Freddie, with the help of two other people, grabbed Joe and took him off Ali. "Whoa, whoa, just playing," Joe assured everyone as he stood up. "I figured he thought I was trying to kill him or something, which I could have because from what I remember, his body felt like a woman. He was real soft like jelly, and that shocked me because I'm used to wrestling and doing weightlifting where the body is hard as a brick." According to Joe, Ali felt really, really weak. He felt no strength in the Champ—not wrestler strength anyway. Ali stood up, and he stood next to Joe. And a whole herd of photographers were now snapping pictures, and Ali put his arm around Joe's shoulder. "You were lifting weights when you were younger, weren't you?" Ali joked. Joe claims Ali could tell he was a lot stronger than anyone he'd been in the ring with before.

The action wasn't over.

"Come on, do that again," Ali insisted.

"You're shitting me," Joe responded in amazement "What do you mean, do it again?" So they squared off, and Joe repeated the fake hand and dropped down for a double-leg tackle, taking Ali down again. Ali was lying on the floor pinned and, again, took the whole thing humorously. Ali's entourage members came to the rescue again. Joe quickly assured everyone that they were just playing. "I did it quite hard, and it looked kind of mean," he said. The greatest karate champion of all time, dubbed the Muhammad Ali of karate, was now the center of focus, as the press wasted no time snapping more pictures.

After all the commotion and chaos, Ali sent his representative to approach Joe. "I represent Muhammad Ali, and he would like to invite you to dinner tonight," the representative told him. Joe turned down the invitation, just like he had three years earlier turned down the part in *Way of the Dragon* that his friend Bruce Lee offered him. If he hadn't, I believe that literally nobody would know the name Chuck Norris. Instead, Joe would have been a star. Joe admitted to me that, perhaps, he shouldn't have turned down Ali's invitation, just like he shouldn't have turned down his friend's.

⌒

Ali, although never formally trained in the martial arts of the Orient, did dabble a little, as he had a couple of friends—I would say they were more like associates—who were revered martial artists. On one occasion, one of his associates at Deer Lake training camp who sometimes worked out with him wanted Ali to attend a karate tournament he was hosting. This was two or three years before the Ali–Lewis incident took place.

"Would you come to my karate tournament?" he asked Ali. "There's going to be several thousand people, and a lot of them want to meet you." Perhaps surprisingly, Ali immediately said, "Yes!" Now a lot of times, Ali would say yes to projects and not mean it or would forget about it. So this associate approached Ali's corner man Bundini Brown and followed up. "Look, I've talked to Muhammad. He said he'll come. Can you do me a favor and see that he gets there?"

"What time you want him there and where at?" asked Bundini. The associate told him, and Bundini said, "I'll give you my word he'll be there."

On the day, sure enough, Ali's corner man made sure he attended this event. Both men showed up, and Ali signed autographs and even sparred with some people. One thing Ali stipulated was that his opponents not be allowed to kick below the belt, but you could do basically anything else. Ali, I was told by this associate, did learn how to evade and counter kicks so that he couldn't get kicked. So, the heavyweight champion sparred with karate competitors that day in front of the crowd, and yet it still went the way of the champ. The martial artists could basically do what they wanted, and Ali still beat most of them, according to this associate of Ali. Ali said to his associate, "I wish karate people earned a lot more money. I could get good at this." I mean, honestly, how many world champion boxers would do that now?

Late in the day, Ali sparred a well-known martial arts exponent from that era called Danny Pai, who was winning the sparring fight on points when he kicked Ali above the belt, which was fair enough according to the rules. However, the associate stopped the fight there because he didn't want them fighting for real, sensing that things could spiral out of control. Ali also sparred two other champions and actually beat both of them. Ali was fast, the fastest thing this associate had ever seen, he told me. Whether the brash boxing champion would've made an all-around great fighter or not, like most things, is debatable. One thing that is thought provoking is that if Joe Lewis was able to take Ali down repeatedly, it makes you wonder if Ali would've beaten Bruce Lee in a real fight. Take into account many are of the sentiment that Ali would've literally killed Bruce. In the ring, in a boxing match, no doubt, but in the street, things would've been reversed, I believe. And Inoki would certainly have been too much for Ali in a no-holds-barred real fight.

20

From Martial Arts to Movie Magic

Before I parlayed my sportswriting career into action movie journalism, I already had a platform to connect with those who were involved in the martial arts action movie industry. My work on *Martial Arts Illustrated* meant I could talk with many martial artists who worked in the action genre.

Martial artist Dave Lea, who had pursued Hollywood in the late 1980s and successfully made it as a stuntman, was one such individual. Dave had performed stunts on the 1989 *Batman* film, doubling for Michael Keaton. Dave went on to work on numerous major Hollywood flicks starring A-list stars. It's hard to miss the ponytailed stuntman fighting Sylvester Stallone in *Tango and Cash*, where there's some eye-catching stick work on display, which I'm sure Dave picked up from Dan Inosanto at the Inosanto Academy in Los Angeles, where he frequently honed his skills.

I did a lengthy interview with David that resulted in a major feature. Back then, most stuntmen were based in Los Angeles. I had several friends in the Hollywood stunt business. Both Ron Balicki and Diana Lee Inosanto performed stunts on movies while maintaining their martial arts teaching duties, and I found this combination very appealing. I did get involved to an extent, working with stunt teams as a SPACT, but mainly as a background artist.

There were a couple things in my favor. My involvement in the martial arts media had given me a plethora of contacts and friends. And, of course, now there's more demand than ever for skilled martial artists in Hollywood. Back in the 1950s and 1960s, John Wayne–style fisticuffs ruled the screen, but after Bruce Lee exploded onto the scene in the 1970s, he influenced a whole new generation. Then, later films, such as *The Matrix* and *Kill Bill*, reintroduced audiences to the Chinese style of ultra-fast-fight choreography that's so appealing to watch. Today, in any action movie with fights, you can bet your bottom dollar martial arts will play a part.

Impact, an action movie magazine with offices in the United Kingdom, the United States, and Hong Kong and published from 1992 to 2012, was the premier magazine for lovers of martial arts in movies and action movies in general for as long as it was published. My colleague, Andy Staton, wrote for *Impact* in addition to penning his column in *Martial Arts Illustrated*. It wasn't until I had been at *Martial Arts Illustrated* for six years that I followed in Andy's footsteps, jumping aboard with the *Impact* team. Both publications were owned by the same company and ran from the same offices. Prior to this, it hadn't even crossed my mind that I had a life-changing career opportunity waiting for me right on my doorstep.

Joining the *Impact* team was one of the best moves I ever made in my career. It afforded me a wonderful platform to talk to A-list names outside of martial arts and MMA and to have a behind-the-scenes glimpse into Hollywood. I felt on top of the world.

It wasn't long before I found myself interviewing the Hollywood fraternity, touching on their fitness, training, and everyday lives as well as their glittering careers. Long gone were the days of being merely part of the combat sports press. I was filled with excitement but still composed myself.

While martial arts had been my platform and passion, now I was ready to use them as a springboard to bigger, broader endeavors. Soon, I started to focus on movie personalities, but I also further extended myself as far as boxing and UFC stars were concerned, going after bigger and better interviewees. The last thing I wanted was to abandon my roots, but I was ready to move up.

Now I felt I had arrived. A whole new world of showbiz opened up to me. It was a rush, but it wasn't always stress free. I already had direct numbers for dozens of fighters and managers, but now I was dealing with huge talent agencies, such as CAA, WME, and ICM, which have hundreds of employees and different agents. This is where the multi-million-dollar deals were being made, and the agents can be a nightmare to deal with. You often had to chase them with repeated calls and e-mails for days, weeks, or sometimes months on end. But I was accustomed to this, and as my contact book grew, I found it easier to work around these agents.

Whenever I contacted these talent agents, it reminded me of the movie *Jerry Maguire* with Tom Cruise and Cuba Gooding Jr. The film portrays Cruise as a high-powered professional sports agent, and the amount of yelling and high-pressure tactics in that movie, if anything, is not as aggressive as the real thing.

Managers and publicists have great powers. They are there not only to make sure that their clients receive the best possible deals but equally to avoid being undermined in the media or any deal they secure. When they're canny and protective, it is quite understandable, but it can be frustrating. Fortunately, by this point in my career, I was pretty thick-skinned. Whenever an interview was refused, the usual "Thank you for reaching out to us, but . . ." would make its way over the Atlantic electronically. It was never a good feeling, but it was better than the silent treatment. Rejection is part of life.

Once I arranged an interview with the late David Carradine, who played the title role in Quentin Tarantino's *Kill Bill* movies. Best known for his leading role as peace-loving Shaolin monk Kwai Chang Caine, David came to prominence in 1972 when he took the role that Bruce Lee had developed for himself in the popular *Kung Fu* TV series. On the day of the interview, I called David on his cell phone at the scheduled time. "I can't talk right now!" he barked at me. "I'm in the elevator. Call me back in 30 minutes!" I called him back half an hour later and had a chat with him.

What I found most ironic was that, despite having released and promoted a series of tai chi fitness DVDs, David seemingly wasn't into fitness at all. I asked him how he kept fit and if he could describe his regime. To my great surprise, he revealed he didn't enjoy working out and wasn't really into exercise. He conceded that he was lazy. I thought to myself, *Why produce a series of DVDs promoting fitness when you yourself are not an advocate of fitness through training for a healthy lifestyle?* There's an obvious answer to that, of course. I could also sense there was a cat running around in his house and that David was multitasking while talking to me. I could hear him shouting at the cat. The interview was getting stranger and stranger.

This was the man who not only took Bruce's part from him in the *Kung Fu* series but also played the role in the film Bruce had developed and written titled *Silent Flute* after Bruce's death—a movie that, in case you haven't seen it, was a complete mess. When I asked him about this, though, he flipped.

"Why do people assume the part was originally for Bruce?" he questioned. "It was never intended for him!"—this in spite of the fact that several notable and reliable sources made it quite clear that Bruce was originally considered to play the character David ended up playing. This includes a letter that Ted Ashley, the Warner Bros. executive, wrote to Bruce. In the letter, the executive basically informed Bruce that he had been rejected because the studio thought it was too big of a risk to invest in an unknown Asian actor because they worried the American public would not embrace a Chinese actor. Racism had prevented Bruce from penetrating Hollywood, and they invested in David, who was Caucasian and looked just Oriental enough for the part. David, at the time, had no real martial arts experience and had someone train him for the part from scratch. Nevertheless, the show was a big hit.

Tragically, David died a little over a year after our interview.

I also had the opportunity to interview Hollywood film director Ivan Reitman. When his new movie *No Strings Attached*, starring Emily Blunt and Ashton Kutcher, was being released, I got in touch with the publicists. Reitman has directed some top-grossing Hollywood flicks, with a résumé including *Ghostbusters*, *Twins*, *Kindergarten Cop*, and the not-so-successful Arnie flop *Junior*. This was another phone interview, and I began by asking the director questions relating to his new movie, but then I decided to switch gears in the hope of swaying him to talk about his previous works with Arnold Schwarzenegger. The director halfheartedly answered the first Arnie question or two before mumbling something to his publicist. Then it happened again. This time, the publicist startled me by telling me that there would be no more questions and that the interview was over.

In the morning, my editor had a word with me. Apparently, Ivan's people had logged a complaint saying that the interview was supposed to focus on the new movie but that I had digressed. I explained that I wanted to talk to him about his new film but also about the success he had with Arnold—though, to be honest, I really did just want to talk about Arnold. I was disappointed not to learn more about their collaborations, but I was quickly learning that interviewing those in the movie business was a much different animal than interviewing MMA stars.

One movie star whom I personally wanted to connect with and tried to lock down several times to no avail was Nicolas Cage. Nicolas is a man of taste and has diverse interests, including Bruce Lee, martial arts, and UFC. I was primed to talk to him about his involvement with jiu-jitsu and his former instructor Royce Gracie, who had taught him privately at his home. Among the Hollywood celebrities who had embraced the UFC, Nicolas was one of the most prominent. After he had been mesmerized by the lithe skills of Royce in the first-ever UFCs, he sought out and became a private student of the three-time UFC champion alongside several other celebrities, notably Guy Ritchie and Jim Carey.

Although not known as a martial arts actor, Nicolas utilized his martial arts skills in some of his movies, including showcasing the wing chun system—a style Bruce Lee originally studied before embarking on his mission of self-discovery to devise jeet kune do—in *Bangkok Dangerous*. In fact, I was pleasantly surprised to learn that Nicolas had originally been inspired by Bruce to get into acting.

"When I was eight, it was in the early seventies, my dad decided to take me to the theater, and I saw a movie that changed my life, my world really, because this force was in a movie called *Enter the Dragon*," Nicolas told an interviewer once while promoting one of his new action films. And it wasn't just because of the way the kung fu star moved. Although Nicolas was blown away when he witnessed the famous back flip that Bruce did—which was actually one of only a couple times Bruce used a stuntman—he said it was the star's presence and charisma that called out to him. "I was like, you know, I wanna do that!" said Nicolas. "I wanna be a film actor."

Later, Nicolas discovered James Dean and Marlon Brando, which was a whole other level of emotional acting, but the first idea of wanting to be in movies came from the late martial arts master. Royce told me that Nicolas would phone him, he would go over to his house, and they would lay the mats out and train. The actor was a very coordinated and intelligent student and easy to teach as well as being strong.

I was sorry an interview with Nicolas Cage never materialized, but maybe one day it will happen!

Writing for a leading action movie magazine really allowed me to experience many highs and lows. I enjoyed being part of the entertainment press, but I didn't merely want to write for a monthly action movie magazine; I had a bigger vision. It was time to explore and research the life of one of the biggest names in Hollywood.

21

I'll Be Back

Now that I had been reveling in life as a member of the entertainment press for a while, it was inevitable that I would gravitate more toward all things Hollywood. And the iconic figure whose life I most wanted to dive deep into was the star of countless high-octane action thrillers and family films, Arnold Schwarzenegger. He's the rare celebrity who's succeeded in several spheres: not only has he achieved legendary status as the greatest bodybuilder of all time, then as the biggest action movie star in the world, but he's continued to use that status for good, moving into politics and championing the environment.

Arnold's story is fascinating and equally inspiring. As a young boy growing up in a small village in Austria during the 1950s and early 1960s, he daydreamed about a land afar where people from all corners of the globe emigrated in search of riches and fame. Coming to America in 1968, with $25 and a gym bag and almost no understanding of the English language, he quickly became a famous face in what was then considered by many a mocked sport, popularizing the sport of bodybuilding like never before. To many, he's the epitome of the American Dream—an immigrant who succeeded through sheer hard work.

Then there's his status as the greatest bodybuilder in the history of the sport—just as Bruce Lee is widely acknowledged as the greatest martial arts exponent of the century and Muhammad Ali the greatest boxer of all time. For me, researching the life story of the greatest iron pumper ever would complete the set. Having occasionally contributed to bodybuilding magazines, I was familiar with the sport and its participants, and since I was writing for an action movie magazine, it seemed like the perfect marriage—a merging of my interests.

For my part, I first came to know of Arnold when I went to my next-door neighbor's relative's house and watched the testosterone-fueled action epic *Commando* in 1985. I was 10 years old—too young for that film in hindsight—and I remember one of the neighbors saying to me that Arnold was Mr. Universe. I didn't know what that meant; I thought it was someone like Flash Gordon who literally had something to do with the universe. Eventually, I came to learn it had something to do with bodybuilding (it's actually a smaller competition, often considered a stepping-stone to Mr. Olympia). *Commando* was a good action movie, I thought at the time, little knowing that I would later get to interview director Mark Lester as well as Arnold's costar Bill Duke. So, Arnold took up residence in my subconscious early. Despite this, I hadn't followed his career in great detail, nor did this giant stand out from the rest of the musclemen I admired growing up—I was too engrossed in the martial arts—but I did find his movies quite interesting.

Later, as I immersed myself into his incredible life, I learned that fame and fortune weren't handed to the Austrian on a plate—far from it. Early in his career, doors were slammed in his face faster than they opened. His thick accent, a body that was too big, a name that no one could pronounce, and lackluster acting skills were all hurdles he would have to overcome. The appeal of the "Austrian Oak" may have been his coveted bodybuilding titles and box-office success, but what I found equally appealing was his mind and motivation to succeed—how he pursued business ventures and career goals relentlessly and made a success out of anything he touched. When you study him, no matter what profession you're in, you can take away inspiration and use it as a blueprint to become successful.

From the perspective of a biographer, there are two imperative prerequisites I have in mind when it comes to producing work. First, I want the audience and critics to go away with a sense of satisfaction. Pleasing the reader is of the utmost importance. Second, the caliber and quality of the interviewee are crucial. It's important to do your homework. I decided to get to work.

∼

I started with Arnold the actor as I nailed down the seven-time Mr. Olympia's bodybuilding friends and buddies. Arnold's acting hasn't got him an Oscar, but his determination to succeed in Hollywood was

present in his head the day he set foot on American soil. To begin my
quest, I spoke to his acting coach Eric Morris, who is one of the most
controversial and famous acting coaches in America. If there was anyone who could enlighten me on the work ethic the sportsman-turned-
actor demonstrated to make it in such a cutthroat industry, then I had
to look no further than this man. Arnold told his coach that he loved his
work in the gym, but the kind of work he was most passionate about
was movies. Arnold's coach apparently had great faith in him from the
beginning and told me he had great conviction his pupil would succeed.

"He came in one night very angry," Eric told me. "I saw him sitting
there, and I could tell he was angry. So I got him up onstage, and I said,
'What's going on, Arnold?' He said—in his accent—he had just had a
very disappointing interview with an agent. He said, 'I'm pissed off!
They don't like my accent. They don't like my body. To hell with them!
I'm going to be a superstar.' And everybody laughed and applauded
him. Then he did an exercise in class where he re-created a Christmas
morning in Austria. He was playing with some of his toys, and he
became very vulnerable; it brought tears to everybody's eyes in the
class." I was surprised to learn that Arnold, the epitome of machismo,
had a vulnerable side to him. "He plays all these action picture heroes
where he kills people, but, you know, Arnold is a very, very sensitive
man," Eric added.

Another little-known fact: when Arnold was taking acting lessons,
karate master Joe Lewis was a member of the same class, honing his
own acting skills under the watchful eye of Arnold's coach. I had always
been intrigued by Joe's stories. He'd treated me to some amazing tales
of encounters with Bruce Lee and Muhammad Ali. And I wasn't going
to pass on the chance of speaking to him again. This man could breathe
life into any story. Besides, I felt I could learn something different and
new because Joe had hardly spoken about Arnold publicly. I asked Joe
if he was surprised when his former colleague became a big movie star,
mentioning that he wasn't exactly an obvious box-office draw.

"No, but John Wayne wasn't, either. Bruce Lee wasn't, either," Joe
told me. "That's not what makes money on the big screen; it's your
persona." Joe proceeded to explain to me that it's ability on the screen,
that presence and the unique energy that you project, that captures the
public's imagination.

For his part, Arnold was able to endear himself to the audience because of that special energy and image he portrayed. "I was shocked,"
recalled Joe. "Because, first of all, his accent was very strong. I'm thinking, *What kind of role can he get?* You can only get roles where you need

that accent." As we all know now, Arnold made Hollywood embrace him and refused to take no for an answer, first taking on roles like the robotic T-800 and then other roles where his accent barely mattered.

Next, I asked Joe about his relationship with Arnold, if he socialized with him often, so I could get a glimpse of Arnold's personality through the lens of this martial arts champion. Joe told me they had mutual friends who had brought them together. "Arnold was kind of a unique figure; he was a man's man," Joe explained further of Arnold's personality back in the 1970s. "But he wasn't necessarily somebody you could befriend easily because he was kind of a loner." According to Joe, Arnold was always dedicated to his work. "He didn't really hang out with the guys, so to speak. He was kind of like me. I didn't like hanging out with the guys, either. People didn't think he was real friendly. Then again, it could've been the fact he needed to learn the language."

One subject that I was keen to get Joe's take on was Arnold's link to the martial arts, if any. I asked the karate champion if he had trained the "Terminator" in martial arts because I had seen Arnold featured in an article in *Black Belt* magazine that claimed Joe had trained him. "In the very first paragraph, he said he trained with me and Chuck Norris," Joe said. "Now, I don't know if he said that for real or the magazine just says he said that."

I was disconcerted by what I was hearing. At one point, Joe gave a copy of the magazine to Jim Lorimer—Arnold's close friend and the copromoter of the annual Arnold Classic—and asked him if Arnold could sign it for him. Joe made it clear to me that he's not the type of person whom you might call an autograph hunter but thought it was kind of, as he put it, "neat" that Arnold had used his name in there, so he made an exception.

"Jim threw the magazine in the bin," Joe continued. "If he wants to tell people he trained with me, let him say that." I didn't know what to make of it all, and it left me scratching my head, but I found the whole episode quite interesting if a little ambiguous.

Whether Arnold had any martial arts training outside of films continued to be unclear to me until some years later when I was at Arnold's best friend Franco Columbu's office in West Los Angeles. Franco told me that Arnold has never trained seriously in martial arts. Franco, who had been a competitive boxer in his native Italy, started training in Brazilian jiu-jitsu when the craze spread after the first UFC, but the "Austrian Oak" had other things on his mind.

Arnold did prepare himself for some movies that required martial arts training, however. For example, he took extensive training under stunt coordinator Mike Vendrell when filming *Commando* and mastered the sword under notable Japanese master Kiyoshi Yamazaki to prepare himself for *Conan*.

"I remember once we walked into a magazine office, for *Inside Kung Fu*, and he saw me on the cover of a magazine," Joe, a fervent iron pumper himself, told me. "And he told the publishers, 'Hey, this guy has a good body.'"

Since Joe's friendship with the late Bruce Lee had been well documented, I asked Joe if he had ever discussed Bruce with Arnold or vice versa.

"I was with Bruce Lee from 1967," Joe said. "Arnold didn't get really well known till he beat Sergio Oliva in the Mr. Olympia contest in 1970, so my thing with Bruce Lee did not come up. I mean, Bruce Lee has a lot of fans who are famous people. Today, for example, Mike Tyson talks a lot about Bruce Lee. The Klitschko brothers, the famous world champion boxers, think a lot of Bruce Lee. The most famous basketball player in this country, probably the best basketball player in the world, Kobe Bryant, is a Bruce Lee fan. So it's kind of odd talking to Bruce Lee about other famous people when he was going to become probably more famous than they are." This answer was good enough for me.

Speaking of Bruce Lee, as I was researching Arnold's life, I interviewed Hollywood executive producer Andrew Vajna, who worked on some of Arnold's most successful movies. Researching the interview, I realized it was the same producer who had offered Bruce a two-film deal before the kung fu star passed away. I thought I'd hit the jackpot. I had been aware that a Hungarian film producer had made the offer to Bruce prior to Bruce's untimely death, and Andrew revealed to me that he had bought Bruce the house in which Bruce lived in Hong Kong at the height of his fame as part of the advance payment for a movie they were discussing.

Unfortunately, the producer would never get to work with Bruce. He went on to produce several action movies, including *Rambo* with Sylvester Stallone, a couple of the *Terminator* movies, and *Total Recall*, all of which were extremely successful at the box office. Originally from Hungary, Andrew was an aspiring filmmaker and partnered with another enthusiastic filmmaker, Mario Kassar. Both men dedicated themselves relentlessly to their craft and in due course made their mark in Hollywood.

I found Andrew's story inspiring. He had come from an Eastern European country and pursued his dream, eventually conquering Hollywood, but remained a very nice gentleman who made time for me. Mario, originally from Beirut, Lebanon, had bought the rights to Bruce's first movie—one of the first foreigners to do so—for parts of Middle East. It was interesting to learn of the Bruce Lee connections both of these big Hollywood executives had who went on to work with Arnold and Stallone. I have often contemplated what movies Bruce would have made and whom he would have worked with. For film fans, a partnership with Stallone or Schwarzenegger could have been phenomenal.

How do Bruce and Arnold compare? Of course, both were physical specimens, but one was a fighter and the other a bodybuilder. One story that has stayed with me ever since I was a young teenager is from when I was walking to the weights gym one Saturday morning with my friend. We were talking, as we often did, about the man we idolized—Bruce Lee. He chuckled, saying that if Arnold got hold of Bruce in a fight, he would tear him up. I'm thinking, *What the heck?*

I could see it in his eyes as he made this (what I felt was) somewhat demeaning comment. My friend was of the opinion that someone like Bruce could never defeat a man of Arnold's stature, a true behemoth. As much as I was an admirer of bodybuilding athletes (and Arnold was just one of them, no more and no less), I refused to embrace my friend's opinion. His opinion reflected the classic "bigger is always better" philosophy, one that seemed to be quite prevalent at the time before the tremendous explosion of Gracie Jiu-Jitsu.

Since the sport of MMA has enjoyed immense success, it has become part of Arnold's annual expo, simply dubbed "The Arnold" by many fans. Arnold approached Relson Gracie to start the Arnold-Gracie World Submission Championships at the event in the early 2000s. "I just love to watch the fights," Arnold, who has taken a real shine to the sport of MMA, once remarked. "I think they're very entertaining, and you get inspiration because they're in extraordinary shape."

On other occasions, this champion bodybuilder admitted that MMA was his favorite sport to watch. Whether he meant it or not I couldn't say because Arnold had learned the American marketing strategy of saying things to get the public's attention. Arnold said that despite the fact MMA is a sport, in equal measure, he perceived it as show business. He showed his appreciation for the athletes and personalities, equally impressed by the fighters' intellectual skills and their technical brilliance. He remarked, "They can all talk very well, they can explain what they've done, why they won, why they lost."

Like Bruce, Arnold used his sport as a platform to pursue a film career. And just as the martial arts had been kicked into popularity by Bruce Lee movies, Arnold was hugely responsible for elevating the sport of bodybuilding, making it more acceptable and fashionable to have muscles and train with weights. Every action movie star now works out and strives to attain an aesthetic look. In the years after Arnold's success, it became the norm for a Hollywood action hero to strip to show his physique on film. Bruce, who had an invincible aura, paved the way, and Arnold followed a decade later.

⌒

Arnold's career trajectory took another turn when he stepped into the political arena, eventually becoming the governor of California. But this immigrant wasn't content. In the back of his mind, he was of the belief that he could reach further heights and contemplated running for president, a prospect that gave me goose bumps. Unfortunately, the U.S. Constitution prevents foreign-born citizens from holding the nation's top job. But if the opportunity were to present itself, I feel he would prevail, landing the job of president of the most powerful country in the world.

When you are exploring the life of a public figure, be it a fighter, sportsman, or entertainer, you can't leave out his best friend. But when I interviewed Franco Columbu over the phone, I had a rather bizarre encounter. We got talking, and I asked him whether a competitive dynamic existed between them when training. Franco has a very strong accent, being an Italian. Apparently, he misunderstood me. Mid-conversation, he suddenly told me to call him back later, giving me the impression that something urgent required his immediate attention. I called him back several times, but he didn't answer the phone.

When I finally did get through to him, he hung up on me, but I'm a persistent bastard, and he was going to see this firsthand. I got through to him again, and when he answered this time, he said I should call him back later. The sudden U-turn left me bemused. I thought to myself, *Have I said something wrong? Was he upset?* Then it dawned on me: perhaps he thought I was trying to talk about his best friend's controversial past.

At the time, Arnold had a sudden and drastic fall from grace because of his personal life. A segment of the public abhorred him. Speculation ran rife about events in his personal life, but in no way was I pursing that route. That was never my intention, nor did I ask him anything having to do with Arnold's personal life. Franco's apparent lack of understanding brought the interview to an end before I could squeeze in everything I wanted to. It may sound bizarre, but I'm sure one of Arnold's close friends simply thought I was a tabloid journalist. I had interviewed Franco just over four years before when I was in Los Angeles, and he was a very nice man.

I have always endeavored to refrain from embellishing my subjects for the sake of sensationalizing them, something that many journalists and biographers are only too happy to do. I never really had an interest in treading that path. A lot of writers would gravitate toward the controversial side and exploit it because controversy sells. No story gains traction quite so rapidly in today's media frenzy environment than one that tears down an A-list celebrity, even if it's the death knell for a star's career. The pleasures and perils of the celebrity lifestyle became obvious to me as I investigated it. I learned that the media create a buzz or hype to fuel interest but can just as quickly tear you down. The stories regarding Arnold's father were his own personal life; I had no real interest in putting them in the spotlight. I was having none of that. Besides, I had been influenced by writer John Little—a Bruce Lee historian and biographer who actually wrote for the bible of body-building, *FLEX* magazine—who glorified Bruce Lee to the max and wouldn't print a word against him. I think his influence rubbed off on me and shaped my own approach at the time.

Arnold once said, "We all like to be liked, loved, appreciated, but some like more than that. I'm one of them." His words have been embedded in me ever since I heard him say them in an old documentary called *Total Rebuild*. The former governor of California became a motivator and an advocate of self-help and a beacon of hope to young men like myself looking for inspiration. Arnold had become an influence on me with regard to capturing my dreams more so than his physical attributes and high-octane movies. Interestingly, I also learned that Arnold's father always favored his elder brother—this somewhat struck a chord with me. Arnold's first-ever girlfriend, Barbara Outland Baker, told me that Arnold's father believed his younger son was useless and that Arnold's brother was not only a better athlete but also a better person overall. I believe this motivated Arnold further to defy the odds and prove he was worthy and could succeed. And succeed he did, as he took the world by storm and achieved the ultimate not only in a physically demanding sport but in the entertainment and political arenas as well.

22

From Hospitality to MMA Chaos

By the end of the 2000s, there was a new breed of athlete making waves in Hollywood—UFC stars. Randy Couture's acting chops may have come as a surprise to many UFC and action fans, but among the UFC fighters who crossed over into Hollywood, he was the first prominent personality to have a larger impact. In 2011, the UFC champion was working on *The Expendables II*, filming in Bulgaria with an all-star cast. On his way back to America after filming finished, Randy stopped by the United Kingdom for less than a week to hang out and do some publicity and promotion, which I arranged. For my team, this worked out perfectly.

We stayed at the Jumeirah Hotel in Kensington, London, for several days before touring around the country. Kensington and Knightsbridge are full of affluent Arabs, many of whom come to the capital to escape the baking-hot summer months in their own countries. On this occasion, we were guests of DJ, the personal assistant to the crown prince of Dubai, Sheik Hamdan bin Mohammed Rashid Al Maktoum, who had profound passion for adrenaline-fueled sports. Although I never got to meet the crown prince, he was aware of my work. The Jumeirah is frequented by well-known personalities, and it was expensive as hell, but our host had made it explicit to us and his staff that everything was on the house for us. My team, all of whom were my personal friends, wasted no time indulging in the small sliced cheesecakes, which would normally cost £12 a slice, and anything else they could get their hands on.

In the late evening, we congregated in the restaurant on the ground level of the hotel. The ambience was that of the kind of very expensive establishment that only well-off people would frequent. As we sat there gazing at the sophisticated menu, DJ asked Randy what he desired from the menu and recommended Kobe steak. The UFC champion was unfamiliar with the dish, so our host proceeded to explain how they breed the cattle in Japan. They don't let the cattle run around in the field, which prevents the cattle from developing big muscles, which can have an adverse effect by making the meat too tough. Instead, the cattle are pampered from a young age and massaged with milk. My friend Seyfi, being curious, asked if it was halal. To his amusement, DJ started snickering, and his Muslim friends from abroad joined in. They advised Seyfi to have the fish instead.

At the dinner table, we talked about the UFC and anything and everything besides. DJ was an interesting individual, very inquisitive, and it didn't take me long to learn of his profound passion for the martial arts and UFC. He was on the committee of some karate and tae kwon do organizations in the Middle East and had competed in karate tournaments as part of the team from the United Arab Emirates. This man was on a mission to get karate into the Olympics. He was quite well versed in the subject, and I was pleasantly impressed by the enthusiasm he showed. All the white uniforms he had competed in were framed up, he told us. I came to learn that quite a few Middle Eastern royals have competed in martial arts, including a princess who competed in the Olympics in tae kwon do and several other royals who have done well in Brazilian jiu-jitsu tournaments. It dawned on me that these royals took their hobby very seriously. As for DJ, he was a pleasant person to be around. I was rather surprised at his sheer humbleness considering his position.

The conversation continued as we sipped on our soft drinks while others enjoyed forbidden (and expensive) wine. The service was impeccable and was lavish to the extent that we almost found it too pampering. The waiters were on you before you could even open your mouth, and your glass would be filled up before you even placed it on the table. As the night progressed, DJ pulled out a small color booklet—16 pages or so—filled with images of him and the prince, included images of them practicing martial arts. "Maybe we could work on a project in the future," I said to DJ, trying to get a reaction—a feeler. I got a sneaky smirk back, indicating that a potential opportunity was certainly on the "menu." This felt like a huge opportunity to potentially collaborate with Middle Eastern royalty in a larger capacity pertaining to combat sports, and project ideas started to run through my head. Looking back, I think I was running before I could walk. That was my problem—I'd get too interested in new projects with little provocation—but I was enthused by the possibility of joining forces with these people. After all, we shared a mutual passion, and I was in a position to bring something to the table their money couldn't always buy. And these men weren't short of money; they lived a lifestyle most could only dream of. For my part, I had great conviction that I could come up with the goods and create a win-win situation for both parties. Sadly, I soon found myself disenfranchised of an opportunity to present and pitch any idea.

In Dubai, MMA stars are treated like kings. It's not uncommon for a royal to hand over the most lavish of gifts, such as a watch worth $200,000, like the one the prince presented to former UFC welterweight champion GSP. DJ invited Randy to Dubai through me, and so I joked with Randy, telling him that he'd be receiving a $200,000 watch gift from the royal family. Randy, a gentleman and not one to take advantage, just laughed it off and didn't seem to be bothered about receiving any sort of gifts. That said, he wasn't devoid of financial concerns: I had once asked Randy if the UFC should be paying fighters more, and he said, "Yes, not just in the UFC, but mixed martial artists in general should be getting paid better across the board in other organizations. The top boxers are making $20 million to $40 million for a fight. On the other hand, the top mixed martial artist in the UFC makes $500,000 per fight. As one of the top fighters, I'm certainly not complaining; the money I've made in the sport has been a great way to earn and make a living. But, at the same time, compared to other professional sports, it's paying low level compared to other professional athletes."

He also added that wrestlers don't have a professional outlet for the sport once their amateur careers are over. Professional wrestling, as everybody knows, is entertainment, not a real sport. "Boxing, both at amateur and professional levels, is a sport, and MMA is a sport," he said. "Olympic and amateur wrestlers have no real outlet to make money. You can see more and more Olympic wrestlers making a transition into professional MMA." Randy had wrestled for the U.S. team, and it wasn't until the age of 37 that he started fighting in the UFC, but he expected to see more young wrestlers make the jump as they saw the rewards being offered.

Excited at the prospect of a potential Dubai visit, I told Randy to keep me posted of his availability so that we could grab some publicity and chill with the royals. Unfortunately, his hectic schedule and filming came in the way of making that trip materialize. It would have been a great experience.

One thing I learned about DJ and the royals is that it takes a long time to earn their trust. I don't blame them. Given the position they are in, worth billions of dollars, it wouldn't be uncommon for people to try to take advantage of them. I would be lying if I said it never crossed my mind, but in my case, I was less interested in money and more keen to be given an opportunity to work with these people.

Although I had struck up a certain level of rapport with DJ, I found him to be somewhat cautious later on as he started to avoid my calls—which, looking back, might have been a bit too frequent. Given our mutual appreciation for martial arts and MMA, I thought it made perfect sense to work together. I knew this individual had met and dealt with many highly influential and eminent figures around the world, including presidents, kings, prime ministers, actors, and athletes. He's experienced life and people from all cultures, and I was merely another guy. His reticent attitude left me rather disappointed, but at least he was an affable and hospitable person who always showed us respect.

⌒

The next morning, I wasted no time phoning world heavyweight champion David Haye's representative to notify them about Randy's visit. David's respect toward MMA had been publicized in the sporting press; hence, he was the perfect boxer to join forces with. David agreed to assist in whatever way he could to help publicize Randy's appearance. I had arranged a press conference at the hotel on the first floor in a nice, spacious room. ESPN and Sky Sports, among other press, were present. David arrived with his representative and a camera crew that was filming footage for a documentary on the boxer.

I had interviewed the boxing champion a couple of years earlier. At the time, he was in Cyprus, so I spoke to him over the phone and hadn't met him face-to-face. He seemed like a nice, down-to-earth guy. But when I finally met the "Haymaker,"he wasn't very approachable. Not that fame had got to his head—if anything, I feel he has been quite humble. He certainly wasn't a diva with a big entourage and was pretty much as normal as a person can be. It emerged that he had once met the UFC champion in Las Vegas when Randy's son Ryan was fighting. Apart from that, David's father had been a martial arts instructor, and David himself had some interest in competing in the UFC one day.

As everyone congregated in the room, I sat with David and Randy onstage, and the press fired questions at the two. Afterward, we organized one-on-one interviews with both of the champions. David broached the subject of acting. He would love to get into acting, maybe joining Randy in *The Expendables* once he hung his gloves up, he told the Sky Sports reporter.

When the press conference kicked into action, I spotted DJ standing in the corner in a moment of solitude with a group of his friends who were visiting from the Middle East. One of them was an ardent student of the martial arts; he was wearing gym clothing like he was there to attend a seminar and glean knowledge from the UFC champion. His enthusiasm was infectious, and he stood out like a sore thumb (my team and I actually ended up giving this fanatic the name "super fan," as he was constantly peppering Randy with questions). The press conference had gone well.

The evening started with attending a high-end establishment in Mayfair for a product launch. DJ's hospitality continued, and he took us to a very posh high-end Japanese restaurant straight afterward. The chauffeurs and bodyguards dropped us off. There must have been a total of 12 or 14 of us. The staff at the restaurant seemed very familiar with the royal representative and his crew. After all, he was an elite client, so they treated him like, well, royalty. After the meal, in which most of us had no clue as to what we had eaten, the bodyguards picked us up again. It was straight to another establishment, one of the most famous celebrity hangouts in London. There was a slight problem—there was not enough space in the cars. So, one of the bodyguards asked my friend Seyfi if he had any cash on him because apparently they never carried cash. Seyfi had to make his way in a taxi arranged by the bodyguard, who assured him that he'd be reimbursed. Seyfi told him that it was fine because DJ had been looking after us. Later at the venue, the bodyguard approached Seyfi and placed a note in the inside of his jacket. When my friend got home, he realized it was a £50 note. He later joked to me that he'd made a profit of £30. I nearly fell over laughing.

The place was packed. The management there were familiar with DJ, so, as usual, he (and we, his guests) would be given VIP treatment at the highest level. We sat and relaxed in our VIP booth while two tall bodyguards stood on each corner, including the one we had named super fan. Randy sat taking in the sights and sounds, but I could tell that, like me, he wasn't a party animal or one to strut his skills on the dance floor. Essentially, it's not my scene, and I'm not the type who frequents such places. Randy had good footwork, of course, but he saved it for the Octagon.

At about 2:00 in the morning, I insisted that we call it a night because I was responsible for Randy, and we had an early morning start. Unfortunately, that didn't go over too well with DJ, as he wanted the party to continue. His displeasure was only too clear, but I would not permit Randy to be out until 4 a.m., as we had work to do the next day. Reveling all night is not conducive to a productive next day when you have work on the menu. So we called it a night, and all of us went back to the hotel to hit the sack, much to our host's dismay.

⌒

Despite the fact we were having a great time, a major obstacle lay ahead of us that would put a dent in my relationship with Randy's manager. We were scheduled to do a promotional event at the BAMMA fight event at the Motorpoint Arena in Nottingham promoting a product of Randy's. With thousands of MMA-mad fans attending the event, it was a perfect opportunity. I had discussed Randy's potential appearance at this venue with his personal assistant Valerie back in Las Vegas. "We do have a fighter fighting in Nottingham on 10 December that Randy would like to corner," she had informed me. "So he is going to push to be there for his fight."Randy's management already had contemplated having him make an appearance at this MMA promotion, a direct competitor of the UFC, and now I proceeded to make a deal with the promoters that stipulated Randy would come and promote his new product and nothing else. He wasn't going to be promoting the organization, as he was still tied up in a contract with the rival UFC.

Perhaps inevitably, it wasn't long before the BAMMA PR department sent out a press release with the massive headline "Randy Couture Heading to BAMMA!" *What's going on?* was my immediate reaction. Valerie and Randy's manager back in America didn't waste any time contacting me, warning me that Randy was still under contract with the UFC and that the press release was certain to put a further dent in his relationship with the UFC. Randy was not allowed to promote any other MMA promotion while still in contract with the UFC, even though he wasn't actively fighting. BAMMA, meanwhile, had worded the headline so that it gave the impression the UFC star was heading to their promotion to fight or promote it—both of which were nonsense.

Things escalated quickly. Randy's manager was now getting involved and furious, apparently having emergency meetings with the
UFC. It's no secret that the UFC's relationship with their biggest star
was not exactly rosy by this point, something I mentioned earlier. They
had had disputes concerning certain issues in the past and were far
from being the best of buddies by this point. The contentious relationship fighters have with promoters and companies is nothing unusual
at all. It's typically about money. Fighters want more money; promoters want to pay them less money. Really, it couldn't be simpler.

Now, though, my master plan was in peril. The thought of Randy
not making an appearance at the BAMMA event, the event that was
going to benefit us the most, was a daunting prospect. This was terrible
news for me.

Shortly afterward, I received a message from Randy's manager.
"Randy's potential promotional involvement with any promoter outside of the UFC is probably a technical breach of his contract with the
UFC," he said in an e-mail. "We have very specific rules for what he
can and can't do with other promotions. Until his contractual relationship with the UFC changes, which I am currently negotiating, he is
bound by those existing obligations." He also made it clear to BAMMA
that the appearance and marketing related to the appearance at the
BAMMA 8 event would, most likely, put Randy into a technical breach
under his existing contract with the UFC. According to the manager,
he was in the middle of transitioning that relationship into a retirement
status, making things even more delicate.

"I was shocked to have seen the press release hit the media yes-
terday morning—especially since I had just e-mailed Neys last week
regarding the plan schedule for BAMMA 8," the manager continued.
Ney was a staff member at BAMMA who, I assume, dealt with in-
voices. "I think I have made my frustrations pretty clear in the last 24
hours, even to random passers-by on the street." By this point, I was on
the verge of losing my temper. Next, the manager said that, in terms of
going forward, he had not decided on the best plan and that it wasn't
his style to do something without telling all involved first. It was hard
for him to pull back the press release since we had already mounted
a marketing campaign based on it, but the real contractual damage to
Randy had the potential to occur at or around the event, he said, so
a lot would depend on a conversation he intended to have with the
UFC. Coming up with a creative solution was something he was working on, he told me, promising he would keep everyone in the loop. "By
the way, now would be a good time for BAMMA to pay the remaining

amounts due Trigg," he wrote in the e-mail. "Neys has the invoice." Allegedly, BAMMA was delaying and not paying some fighters on time. Still, that was between those two parties, and I had no interest in their previous business dealings.

Next, Ashley, the BAMMA promoter, frantically informed me they couldn't get hold of Randy's manager. Apparently, the manager wasn't responding to e-mails and phone calls, so Ashley had no further details on proceedings. He asked me if I could get hold of him so we all knew where we stood in regard to the scheduled appearance. The situation remained precarious. Brimming with frustration, I got on the phone to the manager. Painful minutes ticked away as I sat in my home office in my high-back black leather chair, dialing his cell phone number six times in a row. It was 2:00 in the morning, U.K. time.

It's not uncommon for me to be working into the early morning hours. My typical routine working from home starts at 10 a.m. I'm checking and sending e-mails and making phone calls, ranging from newspaper editors to celebrity representatives, whether I'm securing an interview with a world champion fighter or someone from the Hollywood fraternity. If I'm in the middle of writing a book, I'll spend all day on the project, and I often spend late nights working.

Randy's manager finally answered the call, and I succinctly made things clear to him. I was upset and expressed my concerns. Sometime after that call, the BAMMA rep in the public relations department messaged me, saying, "To be honest, this sounds like a complete mess. In no way does either of these articles sound like Randy promoting BAMMA. They are very clear on stating that Randy is signing his product at BAMMA. Any issues you have with Valerie and the manager need to be sorted out between you. We simply cannot issue any sort of retraction without causing major embarrassment to BAMMA."

Finally, BAMMA and I agreed that no further announcements would be made and that it was still possible to have Randy make the scheduled appearance. It was still uncertain whether he would appear. By now, Randy's manager was not responding to any e-mails, and there were only a couple of days left before the event, prolonging my agony. He wouldn't say yes or no or even that he would be getting back to us with a final solution. The guy had done a vanishing act. Not knowing what action to take, I conferred with Randy to establish the best course of action. Randy said he was cool to go ahead at any rate, so we plodded on. It was time to hit the arena.

When we got to the arena, the fights had already started. We set up, and we had people passing by and meeting Randy as they spotted him. It was open space, so we had security controlling the large crowd. Andy, being the head of my team's security, did a kind of side-to-side seesaw action simultaneously controlling the large crowd (which was funny), and we had a good laugh afterward. By the intermission, a large crowd had clustered around Randy, and it got rather crazy. I asked Randy if he wanted to sit down, but he said he was okay. I had him work his ass off and sign autographs for more than two hours nonstop. I could tell after the two hours he wanted to call it a day, but I was insistent in carrying on for a little longer. I wanted to reach my target. I could sense Randy was somewhat tired, but, boy, did I make him work that day.

Finally, I spotted the BAMMA rep walking toward us. He had two people with him—one on each side like bodyguards. Smiling and relieved, he said everything was cool now. I acknowledged him and decided to let it slide, but in the back of my mind, I had negative thoughts flooding in. A couple of months later, he would be at the center of another controversial hiccup that involved Randy, his manager, and me. The trouble with the BAMMA guy, far from being over, had just started.

Fiaz at 10 years old. *Courtesy of the author*

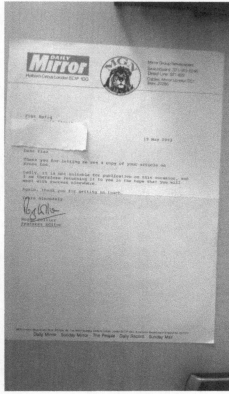

First rejection letter from *Daily Mirror* newspaper, 1993. *Courtesy of the author*

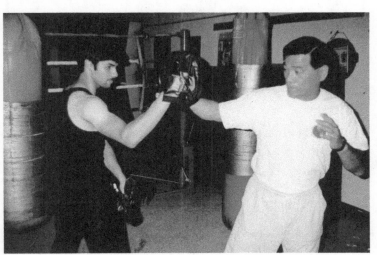

Los Angeles at the world-famous academy with Bruce Lee's original student, 1996. *Courtesy of the author*

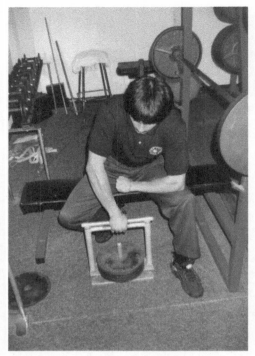

Using Bruce Lee's original grip exerciser at the academy, 1996. *Courtesy of the author*

With UFC creator Rorion Gracie at the Gracie Academy, Los Angeles, 1996. *Courtesy of the author*

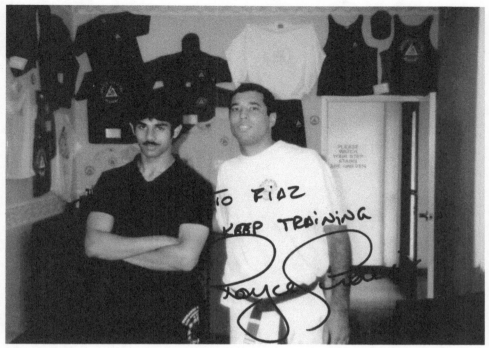

With the first ever UFC champion, Royce Gracie, training at the Gracie Academy, Los Angeles, 1996. *Courtesy of the author*

With friend and Dan Inosanto's son-in-law, Ron Balicki, at his home in Los Angeles, 2002. *Courtesy of the author*

At the Inosanto Academy with Bruce Lee's number-one student Dan Inosanto after a training class in Los Angeles, 2002. *Courtesy of the author*

With the Close Protection firearms training team in Sweden. *Courtesy of the author*

Bodyguarding a world-famous personality in his home. *Courtesy of the author*

Dinner with friends Diana Lee Inosanto and Ron
Balicki in Los Angeles, 2003. *Courtesy of the author*

After a training session with Bruce Lee's original student, Larry
Hartsell, in his home garage, 2003. *Courtesy of the author*

Chuck Norris at a party, Los Angeles, 2003. *Courtesy of the
author*

At a party with Bob Wall, famous for playing a villain in Bruce Lee movies, Los Angeles, 2003. *Courtesy of the author*

Assisting UFC legend and friend Royce Gracie for a magazine photo shoot, Los Angeles, 2005. *Courtesy of the author*

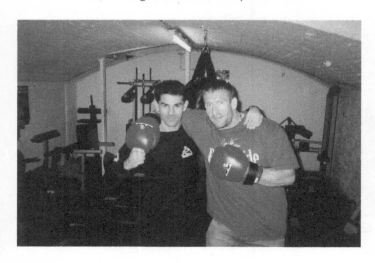

At the world-famous Temple Gym with six-time Mr. Olympia Dorian Yates, 2005. *Courtesy of the author*

At martial arts magazine editor Bob Sykes's house,
Huddersfield. *Courtesy of the author*

After interviewing Arnold Schwarzenegger's best friend, Franco Columbu, in
his office for a documentary, Los Angeles, 2006. *Courtesy of the author*

Bruce Lee's Hollywood Walk of
Fame star in Hollywood, 2006.
Courtesy of the author

After interviewing NBA legend Kareem Abdul-Jabbar for a Bruce Lee documentary, Long Beach, Los Angeles, 2006. *Courtesy of the author*

With UFC champion Mike Bisping after a meeting. *Courtesy of the author*

With Andy Farrell and UFC legend Chuck Liddell. *Courtesy of the author*

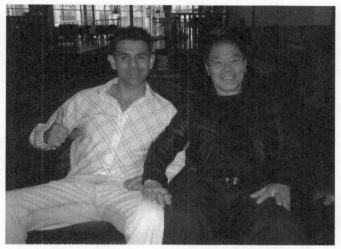

Hanging out with Bruce Lee's childhood best friend, William Cheung, 2010. *Courtesy of the author*

With Mike Tyson in 2010. *Courtesy of the author*

With close friend Diana Lee Inosanto, Bruce Lee's goddaughter, 2010. *Courtesy of the author*

With good friend and Mike Tyson's sparring partner, Joe Egan, at a dinner event, 2010. *Courtesy of the author*

Press conference at Jumerah Hotel, Kensington, London, Fiaz, David Haye, and Randy Couture, December 2011. *Courtesy of the author*

Dinner with DJ (personal assistant of the prince of Dubai), Randy Couture, Andy Farrell, and Fiaz, December 2011. *Courtesy of the author*

New Year's Eve party with close friend and Muhammad Ali's daughter, Rasheda Ali, at Randy Couture's home, Las Vegas, 2011. *Courtesy of the author*

UFC legend Randy Couture's house in Las Vegas, New Year's Eve party, 2011. *Courtesy of the author*

Randy Couture's home garage in Las Vegas, checking some of his "toys" out with him and his partner, December 2011. *Courtesy of the author*

MMA World Expo in New York press conference, Randy Couture, promoter Paul Paone, and Fiaz, 2011. *Courtesy of the author*

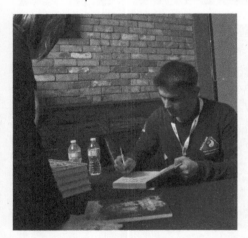

Fiaz book signing while on tour with UFC champion Randy Couture in Canada, March 2012. *Courtesy of the author*

With Hollywood martial arts action star Jean-Claude Van Damme, at an exclusive dinner event, 2015. *Courtesy of the author*

BBC Studios being interviewed on BBC Radio, 2015. *Courtesy of the author*

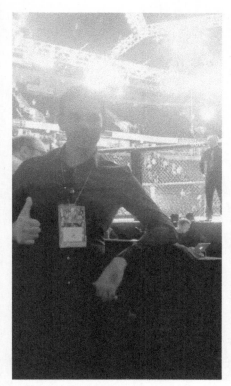

M.E.N. Arena ringside press member at UFC 204—Bisping versus Henderson—2016. *Courtesy of the author*

Warner Bros. film studios on the set of *Jason Bourne* starring Matt Damon. *Courtesy of the author*

At an event in 2016—Arnold Schwarzenegger on the podium. *Courtesy of the author*

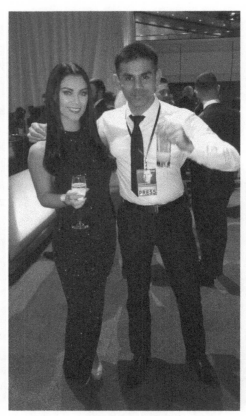

At an exclusive Arnold Schwarzenegger dinner
event in a VIP room with reality TV star Cally
Jane Beach, 2016. *Courtesy of the author*

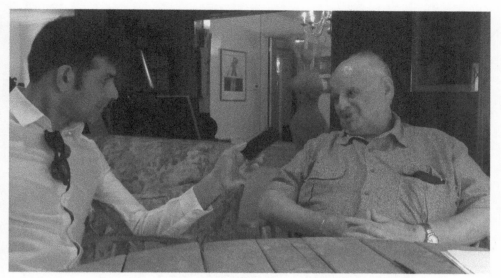

Interviewing *Enter the Dragon* producer Paul Heller at his home in Beverly Hills, 2017. *Courtesy of the author*

Having lunch in Las Vegas with good friend Rasheda Ali, 2017. *Courtesy of the author*

At a film premiere with actor Josh Hellman, who played Lenny McLean in his biopic, London, 2017. *Courtesy of the author*

In a Las Vegas dinner meeting with former UFC bantamweight champion Dominick Cruz, 2017. *Courtesy of the author*

At Paramount Studios in Hollywood, 2017. *Courtesy of the author*

Author coffee meeting with his agent Charlie. *Courtesy of the author*

With Underworld's notorious figure, Freddie Foreman, at his home in London for an interview, 2018. *Courtesy of the author*

Interviewing Michael Jackson's brother, Tito Jackson, 2018. *Courtesy of the author*

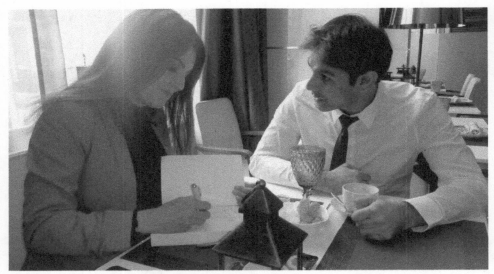

With ex-wife of sportsman-turned-prime minister Imran Khan, London, 2018. *Courtesy of the author*

Creed II red carpet movie premiere, with director Ryan Coogler in the background, 2018. *Courtesy of the author*

Interviewing Dolph Lundgren on the red carpet at the *Creed II* film premiere, 2018. *Courtesy of the author*

At the Ali Center in Louisville, Kentucky, with Rahaman Ali announcing the book, 2019. *Courtesy of the author*

With Muhammad Ali's brother Rahaman at his home in Louisville, Kentucky, 2019. *Courtesy of the author*

With NFL sports legend Jim Brown at his Hollywood Hills home, 2019. *Courtesy of the author*

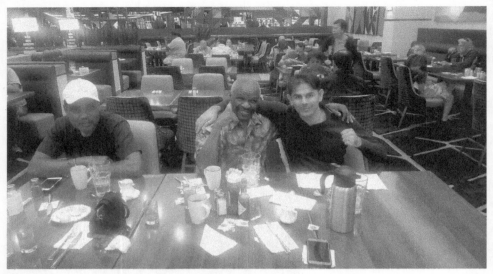

Having lunch with Floyd Mayweather Sr. and Ron Brashear in Las Vegas, 2019. *Courtesy of the author*

Checking out *My Brother, Muhammad Ali* in a bookstore, 2019. *Courtesy of the author*

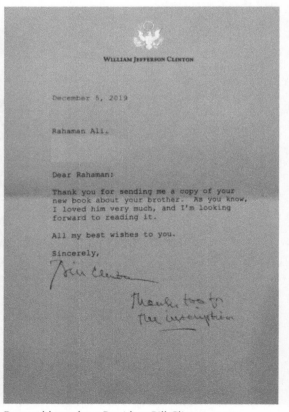

Personal letter from President Bill Clinton sent to Rahaman Ali about Rahaman's and the author's monumental book. *Courtesy of the author*

23

Adventures in New York

In late 2011, I got in touch with Paul Paone, the promoter of the MMA World Expo in New York, which was going to take place on December 17–18, with an idea. At the time, MMA fights were still illegal in New York, and so fans had to settle for attending nonfight events or venturing to neighboring states. It wasn't until late 2016 when the UFC finally ended their long journey to legalization in one of the boxing centers of the world. The UFC held its first New York show on November 12 at Madison Square Garden and came to the city in style, as none other than UFC's golden boy, Conor McGregor, headlined UFC 205. McGregor knocked out Eddie Alvarez in round 2 to claim a historic second title, making history as he became the first fighter to hold two belts simultaneously. UFC 205 reportedly broke the pay-per-view record with 1.65 million buys and would cement McGregor's reputation as an all-time great.

That was all for the future, though. Back in 2011, I secured Randy's appearance at the MMA Expo. Considering the fact that Randy was the biggest name in the UFC at the time before the emergence of McGregor and, to a certain degree, the clout I carried because of my position, I wasted no time requesting certain privileges from the promoter. In addition to Randy's and my airfare and accommodation, I requested an additional flight and accommodation for my friend Elbiz. It didn't take me long to convince the promoter. He complied with my request and booked all three of us at the W Hotel. Paul was a gentleman and easy to get along with, the type I'd go the extra mile for.

One of my close friends from the United Kingdom, Joe Egan, had mentioned to me that he was going to be spending Christmas in New York visiting his sister. Always endeavoring to help my friend, I got him to be a special guest alongside Randy in the Big Apple. Neither of us was aware of the trauma Joe would suffer on his stateside trip, or I'd never have arranged his appearance.

Back in those days, I was the proud owner of a very basic cell phone. I never really embraced modern technology and certainly never wanted a posh new phone or the latest model. Back then, I didn't even know what the hell an app was; it was all just too damn sophisticated for my liking. By 2011, I'm fairly sure I was the only guy in my business with a phone so old that you could no longer purchase it in a store.

By the time I arrived in New York, my battery was completely dead and ready to be buried. Still, I wasn't ready to offer it to the grave just yet. Unfortunately, my charger had been left behind in the United Kingdom when we were touring with Randy, so now I was trying to get hold of a charger to connect with the world again. At first, I tried the hotel desk, only to be told that they had any number of chargers but none were compatible with mine. Next, I went to several phone stores, but they told me it was an old phone, so they didn't stock these chargers and batteries anymore. I was completely cut off from the outside world.

Joe had the hotel address, but he had no clue of what anyone's room numbers were. He had been trying to get hold of me but obviously couldn't, and when he arrived at the hotel and asked for me, the hotel staff wouldn't disclose our room numbers to him. To say that Joe was furious would be an understatement. Eventually, he ended up spending a fortune calling England from his cell phone trying to find out if anyone had made contact with me. Meanwhile, I was curious as to why Joe hadn't linked up with us when he had the hotel information. While all this was happening, Elbiz, Randy, and I stepped out for lunch in a small Italian restaurant not far from our hotel. We had ample time to relax, but it was business that we were there for, so we weren't going to deviate too far from our main objective. In the hotel lobby, people would often recognize Randy, walk up to him, and take pictures with him. The doormen had recognized him, too, and we made sure they got a few photos. After some time hanging out in the lobby, we stepped outside, ready to be picked up and taken to the venue. Suddenly, an unmarked police car pulled up with a brash, fairly well built guy who knew the doorman. Talk about being loud, this guy was a rocket. He was yelling at Randy like a lunatic. It sounded more like he was offering Randy out for a scrap as he sat in the comfort of his warm, cozy seat in his car—but he was actually just being sarcastic. To the passersby, I'm certain it looked like something nasty was brewing. This cop looked and sounded like the actor Mike Starr, who was the big bully in a Steven Seagal movie and led a team of bodyguards in Kevin Costner's *The Bodyguard*. For some reason, this guy always played a big fat bully and got nailed by the star.

This cop came across as a stereotypical Italian American. Pretty soon, he said something that sounded somewhat derogatory to Randy but was apparently meant in jest. The doorman, coming to the rescue, said something to his cop friend along the lines that he couldn't speak to Randy in such a disrespectful manner. Not listening to his friend's words, the cop said he could do what he wanted as he flashed his badge. Randy, not one to trade verbal barbs, laughed it off. He never took these types seriously. In fact, he had told me once, "I don't like confrontation." The fat cop sped off in his car like a rally driver. We stood outside in the freezing cold until Paul's brother picked us up, and we made our way to the venue, unfortunately without Joe, as we never did manage to meet up.

∽

The MMA World Expo was far from the caliber of the expos that the UFC promoted. It was sparsely attended in comparison to the UFC-organized expos and didn't attract the same quality of talent. There were the usual booths promoting their brands, clothing lines, and Brazilian jiu-jitsu and MMA seminars and tournaments taking place, but the highlight of the day was Randy's appearance—he had top billing. The New Yorkers were thrilled and looking forward to meeting their idol, and it was reflected in their expressions when they eventually came face-to-face with the champion in the cage. Randy was unsurprised, as he always believed that there was a wider audience beyond the confines of the UFC brand. "It's not just about the UFC, but the sport of MMA," he told me once. "The UFC is only part of it."

No MMA expo is complete without having prominent names and fighters of repute in attendance. At this one, I spotted Phil Nurse, a Thai boxing instructor who had left Europe to set up a gym and promote Thai boxing in New York in the mid-1990s. When Phil spotted Randy in the cage, he ran up to us sporting a little kid's smile and shook Randy's and my hand like an excited teenage fan. Phil has done a great job promoting the art of eight limbs in America and trained

several UFC champions, including one of his prize pupils, GSP. I think
he made a good move because it was perfect timing to go over the
pond to spread the sport, a sport that had exploded in Britain with the
help of five Thai masters who had immigrated to Britain in the late
1970s. The American market, beyond doubt, had always been there to
be penetrated. Phil, a student of the famed Master Sken, had seen the
opportunity to tap into a huge market and grabbed it with both hands.

After Randy finished meeting people, Randy, Elbiz, and I stepped
outside the cage and spotted Matt Serra signing autographs. There
was a long line of fans waiting to meet him. As soon as "The Terror"
spotted Randy, I recall him jumping out of his seat like a pin had hit
his ass. "Hey, it's Randy Couture!" he yelled. We had a short chat with
the former UFC welterweight champion, who seemed to be in a jovial
mood and was in awe of Randy. It was good to meet Matt, who had
fought some elite champions in the welterweight division, including
Matt Hughes and BJ Penn, and shocked the world by knocking out
GSP to take the crown. His instructor Renzo Gracie was giving a seminar nearby, and we said a quick hello to him too.

Next, I was introduced by Randy to another gentleman, Mark Garrow, a Jewish Canadian who had an MMA TV media company. Clued
up when it came to business, he was the spitting image of Billy Crystal
and even sounded a little like him. Mark and I got on right from the
start. We talked about working together in Canada in the near future.
He had worked with Randy before, so we had a great starting point to
build a rapport.

The promoter had assigned his younger brother to take care of us
for the duration of our stay in New York. He would drive us around,
escort us where we needed to be, and give us a tour of the city.
Strangely, this man was the spitting image of Royce Gracie's cousin
Rodrigo Gracie. Apparently, I was seeing many famous doppelgangers
at this event. An extroverted guy, he was always joking around and
eventually decided to take us to a nightclub. Elbiz, Randy, Mark, and
several others and I packed into two cars.

It was surreal hanging out with the UFC legend in New York.
As we approached the entrance to this nightspot, the bouncers immediately recognized Randy. "The Natural" was in a joking mood; he
even went for a half-speed double-leg tackle on the big giant African
American bouncer, who must have weighed at least 280 pounds. It
was hilarious as this giant tried to sprawl on the wrestling legend. The
champion may have been in a mellow mood, but I knew that Randy
wasn't someone who took substances to get high. He had a clean-cut

image. Fighters like him didn't need to slip down the substance abuse road to get a kick out of life. Competing in an adrenaline-fueled combat sport is their high.

The club was an old red-brick building, but inside, it was packed out with night owls. It was heaving with bodies of all colors and creeds, so packed that you had to really squeeze through to get any-where. Fortunately, Paul's brother had secured a VIP area for us, and to my great surprise, there were quite a bit of Asian Indians already in the joint. Clubbing isn't my scene, as I've already mentioned, but Elbiz was in his element partying, as he has always been a crazy party animal not shy to strut his stuff on the floor. Randy had more of a laid-back approach, as most of us did who were there with him. He enjoyed a sit-down and just having a good time watching others revel.

When it was time to leave, at around 2:30 a.m., we made our way outside, and some of us got separated. Although this club wasn't huge, it was like a maze; if you weren't familiar with the layout, you could very easily get lost. I had no form of communication with the group because my phone was out of commission the day we landed in New York City. Suddenly, I found myself in New York in the early hours of the morning in, from what I could tell, a not-so-good neighborhood. In a situation like that, all sorts of things start going through your head. Being robbed or attacked with a knife or at gunpoint felt like it wasn't far away that night. A trick I often used to employ was to put almost all my money in my sock and maybe keep $20 in my wallet in case I did become a victim, but, finally, I got a taxi to take me to the hotel.

All in all, New York was great. We had fun. I had always been a lover of the West Coast—Los Angeles in particular—but now had a newfound respect for the Big Apple, even if I had previously visited this bustling city several times before. And there aren't many better ways to see it than alongside a UFC star.

24

Las Vegas

New York was fun, but Las Vegas wasn't far off. Famed for being the boxing capital of the world, Las Vegas is also the spiritual home of the UFC. The original creator of the UFC, Rorion Gracie, had sold the UFC for $2 million to SEG in 1995, who later sold it to Zuffa in 2001 for the same amount. Zuffa built it up to a billion-dollar business. The Ferreita brothers, who owned the UFC at the time, happened to have business interests in Vegas, and after taking Rorion's revolutionary concept from its small beginnings to a global phenomenon, the company prided itself as being one of the biggest sports companies in the world. In late 2016, the Ferreita brothers sold the UFC to WME-IMG for an astounding $4 billion. WME is one of the largest Hollywood talent agencies, representing a plethora of A-list stars—a nice bit of synergy, as reportedly more than 19 A-list personalities and Hollywood stars have shares in the UFC.

In an effort to keep the momentum going with Randy's promotional activities, I was heading to see him in his hometown, jetting off to Sin City less than two weeks after the New York trip. I had never visited this desert city in Nevada, but I had heard quite a bit about this place, famed for its vibrant nightlife and a hub for gambling and combat sports.

I was quite surprised that downtown didn't look as big as I had expected. It's nothing like Los Angeles or New York—two truly huge cities. The world-famous MGM Grand Garden Arena Caesars Palace is one of the main attractions. This is where the big boxing fights take place. It transported me back to being a kid watching on TV Marvin

Hagler and Sugar Ray Leonard—the classic fight at Caesars Palace. Now, of course, it is the home of the UFC, and many big UFC fights events seem to have taken over. I feel UFC couldn't have picked a better place than Vegas.

Although I was more acclimated to Los Angeles, the city I mainly frequented, I felt at home in Vegas. I was there as Brock Lesnar and the Dutch sensation Alistair Overeem were headlining UFC 141, an event that marked Brock's return to the sport after being out for a year due to an injury. Brock had defeated Randy in Vegas three years earlier at UFC 91 and then lost the title to Cain Velasquez, and many believed that his return against Alistair was premature and market driven. Nevertheless, the bout garnered more than a million pay-per-view buys. UFC fans wanted to see this giant fight, and the former pro wrestling star filled arenas. Proving many people right, the Dutch giant beat the former WWE superstar with a first-round knockout.

While in Vegas on a trip from Manchester, I had a chance encounter with a familiar face, bumping into Kerry Kayes and his wife. Kerry, the former conditioning coach of Ricky Hatton, Rampage Jackson, and Mark Coleman, is a former bodybuilder and a thoroughly nice guy. He recognized me immediately because I had met him several times before. We exchanged pleasantries and had a quick chat.

Next, I accompanied Randy to a gun store. Yes, a gun store. He was meeting fans there, far from an unusual event in a country that's obsessed with firearms. It was quite weird seeing the staff at the store wearing guns and pistols as they served customers. In America, not only are the police armed, but many security guards are, too. Look at the United Kingdom: gun crime is very low, and even the police don't carry guns. If there's a firearms incident near where I live, the closest armed response unit is 12 miles away back at police headquarters. In American, shopkeepers can have big guns under the counter, so if they get robbed, they are armed to defend themselves. It's quite a culture shock when you're coming from another country such as mine.

I had arranged to meet Rasheda Ali, Muhammad Ali's daughter, who also resides in Las Vegas. I had interviewed her once before on the phone, but I had never met her.

Eventually, Rasheda pulled up in her four-wheel drive. When I got a glimpse of her for the first time as she walked toward me and we greeted each other, I was mesmerized. My first impression was, *What a wonderful smile, jovial personality, and happy-go-lucky person.* I could barely contain my enthusiasm. There was a classroom in the gun store where we sat down to have a long conversation, and it felt like I had known her for eternity. Rasheda is the fastest friend I have made as far as public figures are concerned. I couldn't believe I was in the presence of Muhammad Ali's daughter. I rarely get starstruck, as my work involves meeting many well-known people, but suddenly, I was transported back to the feeling of being a young teenager. I was awestruck. Over the years, I have interviewed many personalities, but if you were to ask me who has been the most mesmerizing person I've met, I would say Rasheda Ali is somewhere near the top spot.

As we sat there for more than an hour chatting away, Rasheda told me about the gun culture in America. Anyone could have access to a gun, she told me. And gun violence and its effects and consequences were something that she had witnessed firsthand while growing up in Chicago. Her cousin was shot as an innocent bystander during an event in 1997, and many other people had suffered their own losses in this mad culture. Finally, the interview was wrapping up, and I told Rasheda that I was going to be with Randy at his gym the following day and that she should come. Not only did she show up, but she brought her husband, Robert Walsh, and her two kids, Baggio and Nico. I introduced her to Randy, and we had a great day.

꒰꒱

That wasn't the end of the party in Vegas, either. Randy had invited me to his house for a New Year's Eve party, so I asked him if it was okay if I asked Rasheda to come, too. He said it was fine, so I phoned her and invited her and her family to join us in our celebrations.

Randy lived in a suburban gated community in the outskirts, Foothills at Southern Highlands, in a million-dollar home he bought a few days after his victory at UFC 68 on March 3, 2007, when he dispatched Tim Sylvia to take yet another title. This 3,700-square-foot mansion had four bedrooms, five bathrooms, and a swimming pool. After I'd taken it all in, Randy introduced me to his partner, Annie, who was gregarious with a very extroverted personality. A couple of MMA and UFC fighters were in attendance, including lightweight title contender Tyson Griffin. We made ourselves feel at home and chatted away in the kitchen and living room with Randy and others and helped ourselves to the food.

As the night wore on, my two companions and I checked out some hardware in the garage with Randy and Annie. It turned out that Randy had an extraordinary collection of guns of all shapes and sizes. Randy had been in the U.S. armed forces and had been stationed in

Germany, among other countries. I wasn't all that familiar with all the technical jargon, but one of my companions was and said that Randy clearly knew his stuff. Randy was living the good life. He had made a name for himself around the world and been the best fighter on the planet and was making a great living as a professional sportsman. Yet I never did see any of the fame get to his head.

By the time we finished checking out the guns, the house was quite full. Rasheda, her husband Bob, and their two kids arrived late. I found her kids to be shy and reserved but well mannered. One thing that I shared with Rasheda's family was that I didn't drink because of my religion—neither did they, so we stuck to soft drinks. I was curious about American Muslims, so I asked Rasheda about her thoughts on Islam and bringing up her two boys in a Western country. She told me that she was often judged because she didn't wear a head scarf but still endeavored to go to the mosque for her Friday prayers. In an effort to console her, I told her there will always be criticism and people judging others and commended her for her faith. She had grown up in the windy city of Chicago, and her mother, Belinda, was not a convert; she was a born Muslim. So Rasheda, her twin sister Jamillah, Maryum, and Muhammad Ali Jr. were all born Muslims.

I had a long conversation with Rasheda and couldn't pass up the opportunity to ask her what her famous dad was like when she was growing up. Ali's swagger inside and outside the ring made him a larger-than-life sportsman. I asked if she had any intriguing anecdotes from home life.

"We visited him every summer," she told me. "We were driving around in California one year when my dad ran across a family who had lost their home and didn't have a place to stay. My dad brought them home with him and fed them and gave them money." Ali was known for this kind of act, for helping random strangers, and often gave away money to the poor and homeless, something he continued to the end of his life. "We were all frightened at the time, of course," said Rasheda, "Because we were like, *Oh, you don't know these people. But my dad didn't have a care in the world.*"

For her part, Ali's daughter has done her bit for charity by promoting awareness for sufferers of Parkinson's disease and charity work on the public speaking circuit. "I think my father did what most people should do with their celebrity status: help certain causes," she told me. "He has helped fight against obesity, illiteracy, racism. One of his legacies has to be the gift of giving."

That wasn't all we talked about, however. Rasheda shocked me when she told me that when she was younger, she wanted to be a professional wrestler. Her brother, Muhammad Ali Jr., had also revealed to me his affinity for professional wrestling. It seemed like the Ali family were huge wrestling fans. Ali's fascination for professional wrestling fueled his own career. He famously got the idea of being bigmouthed and a braggart after seeing Gorgeous George wrestle in Las Vegas and realizing that people would pay to see a loudmouth being shut up. Of course, in time, Ali became known as much for his antics outside the ring as his boxing brilliance. Ali Jr. actually told me that his hero was Hulk Hogan. Hogan was somebody I also watched and somewhat admired when I was a kid, but I grew out of it and no longer had interest in WWE and its antics as an adult.

Years later over lunch in Las Vegas, I asked Rasheda about the hard time Muslims were having in America. Of course, it's never been popular to be a Muslim in the land of the free. "My dad always told us whether it's about terrorist attacks or something else, the world will always have misconceptions about Muslims," she told me. "But he also told me that true Muslims aren't terrorists. Our religion is a religion of peace—that's what it means, peace." Ali, for his part, never stopped propagating this fact. Intelligent people have the capacity to understand this about Islam, but there are a small percentage of people, just as with any other religion, who take whatever scriptures they read and distort them. Unfortunately, in the religion of Islam, there are clearly some bad apples, and sometimes it feels that the whole world is showcasing the religion as a bad one. So, Rasheda told me, it's our job to do the best we can to be great representatives of true Islam and inform people that if you are intelligent and read about it, you will come to the realization that it's a religion of peace.

"Most people really don't want to believe that or may not have done their research," she told me. "They rely on the internet, and they'll believe the worst from the media. So I think those people need to take time and learn about not just Islam but other religions they may not be familiar with." She proudly told me that her dad loved everyone regardless of their race, creed, or religion, and he taught his kids to do the same. Ali wasn't perfect, but I think for the most part, he was sincere, and he did showcase the great values the Muslim religion teaches.

Undeniably, we are living in critical times right now. Rasheda's mom and brother were stopped by Transportation Security Administration officers as they were returning home to Deerfield Beach, Florida, from attending a Black History Month event in Jamaica in 2017.

"The officers interrogated my mom and brother separately for nearly two hours asking illegal questions like, 'Where did you get your name? Are you Muslim?'" Rasheda told me. Their passports were in order and verified, and no questions relating to documentation issues were even asked, according to Rasheda. "I feel that our new appointed U.S. leader [President Trump] has taken us back nearly 100 years."

Rasheda believes that if her dad were here today, as difficult as it was for him to speak in his final years, he would go on national TV to let people know that what's happening to us is horrible and that the Muslim religion is one of peace. In his time, the three-time heavyweight champion was quick to inform the public of the misconceptions facing his religion and constantly spoke against bigotry and racism in this country. We should all remember that today.

25

Canada: MMA Mad

I had set up another trip overseas to accompany Randy Couture, this time to Canada, but first we had another American city to jet off to. The annual wrestling event and expo was taking place in St. Louis, Missouri, so we negotiated with the organizers to bring Randy over as a special guest. In March 2012, I flew to St. Louis, and after a brief stop, we flew to Toronto. At border control, I was hit by a barrage of questions, but honestly, compared with what I was used to in the United States, it almost seemed like a reprieve.

The Canadian MMA scene is huge. Canada's population is only a tenth that of the United States (and half that of the United Kingdom), and yet, at one point, Canada boasted two of the largest attendances in UFC history. Randy had fought in Toronto at the Rogers Centre at UFC 129 on April 30, 2011, breaking the attendance and gate records as more than 55,000 fans witnessed Randy being knocked out by Lyoto Machida via a *Karate Kid*–style jumping front kick to the face. The gate was $11 million, while the pay-per-view buy rate cleared the 800,000 mark. Supposedly, Steven Seagal had worked with Lyoto after the action movie star and aikido specialist had also associated himself with Anderson Silva. How much he actually contributed to their victories is questionable, but if these Octagon warriors are happy to be associated with him, I guess that's fine by me.

Back in New York, I had asked Mike Garrow of Fight Network TV why MMA was so big in Canada and bigger than in the United States. It was beyond my comprehension—was I missing something? He told me it was simple: Canadians love ice hockey; in ice hockey, fights always break out; and Canadians just love to see fights and brawls. I wasn't sure about that, but I guess it was a reasonable explanation, and it would certainly be foolish for any serious MMA business or UFC athlete to ignore the Canadian market. It had the buying power to be considered one of the powerhouses in the sport, and taking advantage of it was crucial. And so, with this in mind, I made sure Randy was contracted to doing appearances in Canada as part of his promotional obligations with the company I owned.

One can't talk about the sport or the UFC in Canada without mentioning the name GSP. He was the biggest name to come out of Canada, a gentleman and a scholar who also happens to be one of the most dominant champions ever to grace the Octagon. After great success in smaller MMA events, GSP made his UFC debut in January 2004 at UFC 46 at the Mandalay Bay Event Center in Las Vegas, then went on to have a string of victories over some of the best fighters in his division, including dominant wins over then-champion Matt Hughes and the highly regarded BJ Penn. After brutally avenging his only losses and remaining undefeated as a champ and then returning to take the middleweight belt from Mike Bisping years later, the former UFC welterweight champion is considered by some the greatest of all time. He made it look pretty easy as he destroyed every opponent put in front of him, but his route to the top was anything but simple.

"There was a time in my life when I was studying in school and working three jobs at [the] same time," GSP told me in an interview at one point. "I was bouncing in a nightclub, working in a floor roofing place and in a government program for teenagers at school." At the Montreal nightclub, he was working with guys who were imposing and strong, most of them happy to put their fists up at the first sign of trouble, but the soft-spoken fighter never resorted to violence if he could help it. He told me, "I always thought the best way to take care of the problem was talking, so that's what I did most of the time to sort out problems."

Like many at the time, GSP's knowledge of the sport of MMA was limited. In Canada, hardly anyone knew what Brazilian jiu-jitsu was because it had just emerged. Seeing the early UFCs, GSP pursued the art doggedly. He had always been very good on his feet because of his Kyokushin karate training, and after adding Brazilian jiu-jitsu at age 16, he progressed quickly. His knowledge of ground fighting was limited, of course, but he was very strong, so he would often power out of submission attempts from his opponents on the mat. It's also interesting to note that at the time, the sport was illegal in Canada. He was competing in secret no-holds-barred competition that permitted open-hand strikes on the ground. GSP had four amateur fights, prevailing in every single bout. This teenager was fighting adults before he made the transition to fighting on a professional level.

GSP revealed to me that he's not one of those competitors who fight because he has no choice. He fights because he loves to fight. If he wanted to pursue a professional career doing a nine-to-five job, he told me, he could have gone in another direction because he has a diploma to fall back on. "The morning I wake up and I'm not happy with my job, then I'm going to do something else," he said. "If I didn't fight in MMA, I could have been a professional trainer." That, of course, would have been a huge loss to the sport of MMA.

⌒

Back on our schedule, Randy had a three-city tour to do, including stops at the Xtreme Couture gym in Toronto and another gym owned by former UFC fighter Jeff Joslin in Hamilton. Our third port of call was to be in Quebec, where the trainer hosting Randy had already hosted GSP, among other prominent names. Randy and I were welcomed by the owners of Xtreme Couture, a franchise Randy had started, who seemed like nice people who simply loved MMA. The Xtreme Couture gym was massive, and dozens of fans were at the meet and greet. Something that caught my eye was an Asian—when I say Asian, I mean Indian—girl fan. One thing I've learned about MMA is it attracts a huge variety of people.

After the Xtreme Couture appearance, we made our way to Hamilton, where there were 130 people all eager to meet Randy in a restaurant. We had a lot of fun, and everyone seemed to be enjoying themselves in a great night of entertainment with food and music. After an extensive question-and-answer session with Randy, he posed for pictures and signed autographs. The whole event lasted two long hours. Again, Randy was a trooper. He was on his feet meeting fans for two hours without taking a break, and, moreover, he would pause and smile for a picture with every single fan. He was very conscious about representing his image in the best way possible, and the fans meant everything to him.

The atmosphere was relaxed, and I was elated with our reception despite the fact that exhaustion had set in. For fighters and athletes, traveling the world and experiencing different cultures is one of the best parts of the sport, and it was a privilege to be in the same position as a sportswriter and member of the media.

After the event, a black limousine was waiting for us, and Jeff, Randy, I, and several others jumped in with more drinks and pizzas for the ride. It was great to be treated well. Not that we had demanded special privileges, but Jeff was amicable and made us comfortable. I had been a fan of America all my life, but now I was converting into a Canada lover.

I was going to head back home, while Randy was flying out to Quebec for the final leg of his promotional tour in Quebec. The feedback from the host and Randy himself was that it went well and Randy enjoyed it. I had made it clear to the promoter that the remaining money had to be wired over to me before Randy could make the appearance, telling him that if he didn't comply, Randy wouldn't show. Knowing the risks associated with requesting payments after an event, I had made it clear to Randy to make sure the promoter deposited the money into my account, but the promoter promised that he'd pay me afterward, leaving the situation precarious. Nevertheless, I decided to trust the guy. Boy, was I naive.

cᒋ

When I got back home, disaster struck. By now, I was used to having problems squeezing money out of most of these promoters, but we had fulfilled our obligations and made appearances, and they had used Randy's name to get people in. Yet, when it came to fulfilling their part of the bargain, false promises were made, resulting in nonpayments.

I was, to a great degree, to blame. I had to stop breaking my own rules; I had to keep a mind-set of an astute businessman. I understand that putting on events is not easy, but a good promoter will succeed if he does his job well. Most agents and managers demand to be paid in advance in most cases on the understanding that if a promoter wishes to host a big name, he should have the capacity to make it a success. Marketing, advertising, and the power to get the crowds in are the promoter's responsibility. If you can't do the job, you don't take on the task. Famous sports athletes and their agents don't care whether you get 100 people or 1,000. Essentially, the fee is fixed in most cases. I've had promoters approach me asking if they could have Randy at their place and give any revenue they generate to the fighter. That's not how it works, I told these guys. Why would a star name risk that? The promoter gets a famous name at his event, so it's a win-win situation for him, but what if nobody shows? A sports and entertainment personality is a commodity, and a value is placed on him, which he needs to keep. If it were that easy, then everybody would be doing it—no risk attached.

Regardless, I was furious and stunned when two of the promoters decided to hold back the remaining money they owed. Jeff had paid me, but the other two were the problem. They were cheating me and the UFC champion. When I told them in no uncertain terms that my legal team as well as Randy's would need to be involved, as the promoters were also withholding from him, one promoter vowed that payments would be made in several installments. In the event, both of the promoters who were in breach sent some money but not the pledged amount, so the disputes remain unsettled. The mishap taught me a salient lesson: always make sure the payment hits your account, every single cent, well before an appearance. And never listen to a promise made by the other party.

Sensing no payment was readily forthcoming, I wrote to Randy's personal assistant. "Just want to check what your relationship is with this gym in Canada. I want to let you know that their behavior has been unacceptable. They promised me numerous times that they'd make the final payment, but the organization then completely ignored my requests and e-mails. It's somewhat embarrassing that they would do this. The reason for this e-mail is to merely inform you, not for you to deal with the matter, which is a matter I'm dealing with." Randy had done events at this gym before, I knew, but I continued, "Have you had money problems with them in the past? I had a feeling you may have. Because they have not paid, this is something you should take into account in the future if you decide to do anything with them; otherwise, it's sending the wrong message. And they may feel it's no big deal. Remember, it's not just about stealing from me but stealing from Randy." I was absolutely stunned by the whole fiasco. It never crossed my mind that a reputable, well-known gym that had ties with my client would even dream about ripping us off.

The sad fact is, these problems are standard. I have heard countless stories pertaining to athletes or entertainment celebrities having problems with squeezing money out of a studio or a promoter. When you're the unfortunate victim, you may think you're the only one, but when it comes to money, believe me, you quickly see people's true colors.

All in all, though, the Canadian experience was great—other than the fact that two promoters had ripped us off. Maybe fortunately for me, I was oblivious to what lay ahead. Another fiasco was on the cards. It was none other than the former BAMMA employee who would be responsible for this next bizarre episode.

26

The Massive MMA Fiasco

While I was in Canada, a massive MMA Expo, the MMA Live Show, was being organized in the United Kingdom by the same former BAMMA staff member I had already encountered. He had partnered up with a man who promoted a martial arts expo annually and who eventually ended up in prison for fraud.

I wasn't keen. The chaos and commotion I had experienced six months earlier relating to Randy Couture's appearance at BAMMA left a rather sour taste in my mouth. Then again, the show promised to be an unforgettable experience dedicated to the sport of MMA. The show's advertising boasted that they were bringing 40 fighters and MMA personalities from around the globe to the United Kingdom, featuring a mix established of fan favorites, legends of the sport, champions and stars, as well as athletes who were making a name for themselves, all set to congregate under one roof in May 2012. This was the big one! Well, that's what the promoters were claiming.

The organizers had approached Randy via his management offering him a package deal that was enticing and hard to refuse. I had spoken to and advised Randy's personal assistant, Valerie, emphasizing that Randy should make an appearance at the Seni show instead, a combat sports show that was taking place a month later in Birmingham. I knew and had worked with the promoters of Seni before, but now, the UFC legend was being offered a lucrative deal, and his people—his legal and management team—were drawn to it like a moth to a lightbulb. Consequently, my advice was dismissed. So what do you do when plan A goes down the drain? You activate plan B, of course. I

185

always have a backup plan; it can steer you out of a mess. It occurred to me that maybe we could tie something in with the MMA Expo even though I wasn't personally keen on working with the promoters.

So, I liaised with Valerie and also the MMA Live Show's organizer. The idea was to tie in a slot at the show for Randy to promote him and his product, an idea I floated with the promoter. I was acting in good faith, so I was stunned when the organizer gave Randy's management the impression that I was interfering with matters. I was on the edge now and very distressed. But in situations such as this, it's imperative to have self-control. So I composed myself.

I never really dealt with Randy's lawyer and manager; I dealt with Randy directly and with his personal assistant and literary agent and had dealt with his lawyer only six months before when all the commotion and chaos linked with BAMMA was going on. Randy's lawyer succinctly told me that they were being offered a large sum of money and that they didn't want the deal to be jeopardized. Essentially, he was saying that I could potentially put a dent in a good deal. Sensing that the whole thing could spiral out of control, I left it to both parties to negotiate, but I voiced my concerns to Valerie, advising her to request an up-front payment if Randy was going to make an appearance.

Shockingly, at least to some people, five days before the show, the expo was abruptly postponed. The official website of the show changed to include a press release saying that the show had been postponed until October 20–21 due to circumstances beyond the organizers' control. Now, a whole host of MMA athletes had been scheduled and advertised to appear at this so-called massive expo, and what's most bizarre is that many fighters' reps said they had found out about the cancellation online. Following this, they attempted to make contact with the organizers, but again, the response they received concerning the unexpected U-turn was unacceptable. When some of the managers and lawyers demanded answers and a logical explanation from the promoter, he came out with feeble excuses.

"We would like to apologize to any fans we've disappointed for postponing the show, and we would like to thank everyone for their support and understanding, as we are deeply disappointed in having to make this decision," the press release read. Understanding? No one could understand these two, who, it turned out, had been misleading a lot of people.

As speculation about what was happening was mounting, certain individuals who had been duped felt the promoters were holding back on information because they simply had no valid explanation. Valerie told me that she was trying to work things out with the promoter, who had asked Randy's legal team to bear with the organizers while they came up with an amicable resolution. Not being convinced, I made it clear to Valerie to make sure the promoter flew Randy over regardless, as I had Randy's itinerary planned out to promote the second leg of his European tour. I also said that if the promoters had already paid Randy the negotiated fee in advance, he should hold onto it tightly and have them fulfill their obligations. Inevitably, many of the lawyers who managed and represented some of the top MMA fighters set to appear were now seeking damages for breach of contract as things started to further spiral out of control. One manager who had negotiated for a bevy of fighters to appear said that the promoters had deceived him— and everyone else for that matter. The show's promoters had not only left the athletes and thousands of eager fans out of pocket but also put everyone's schedules in chaos. Some fighters, no doubt, had refused other work due to their calendar being full.

Randy was to be paid his appearance fee a week before the show, but it didn't materialize, so there was nothing he could do other than wait to see how things would unfold. Clearly, there was no money to pay the fighters. My guess was that the promoters had gambled that with all the top MMA stars, the show would attract major sponsorships and ticket sales, which would generate a huge amount of revenue, and were oblivious to the prospect of their plans failing. It soon came to light that they were banking on securing a sponsorship from the film production company Lionsgate, the company behind *The Expendables II*, through Randy's lawyer, as Randy was one of the stars of the movie. The problem is, assuming can often put you in a lot of trouble. And, boy, they were in trouble, and only providence could save them now.

Figures kept deflating. Things felt futile. To further illustrate the scale of the deceit, one of the promoters had apparently called Randy's lawyer boasting that the show had already sold tickets in the region of 24,000 and that they were expecting that number to increase by 25 percent by the end of the week. These are huge numbers for an expo. If I hit those numbers, I'd be filthy rich. They also bragged to one MMA manager that the major sponsors they had been pursuing were now on board. "They were front-loading this event, and they were looking to bring in a sponsor," one disgruntled manager reportedly said. "My belief is that they didn't have the funds."

I think it was clever of the promoters to declare that the show was postponed because of unforeseen circumstances beyond their control, although they knew very well there wasn't going to be a show at all. It was just a feeble excuse to save their asses. The fact is, it was doomed from the word go—or so I believe. Not surprisingly, the organizer who I had dealt with for the BAMMA event once again blamed his copromoter. The latter, according to him, had sent out a press release without his approval. "I was assured Paul and his team were going to speak to every fighter, manager, member of staff, and exhibitor involved before the press release went out," this guy wrote in his statement. When I read that, the anger started to boil inside me. This was the same guy who had played the finger-pointing game with me more than once.

Looking for a way out, he next claimed that he had no final say in the postponement of the event and that his own company worked in partnership with the copromoter's company. The excuse was that a major contractor had pulled out, which made it impossible for the show to proceed, according to the promoters. What left people incensed, though, was the fact that no specific details were given. The collective thinking was that the promoters simply didn't have the ability to run an event of this magnitude. With the amount of money the organizers were promising the big stars, as I said, it wasn't going to be easy to generate the required sum. It was beyond their capacity.

It was time to implement plan B. I was still hoping to get Randy over to the Seni show. Unfortunately, after several discussions, it didn't pan out because of a scheduling conflict. Randy always had a hectic timetable, as he was filming and making appearances all over the place. So we never did nail down another date or recover from that fine mess. From then on, it was a downward spiral for me, ruining any hopes of returning to normality.

27

I'm No Terrorist

After the MMA Expo fiasco, my life took a turn that included my becoming involved with a few charitable causes. These days, I see charity organizations and events taking place everywhere I turn, but until relatively recently, I had not gotten involved to any degree. It wasn't until I attended an event in December 2010, coinciding with the release of a musician's debut single, that I got a real taste of charity work. The experience I had changed my perception about charity, and a seed was planted in my head that has stayed with me ever since.

They were raising funds for Palestine and Syria, and I was able to help as a professional writer. It also gave me a platform to promote the icons of sports who impacted pop culture at most of these events. Since then, I've come across many events raising funds, particularly for the Middle East but also for Africa or other good causes, and I'll often take part. I've never really been inclined to have political views, and I was never an ardent or casual follower of any political cause. The Palestine and the Middle East situation have been going on for longer than we care to remember, and I doubt they'll be resolved in my lifetime. And yet, over the years, I was, along with so many others, exposed to the outpouring of sorrow via not only the media but also people directly affected by these issues. There was a period when my naïveté led me to believe that the Palestinians were unfairly attacking innocent people. Since then, I've learned that the truth is a little more complicated.

What first got me pondering was an incident when I was in Los Angeles many years prior to the musical event. I was being picked up by a representative of a notorious but retired fighter whom I was in the process of negotiating and working with. This woman, who was obviously aware of my background as a Muslim, wasted no time in expressing her views as her husband drove. "How can these Palestinians launch bombs in Israel and blow people up!?" she questioned me angrily. I thought, *Why is she ranting at me? What's that got to do with me?* It wasn't until later that I realized she was an American with links to Israel via her heritage. This woman was painting everyone with the same brush, but she needed to change her brush or her target. I was no threat, nor was I responsible for these atrocities. At the time, I was still of the opinion that what was happening in Palestine was wrong but barely knew anything about the issue.

Like I said, even though I'm not one for having strong political views, I will say this now: injustice is being done in certain parts of the world, and when the media show only one side of the story, it doesn't help. As a matter of fact, it's a dangerous thing to do. It seems that when one party does something horrific, there's an outrage, but when part of the mighty West goes out, killing millions of people who are more or less innocent, then this doesn't register on many people's radar. Double standards are rife. It took me a long time to comprehend this, but now it's fully sunk in.

Anyway, this woman kept on raving and ranting. I eventually realized that I had made one of the biggest mistakes of my life by getting involved with her. She was very difficult to work with. So, this little episode planted a small seed that eventually grew in my brain.

More astounding though, was the day I had a visit from the U.K. Special Branch. I was out for the day, and when I came home, I was told that two plainclothes police officers had paid a visit and left a message, saying they would be back. I was left with my imagination flying all over the place. *What could this be all about?* I thought. Later that day, there was a knock on the door, and two plainclothes officers were standing right there in front of me as I opened it. They asked me if I was Fiaz Rafiq, and I confirmed my identity. They politely asked if they could step in to have a chat with me. Trying ever so hard to keep my demeanor intact, I let them in. Well, what choice did I have?

Bear in mind that at the time, the situation in the Middle East was precarious to say the least. A certain Middle Eastern embassy in London and the British government had received ongoing bomb threats from terrorists, and things were hitting fever pitch. These days, the word "terrorist" has apparently become synonymous with us Muslims, but back then, I was curious what this was all about as a sense of agitation set in. I hadn't robbed anyone, so what were these men doing in my house? Dismayed at the prospect of being locked up for something I hadn't done, I sat on the edge of my seat, waiting for the worst to unfold. "It's nothing to worry about," the officer assured me. "It's just about a phone call." I thought to myself, *What the hell is going on?* "You made a phone call five months ago inquiring about firearms training," he continued. "The individual you contacted is an ex-police officer, and he was suspicious and reported you."

I let out a loud laugh, slouching back on the couch. Oh, God, was I relieved. I wanted to jump up and down. The fear that had gripped me left my body faster than it had arrived. I told the officers that I was a professional working in the media, a sports journalist who wrote for the number-one martial arts publication in the United Kingdom, and that I had a bodyguard qualification, also known as Close Protection and Executive Protection. I showed the officers my Close Protection credentials and copies of my work in various magazines. I proceeded to explain that I had been, at the time, scouting for bodyguard courses that had firearms training as part of the syllabus, planning to add an additional qualification to my résumé. I already possessed a Close Protection licence.

I was no terrorist. And I wasn't going to be called one, hell, no! What I found amusing was the fact that years earlier, I had been one of the Close Protection operatives assigned to the Middle Eastern embassy in London, working for a country that was an ally of the West. I had been one of two such operatives at the embassy when it was on a code red alert receiving bomb threats from terrorists, and now I was being accused of being a potential terrorist. To be perfectly honest, even though I had been fairly composed while carrying out my duties, which included surveillance, naturally there was a twinge of fear running through me. It was Christmastime—perfect time to target—and the chances of getting blown up were pretty high. You ask yourself, *Is it worth risking your life?* I don't think so. But that was my first Close Protection assignment, so there was no way I was going to bypass the offer. Getting your foot in the game is hard enough, and to decline an operation could be career suicide—no pun intended. So I had no hesitation in accepting the assignment, even if it meant putting my life on the line. Given the fact I had taken risks throughout my life, one more risk wasn't going to make much difference. Besides, sometimes in life, you have to pursue adrenaline-pumping situations for the sake of the thrill.

The two officers apologized and left convinced of my innocence. I can't remember if I offered them tea, but I don't think they deserved a glass of water, never mind a nice cup of tea after what they had come to accuse me of. However, I wasn't quite rid of "Mr. Columbo" and his sidekick. Following this unexpected visit, several months later, I got a visit from the same officers. This time, they wanted me to come aboard. They were looking to make a new "friend" and asked if I would work for law enforcement as an "interpreter." Apparently, what they were really asking was whether I would be willing to spy on people for them. I wasn't game, nor was I ready to play James Bond.

I kindly declined, saying I doubted I could accept the "interpreter" role because I was inundated with my media work. Still, one of the cops left his card and said if I changed my mind, I should call him. I never did, though I was quite flattered. Months earlier, I had been suspected of criminal activity, but now the same law enforcement organization wanted me to be a part of the "team." Nah, no thanks! You do your own dirty work.

∽

Government authorities like that never got off my back, especially the Americans. Whenever I visited America, without exception, I would get stopped and harassed for up to three hours, which made my life hell. Los Angeles, New York, Las Vegas, wherever and whenever I landed, I would be victimized like a potential terrorist.

Apparently, I was on Department of Homeland Security's "list." Homeland Security is a department of the U.S. government with responsibilities in public security. Every time my passport was scanned or my name fed into their system, alarm bells rang, meaning I needed extra security checks. I had proved my identity time after time, confirming that I was a professional working in the media. Not only was I working for a national sports-related magazine, but I was working with high-profile martial arts and UFC personalities from the United States and had a track record of doing it. Moreover, I got into the habit of carrying two of my expired passports with me, along with the current valid one, just to prove my ID. But, no, the authorities just had to waste my time and treat me like shit.

The first time I got stopped in America was when I was on my second trip to Los Angeles in 1998. They spent hours detaining me. They finally told me that because I had overstayed by one week on my first visit two years previously, I now automatically required a visa. I was beckoned to an area where they grilled me with extra questions, and one immigration officer kept looking at me and my picture in my passport. He kept asking if it was me in the picture, which only proved to annoy me more. I wanted to scream at him. He was hoping I would trip up, but how could I trip up when I had nothing to conceal? I later learned that this officer had been on a TV show about immigration departments at American airports. While all this drama was going on, a couple of officers joked to me that he was the guy who dealt with the case of a Chinese woman who married an old white guy. No wonder he looked familiar.

My interrogation continued. I got to talking with one of the officers, who looked like Tom Selleck, about martial arts, and he seemed friendly enough. Next, I got frisked and had my fingerprints taken and then eventually handcuffed.

Never had I experienced this type of humiliation before. I felt like a piece of shit. I went through the standard interview procedure where they try to extract as much information as possible and employ trick tactics in the process. No tactic was going to trip me up because I was genuine, even though my demeanor probably made me look guilty as hell. Nervousness was all over my face. I hadn't mastered the art of confidence in these situations as yet. Now I know that officers are happy to make you sit there while they probe into your background, obtaining information from whatever source or means they can. Then they question you again, the same questions over and over, hoping you'll crumble or misremember an answer you've given. In my case, the boredom and the fact I'd been on a flight for 12 hours made this exhausting. It was deplorable.

I didn't get the worst of it, though. Several feet away, there was a tall, skinny, dark-skinned guy with a tanned blond woman who was his partner. They were returning from Australia and were having problems with the authorities just as I was. Unfortunately, the guy got a little hostile as things progressively got worse, and several security immigration officers who actually carried guns had a standoff with him. The officer in charge had a remarkable resemblance to Dan Lee, one of Bruce Lee's original students. I seem to always come across look-alikes whenever I'm in America. This officer had his hand on his gun, ready to draw like you see in westerns before a shoot-out. This guy was ready for action. After some raving, ranting, shouting, and commotion, things calmed down. Thank God, no one was shot. It suddenly dawned on me this was America, where even security personnel carried firearms. It was quite terrifying, especially for someone from Britain where even the police officers don't carry guns.

After similar treatment was repeated on more visits to the so-called land of opportunity, the country I had admired all my life was starting to lose its luster, and I decided to pay a visit to my local member of Parliament. He was associated with a family friend who was a local councillor. He wrote an endorsement letter on his letterhead paper, and so on my next trip when I landed at the airport in America, I figured I could shove this official endorsement piece of paper from the British government in the immigration officer's face. *That has to be good enough for them*, I thought. I'm afraid I was wrong. By now, I had developed the sort of guilty look cops will always pounce on.

As I approached the counter on my next trip to America, I handed over my passport and shoved the golden letter on the desk right under the immigration officer's nose. "Every time I come here, they stop me for hours!" I sarcastically remarked with added venom in my tone. "Here's a letter from my MP." As the guy proceeded to check me out on his screen, he beckoned me to move to the side as he handed me the card we fill out on the plane for immigration. So, now I was back to the routine of waiting in the "special" room, a routine I was more than familiar with. After hours of waiting, when my name was called, I walked up to the desk. Again, more questions were fired at me. In the end, the ordeal would waste at least three hours of my time.

The only time that I did not get stopped was on my first trip to Las Vegas. When I got to the immigration desk in Sin City, the officer was surprisingly okay. I told him who I was and what I was doing there—working with UFC star Randy Couture. This was UFC city, and UFC and fighters were now in the consciousness of the general public. I told him that I got stopped every time at American airports, and he stamped my card and consoled me, telling me it wasn't going to happen this time. I had just broken my record. I couldn't believe it.

⌒

I'd had enough of this terrorist list nonsense, but things came to a head when my American visa expired in 2012 and I went to the American embassy in London to renew it. The visa was for 10 years, and the procedure was always the same: you paid a hefty application fee, drove for four hours to London, waited all day, and felt like crap, as if you had done a 12-hour shift of hard labor. When it was my turn, I went into the designated room, and on the other end of the counter, an American staff member who looked like Mark Wahlberg appeared. I told this Wahlberg look-a-like that I was going on a business trip to a UFC event with Randy Couture in Las Vegas. "In 2006, you threatened the U.S. embassy," this guy fired back at me, taking me by complete surprise. He said he had the e-mails there with him.

Unfortunately, I did write to the embassy expressing my disdain, but I did not threaten the embassy. When I had applied for a media category visa in 2006, I made it clear that I had interviews lined up in mid-September for a Bruce Lee documentary I was working on, so I would want a decision well before that. So, when I received the visa about five weeks late, it royally pissed me off. I basically said in my follow-up e-mail that a lot of Americans lacked much in the way of IQ and always were of the impression they were the best in everything and also said their armed forces were not even the number one in the world. Well, apparently, they decided that I really hated America and its armed forces and was a potential threat to the security of this proud nation.

"You do not threaten a U.S. government institution!" my interviewer boomed at me. Suddenly, it dawned on me this was the reason I was on their list and getting detained every time at the airports. After more waiting, he called me up to the counter again, told me that I would be hearing from the U.S. embassy, and would be able to send the passport to get it stamped. Needless to say, I left the embassy dismayed.

Six months later, nothing. I followed up via e-mail only to be told that they had asked for my passport five weeks after the application and, since I didn't send it in, that I had to now reapply and go through the whole process again. I wasn't pleased at all but made a conscious oath not to express my anger at the American embassy if I ever wanted to step into the country again. In the end, I had to send my friends Seyfi and Tash to Las Vegas to represent me with Randy. Of course, Seyfi loved it, as he was getting an all-expense-paid trip.

In the end, all this hassle about being on the list was because I had a mark on my name for overstaying and also because, according to the Americans, I had threatened their embassy in London and was on the "potential danger" list. The funny thing is, as I said, I had protected their allies' embassy in London when they were getting bomb threats many years earlier when I was forging a Close Protection career. How about checking that out on my background?

When I was flying out to St. Louis to join Randy Couture at a wrestling event, I encountered armed police at the Manchester airport. When I got to the airport, I walked over to the counter, but there was no line. As I approached the attendant, I was told I had missed the check-in deadline. I had to be there at least an hour before flight time, but I was 10 minutes late. I protested that I was only a little late and that the flight had not even left, but the staff would not budge. Next, I explained the importance of my trip, explaining that it was a business trip and not a vacation and that I had to be there the next day, otherwise there would be dire consequences. The attendant wouldn't comply, so I had no choice but to go into seventh gear and got a little hostile. A security guard walked over, and to my further dismay, I was told that I had to change the ticket and fly out the next day.

That was out of order, but what came next was worse. After seeing my "hostile" behavior and deciding I was capable of employing desperate measures, armed police made their way over to me. It was a couple of officers with the kind of machine guns that you usually see patrolling when there's a terror alert. One calmly attempted to reason with me, while the other stood back glued to his big machine gun like Rambo. I explained that I was a combat sports journalist. I was no terrorist, and I felt all this intervention was unnecessary. I was no real threat to the staff or the people around me.

I came to learn the police had checked me out because when I returned, Bob Sykes, the editor of the martial arts magazine, had a good laugh with me. "What have you been up to, Fiaz?" he laughed, needling me as he often did. He told me the police had been checking me out by getting in touch with the magazine. Bob loved chaos and commotion and wasn't going to let this hiccup pass. So, the authorities in America and back home have been on my back forever, but I'll never let it stop me.

᠀

Ever since I can remember, I had been interested in pursuing something different as far as a career is concerned. I have always been ambitious, and I wasn't really going to settle for a normal job. Before I ultimately became a professional writer, a profession that had intrigued me was that of a bodyguard. Another profession that invoked my interest and one that I would have liked to pursue was Hollywood stuntman.

My friend Peter Consterdine, who was a leading authority in Close Protection in the United Kingdom and had some high-profile clients, was the man I turned to back then. Peter, a former national karate team member and advocate of realistic self-defense, advised and encouraged me to do some training courses that would give me the relevant qualifications to pursue a career in this now highly competitive industry. Peter used to run these courses long before I came on the scene and was active on the Close Protection circuit. So, as a young man, I endeavored to take this path with the intention of carving out a career in a field that most people perceive as glamorous. If you're old as me or older, you will remember Kevin Costner's 1992 movie *The Bodyguard*, which was a glossed-up Hollywood portrayal of a celebrity protection officer. Shortly after it hit theaters, young men flocked to courses in the vain hope of becoming the next Kevin Costner. I did the courses many years later, and by then, the students were from diverse backgrounds, including a couple of them with an armed forces background. A lot of these men had no martial arts experience, something that left me stupefied.

Some years later, major changes came into play. With the new government-stipulated rules, I had to retrain, so I redid my training and received my qualification again. As part of the course, we flew to Sweden for basic firearms training. We had actually landed in Denmark, at Copenhagen airport, and took a tram across into Sweden. This was the first time I had seen my place of birth because I had left Denmark when I was only a couple of years old, so I couldn't remember anything about it. Sweden was cold, and the snow blanketed the place. The food was crap, and I was missing home and my comfy bed and home-cooked food, not forgetting my daily routine that I was all too familiar with.

The worst was yet to come, though. We were going to be walking through hell, and only providence could save us. One of the students, who had apparently mental problems, had broken up with his partner when he was on the course and was having problems getting over the split. This guy was not in the right frame of mind to be on the shooting range. We were put up in a camp, like the ones you see in old black-and-white films about World War II, with wooden huts for prisoners of war. Each room housed two students, and this guy was in mine. Yes, of course, it had to be me. Back in the United Kingdom during our unarmed combat training, I had pissed him off a little because in our self-defense training on the ground, I would add extra pinning moves. At the time, this resulted in a bit of a scuffle but nothing serious. The way I saw it, I was merely injecting a bit of reality into the training. This guy was slim and about my weight, but he was pretty tough and solid, so I knew he could look after himself. I could feel his energy. Many times, these skinny-looking individuals are the most dangerous ones. Never underestimate them, believe me, or you'll be in for a nasty surprise.

Now some of the students were refusing to come onto the shooting range. *What if the guy goes berserk and starts shooting everyone?* was the question in our heads. The three instructors, Matt, Gary, and Johan, congregated in a room for an emergency meeting. On the range, there was some fear of the unknown. We felt that our lives were being put on the line, and some even had second thoughts about staying for the rest of the course. We've all heard of the random shootings in

America in schools and shopping malls, and now I wondered if I was going to be experiencing this for real in ice-cold Sweden. The snow was a problem for me, as was the food, and to have the thought of being potentially gunned down was just too damn terrifying. I'd rather live on water and bread than leave this world young. The group made it known to the instructors that it was for the best if the potentially unstable student sat out the gun training part of the course. Take into account that this guy had handled firearms before because he had been in the armed forces. We were using Glock 18 guns, so we knew he'd have plenty of bullets.

After much discussion, the instructors decided that our "friend" would be allowed to take part on the range. This, of course, made the rest of us furious. We were being put up to be slaughtered. We knew who would be responsible for any potential bloodshed, but dead men can't complain afterward. I've never been shot but have friends who have, and I wasn't planning on getting live rounds in me just yet. Thank God, things went smoothly. The instructors had marked out their man and were keeping a very close eye on him. It was a relief to complete the firearms training.

In the Close Protection world, it is very hard to carve out a career. What you have to remember is that you're applying for the same jobs that hundreds of others are, and in the industry, who you know often helps. Most of the work is in the capital. It is very lucrative, too. At one point, there were contracts popping up paying a lot of money. Paying £500 a day, which would amount to £14,000 a month, to go to Iraq and Afghanistan wasn't unusual. Back then, a lot of people didn't even make that much money in a year, never mind a month. I was tempted but decided not to pursue it further. You could go do three or six months and make your money, but then again, you could be blasted to kingdom come on your first day. Taking risks in life is something I'm an advocate of—believe me, I've taken my fair share—but there are times when you have to gravitate toward doing the sensible thing, weigh everything, and look at things from the perspective of the long term. So that idea went out of the window. On the bright side, I could eliminate the fear of being shot or bombed. It wasn't a bad deal after all.

I had a prestigious professional qualification under my belt, which is always great to fall back on. I did eventually go on to forge a professional career in this field, protecting one of the top sportsmen and his family, which was fun, and taking care of some other individuals.

Protecting celebrities wasn't something that particularly invoked my interest as I matured. Taking care of multimillionaire executives and foreign royals and dignitaries is something that was ideally right up my alley. Indeed, like I said, there's big money in it, but often you must be able to travel around the globe if you seriously want to pursue it as a career. Long hours, staying away from home, following protocol, and having the ability to get the job done are all part and parcel of Close Protection. In the past, as I mentioned much earlier in the book, I had done some meager jobs, including general security-related work that included a little bit of door work—the latter hardly worth mentioning. Generally speaking, people are unable to discern the difference between the two professions. A bodyguard's role differs in that they are hired to provide personal protection for an individual or a family, whereas a security officer's role is to deter crime, protecting property or people within a given space; they are not trained to physically protect an individual. In the past, individuals required no training or qualification whatsoever to work as a security officer, and today the training does not cover the specialized knowledge and skill of a bodyguard; the latter is considered a highly respected profession. Furthermore, there's a difference in salary. A bodyguard commands a high salary, while a security officer receives a minimum wage. It's basically like comparing a nurse to a doctor or an army soldier to such elite special forces as the Marine Corps, Navy Seals, or Delta Force. It was interesting to learn that UFC icon Ken Shamrock once went into bodyguarding, and 50 Cent was one of his clients. We had more than one thing in common.

28

From Racism to Road Rage

In life, you sometimes cross paths with people who become regular fixtures, popping up throughout your life. For me, Ronnie Green is one of them. Nicknamed "The Machine Gun" because of his rapid machine gun–style combinations, the five-time world Thai boxing champion is a revered member of the martial arts fraternity. Ronnie is widely regarded as the greatest Thai boxing fighter and champion Britain has produced in the history of this brutal contact sport. Not only is he a tremendous fighter, but he is one of the most self-effacing guys you will ever meet. Ronnie's master is the famed Thai boxing coach Master Toddy. Ronnie was his number-one disciple. Master Toddy later moved to Las Vegas, where he coached numerous famous MMA champions, including Gina Carrano, Randy Couture, Tito Ortiz, Forrest Griffin, and GSP.

Growing up in the Moss Side area of Manchester (Manchester's South Central Los Angeles), Ronnie often experienced racism, which left an indelible mark on his life. I often meet up with him just to hang out, go for a coffee, grab a bite to eat, and talk about martial arts. As much as Ronnie became known for his lethal and brutal fists and feet, he is equally famous for his big mouth. When I say this, I don't mean he is a loudmouth—far from it. It's just that when he starts talking, you have to practically kill him to stop him! But Ronnie has a big mouth for the right reasons. With his focus on giving positive role models to the community, his vision has always been working with the young generation to get them off the streets and involved in the martial arts. He was always trying to get me involved in school programs. Getting involved in inspirational talks for kids in schools and colleges because of my sports journalism background was something he really pushed me toward. Our friend Esmond Francis had a brother who was a victim of knife crime and lost his life, and he now works tirelessly to spread the message, helping youngsters to see the light and steer clear of gang life. Tottenham, an area consisting of large African and Turkish communities, is a knife crime–infested area. The police force is under increased pressure to clamp down on knife crime after a surge in the number of teenagers stabbed to death over recent years. Whenever I stayed with my friend Elbiz at his flat when I was visiting London, whether it was being on a film set or interviewing someone, I often got off the subway there late at night, and although I never became a victim of a crime, it's always in the back of your mind. In America, gun crime is high, but on this side of the Atlantic, the knife rules in London.

In this spirit, both Ronnie and I were invited to a community event in Tottenham in North London as special guests of Esmond. At the event, a documentary film, *One Mile Away*, was screened, highlighting the historic feud between Birmingham's prominent Burger Bar Boys and the Johnson Crew. Among the special guests were gang members from London and Birmingham who were on a mission to tackle the evils of gang culture. The speakers voiced their concerns about gang life. Making a positive change in young peoples' lives was the overarching message.

Ronnie has always espoused the philosophy of bringing people of all colors, creeds, and cultures together. In the long, thought-provoking conversations we've had, he's always stuck to this. I feel he is doing his bit for the human race and community through the medium of martial arts. On this occasion, the event kicked off with a kickboxing demo from Esmond's students. The mayor of Tottenham was in attendance and was given a platform to voice her opinions. "We need education to claw ourselves out of the pit," she addressed the audience. "I like the fact that you have people here who are working so hard with young people to bring them up and show them the right way." As the mayor continued with her edification, some members of the audience, which was 95 percent black, were in despair. The mayor went on to speak about occasions when the black race had been treated wrongly in the past in history and the white man's injustice toward the black man. Next, the audience voiced their opinions, arguing that racism was still prevalent in today's society. Suddenly, I witnessed a change in atmosphere as outbursts continued and the mayor's comments were derided by the attendees.

Sensing a change in the audience's behavior, I also saw the mayor's head turning from side to side in disagreement with the unruly crowd. Things were getting tense. For as long as I can remember, I was of the impression that we Asians from the subcontinent were more prone to racism than blacks are now. Yes, the black community had been subjected to horrendous treatment well before us, but now I thought they were accepted more than us. Black music and entertainers had won the hearts and minds of the Western world, I had believed, and white people had changed. But I was wrong. Perhaps things have improved since the civil rights movements, but the disease of racism is far from beaten.

I witnessed something in the crowd's eyes that day I will never forget. Being exposed to more African American history really put things into perspective and was disturbing to me. I was stunned to learn how black Americans were treated in the slave trade period and how they continue to be mistreated today.

Eventually, everyone settled down. Ronnie was up next as guest speaker and emcee, broaching the subject of role models and how we could be inspired by men like Muhammad Ali and Bruce Lee. Both men, he pointed out—one Chinese and the other black—made a difference and stood up for their beliefs and their people who experienced prejudice.

I refrained from making a speech that day, as I've never enjoyed public speaking. Once I was in Barcelona, Spain, as a special guest speaker at an official Bruce Lee event. Frightened by the prospect of public speaking, a part of me was experiencing fight-or-flight syndrome as I sat onstage. I think it can be traced back to my early childhood, as I felt a twinge of nerves whenever I had to stand up and talk about myself in the classroom. I was never good at that, and my accent only added to the problem. But that day in Barcelona, it was my turn to enlighten the audience and share my knowledge. After all, I was an authority and encyclopedia on the late martial arts master. I had an interpreter, which actually made me a lot more comfortable because I find it a lot easier talking to one person than talking to 100 people at once. I mean, who are you supposed to look at? As all eyes were glued to me, I managed to get through my speech, eradicating any nerves that would get in the way of embarrassing me. I even received rapturous applause in the end. On the second day I was set to deliver a speech, I was feeling a little uncomfortable again, but this time the host was my interpreter. Again, this put me at ease. I was feeling very calm, and confidence had made its way into my soul now as nervous energy made its way out. So I did well. Furthermore, what I can say is whenever I did book signings with crowds waiting in line, I never felt any sort of shyness whatsoever. I was always very comfortable and in control and enjoyed talking to people.

⌒

Ronnie earned and made his mark in the fight world, proving himself in the ring with the best. Outside the ring, he is a gentleman with impeccable manners, and he kept his cool at the event. But once when I was in his company, he almost got into an altercation in the street with a motorist. A former UFC champion friend of mine from the United States was on a seminar tour, so I phoned him to tell him that I'd make it down to Steve Marsden's place in the Sheffield area for a quick catchup. The Marsden family is a nice family, and I was always happy to see them. I rang Ronnie, whom I had introduced to this UFC champion once years ago. Ronnie picked me up, and we set off to Sheffield.

We were in our lane, and this guy was honking his horn and suddenly overtook us. Ronnie, the personification of calmness, the epitome of niceness, love, and peace, suddenly changed into Superman like I've never seen him before as the situation got the better of him. The car was in fifth gear, and so was my friend's adrenaline. He hit the accelerator hard, tailing this guy. The guy hit the brakes, pulled over in front of us, got out of the car, and sprinted toward us. This guy was in his late twenties and looked fairly solid and was taller. Ronnie was old enough to be his dad. Ronnie and I got out of the car, and Ronnie started racing toward the guy. I'm running behind him with a smirk etched across my face trying to keep up. An argument started, and this guy was shouting, raving, and ranting, arguing that Ronnie was in the wrong. As they got closer, I intervened and warned the guy that Ronnie was a five-time world Thai boxing champion to defuse the situation before it escalated. As soon as these words hit the young man's ears, he immediately put himself into reverse gear. "I'm not going to fight him in front of people," he countered, losing his courage.

I couldn't stop laughing throughout this bizarre episode as both men were roaring to rip each other's heads off. This was the first time I'd seen Ronnie really furious. I felt sorry for the other guy. I thought if Ronnie's light is lit, the guy's going to get it and get it real hard. I thought I was going to see a world champion—the greatest kickboxer Britain ever produced in this brutal bone-crushing sport who had knocked out champions all around the globe—in a live altercation right in front of my own eyes. Within seconds, they both calmed down, and

Ronnie transitioned into the calm, caring man I had always perceived him to be as he gave him a hug, which the guy accepted, and the situation was defused.

Ronnie may have hung up his gloves 15 years prior, but his reflexes, power, speed, and accuracy were such that even the current crop of fighters would have a hard time prevailing. Not only had I seen his fight footage, but I had seen him move live. And, boy, he could move fast and hit hard and hit you many times before you even knew what hit you. Some fighters have a mouth, but they can't back it up. With Ronnie, it was the opposite.

As we sat back in the comfort of our warm and cozy car and continued on our journey, in a fit of hysteria I could not stop laughing. Sensing the lighter side of this whole episode, my friend joined in. Despite what I had witnessed, I can say with great conviction that my friend embodies the true spirit of kindness and a nonviolent approach to finding a solution to a problem. In fact, Ronnie has often told me that in the gym and when he was fighting in the ring, some people used to argue with him that he wasn't aggressive enough, that he often was holding back—even though he was beating everyone up and winning. Once in the ring when Ronnie caught his opponent with a devastating elbow to the face, which caused severe damage, he made a pledge to himself never to employ elbows to the face again. He had the capacity to do real serious damage. Although he was a dangerous and powerful fighter, he was compelled to hold back. I feel he's had a natural tendency, despite being a world champion fighter, for feeling empathy for others. Call it a weakness or whatever, but that is something he has been unable to defuse within.

29

Mr. Rocky

Journalism is one of the only professions in which you are paid to learn. There are a slew of opportunities you can take advantage of as a journalist. One of the many merits of being in this position is that it allows you to meet a wide array of public and famous figures. Often, you can spend quality time getting to know those individuals during an interview. Depending on the press exposure, usually they welcome your presence—particularly if you work for a high-profile establishment. And who would say no to free drinks and access to the VIP section at events and ringside seats at sporting events? It truly is a dream job. I have been fortunate enough to be able to do what I love.

Although I had rubbed shoulders with the Hollywood elite on movie sets, there was nothing better than actually interviewing the stars or meeting them in a professional setting. If a major action star is in town, how many would bypass the opportunity to meet him? When Sylvester Stallone was over for two exclusive events in London and Manchester in August 2014, I grasped the opportunity.

I wasted no time getting in touch with the promoters, flashing my media credentials to obtain two Access All Areas passes. Obsessive fans were forking out up to £1,600 for VIP tickets. Compare this to a £200 VIP boxing dinner event ticket with the likes of Mike Tyson.

This was a rare opportunity for me to meet the action hero. Along with my friend Ronnie Green, I arrived at the M.E.N. Arena early. Given the actor's popularity, it was packed with more than 3,500 noisy fans—with one media outlet reporting a figure near the 4,500 mark. We were escorted to the VIP area, where some major TV actors were in attendance. After mingling with VIPs and celebrities, some of whom I knew, and an actor friend of mine who is a cast member of the most popular TV show filmed in the same city, it was time for the show to kick off in the arena. In what is considered true superstar fashion, Stallone arrived late after being stuck in traffic for four hours. The Hollywood heavyweight entered the arena to deafening fanfares and ovations, escorted by military with the *Rocky* tune blasting away. The general vibe, I sensed, was hero worship. Onstage, the audience was treated to a question-and-answer session with Stallone. The crowd was extra exuberant as one man clambered onstage requesting a hug from Mr. Rambo, only to be manhandled off by his bodyguard.

Listening to the star talk about the hurdles he had endured in life was inspirational and empowering for many, although for me, it was merely a repeat of what I already knew. The *Rocky* star had huge obstacles shoved in his face. He is another actor whose background can be traced to combat sports and bodybuilding. His mother was a wrestling promoter. As a young teenager, Steve Reeves, the Hercules movies star and bodybuilding icon of the 1950s and 1960s, became the young man's inspiration. Stallone was a weakling teenager, so in his quest to build his muscles, he started lifting weights and anything he could find, inspired by the bodybuilding legend. He would eventually sculpt one of the best physiques in cinematic history. His slurred speech impediments led to being bullied and made him less of a candidate for transforming himself into an alpha male. His speech problem was the result of an accident at birth that left his face paralyzed, further resulting from nutritional deficiencies in early childhood.

Stallone's story is one of the most inspirational in the history of Hollywood. His upbringing as a kid in contrast to becoming Hollywood's top action star with blockbuster hits is phenomenal. Like Arnold Schwarzenegger's father, his father also never believed in him and always put him down. I'm sure this fueled him to prevail against overwhelming odds.

He further opened up to the audience. A struggling actor, he churned out the *Rocky* script in a matter of three weeks after watching the Muhammad Ali–Chuck Wepner fight on cable TV in 1975.

After the question-and-answer session and a rapturous applause, the VIPs congregated to the VIP area for a meet and greet and professional photos. These fanatics had paid a hefty price to shake the hand of an icon. Stallone walked in with his rep and event promoter from the south. I was sitting at my table, and as Stallone was passing, he pointed to an Arnold Schwarzenegger item on the table and picked one up, smirking as we both shared pleasantries.

Suddenly, his official said, "No, we can't have this." It seemed that although Arnold and Stallone are on friendly terms now and even collaborating, the rep apparently didn't want an Arnold product being promoted at a Sly event. *Here we go*, I thought. It dawned on me that a clash of egos between the two action stars was still prevalent.

After Stallone finished posing for photos, he walked past and stopped by my table again. We shook hands and had a quick chat. I tried handing him a copy of UFC champion Randy Couture's autobiography, but there was a perceptible change in his behavior. I felt perplexed because when promoting *The Expendables*, Stallone, who is now one of the celebrities who owns shares in the UFC, had praised Randy on David Letterman's *Late Show*. "You put all these tough guys, Dolph Lundgren, Jet Li, in a room together, who comes out?" The Hollywood action star proudly said, "If you walked in 10 minutes later, you'd see Randy Couture sitting on top of us having a chocolate fudge sundae." I was aware of the reverence he had for the UFC legend, so I was quite puzzled by his reaction when I tried to hand him the book. After a quick chat with me, his bodyguard whisked him out, leaving many VIPs rather bemused.

Stallone seemed tired—after being forced to smile for about 100 rich fans, he got up and left, leaving many fans disappointed. Those who never got their promised photos with him apparently got refunds. I could see the promoter running around like a headless chicken. He had disappointed VIPs who had missed their once-in-a-lifetime chance to be pictured and mingle with the actor. So the meet and greet went out the window. But all in all, it was a great day for many who had this rare opportunity to see the man in the flesh.

⌒

I learned something very interesting about Stallone when I was researching Ali's life. One of Ali's training partners at Deer Lake revealed to me that Stallone actually was among the boxers who spent time at the camp before anyone ever knew who he was. He said, "He came, yes. He stayed in the bunkhouse; he had nowhere to sleep. This was a year before *Rocky*. He wrote *Rocky* on yellow tab paper in the bunkhouse. He was a normal guy, but he was a boxer." Boxers were welcomed at Deer Lake, and Ali would be accommodating. He'd give you tasks to do. He'd get somebody for you to spar. He would spar you. He added, "Stallone was eating in the kitchen staying at the bunk house, boxing. I think he sparred with Sugar Ray Leonard early on, his sparring partner. Ali was trying to get him work. I think it was Ali was the one who introduced him to the guy who made the movie *Rocky*. I did remember him; there were a lot of people there, they were coming and going. It was full of people [at the] bunkhouse." All this was a pleasant surprise to me. This individual told me to talk to Eddie Mustafa Muhammad, who spent time at the camp and became the WBA light-heavyweight champion. But when I asked Eddie, who lives in Las Vegas now, to verify the story, he said he didn't remember Stallone being at the camp.

Stallone tried to sell the script and was offered $125,000. But he was adamant on starring in the film. The studio refused because they wanted a bona fide star. A couple of weeks later, they offered the broke actor double the amount—$250,000—then increased it to $350,000, but he refused to accept the inflated offer. Would you refuse that kind of money if you were broke with only $50 in your bank account and nothing to your name? Some would take the money and run. Finally, the deal stipulated that he'd receive only $35,000 for the script but get to star in the film. As we know, the *Rocky* franchise became one of the most iconic in cinematic history, catapulting Sylvester Stallone to superstardom.

Fast-forward to 2020. I interviewed Irwin Winkler, the producer of all the *Rocky* films. I was curious about this widely circulated story in the public domain how the then-unknown actor convinced the studio to take a gamble on him. I asked, "Irwin, what can you tell me about the first *Rocky* movie and how Sylvester Stallone convinced you to do the movie with a then unknown?" He said, "Well, the thing which is interesting is he came to me, but he was an unknown actor. And I didn't have a role for him for another film. But as he was leaving the office, he said to me, 'Oh, by the way, I'm a writer.'" Irwin was dubious and told me that he didn't sound like a writer, nor did he look like a writer. Stallone, refusing to take no for an answer, enthusiastically tried to pitch another idea to the producer: "I have a script that I'd like you to read." And he gave the script to the producer, who conceded and actually thought it was well written. Yet Irwin wasn't interested in pursuing it any further. Somewhat consoling Stallone, he said, "Look, I think you're a good writer, but I don't like to do a movie on it." Stallone had another plan, which I would refer to as plan B, up his sleeve. As he was about to leave, he said, "I have another idea." And he proceeded to pitch the idea of *Rocky*. As I mentioned earlier, it was based on the underdog Chuck Wepner, whose boxing heroics had inspired Stallone to churn out the script in a matter of weeks for *Rocky*. So, originally, Stallone had visited the producer to pitch something else.

Stallone said something that Irwin found very thought provoking, something very few people would ever be willing to do. He said, "Look, I don't have any money"—which was true—"and I will write the script for you, but you don't have to pay me. No money! One thing you have to do is once I write the script, you don't have to pay me, but you have to give me the starring role in this movie." This impressed Irwin, and he felt it was very unique. This unknown actor had won over the Hollywood producer, and the rest, as they say, is history.

I asked Irwin whether the film was an idea for the fight-trend kung fu films that had caught the attention of the public several years earlier. "No, not at all," the producer said. "The thing is we never considered it as a fight movie; we always considered it as a love story between him and Adriane. The fighting was just an opportunity for him to show that he could make something better out of himself." This, I must admit, was a complete surprise to me. You learn new things in my game.

Stallone went on to write all the *Rocky* movies and directed *Rocky II*, *Rocky III*, *Rocky IV*, and *Rocky Balboa*. Now, what they did was turn the writing and directing to Ryan Coogler. Stallone was very gracious about it and very encouraging to Coogler, Irwin told me. He was very determined to pass the baton to this young filmmaker. "What surprised me most in my career was we made this movie with a then-unknown Sylvester Stallone, and it won an Academy Award," Irwin said. "It became a world phenomenon. And 40-odd years later, we're making *Creed III*, which will be the ninth version of *Rocky*. It's quite an accomplishment going from 1976 to 2020 still making *Rocky*. The only one I think which has a longer history is the James Bond franchise."

Widely considered the hard man of Hollywood with a heart of gold, Stallone had slept in a bus station in New York for three days, homeless when he was at his lowest. He was unable to pay his rent or buy food. That day at the question-and-answer session, Stallone empowered us with messages of determination, willpower, and holding onto your dreams.

⌒

I had the opportunity to attend the European red carpet premiere of *Creed II*. It was a dark, rainy night. The stars walked the carpet, from Michael B. Jordan and Dolph Lundgren to Tessa Thompson and

Brigitte Nielsen. Numerous world champion boxers were in attendance at the star-studded event. But I think it was Tessa Thompson who was the queen of the night. She dazzled the audience with her confidence and style to carry off her Valentino Haute Couture dress with such grace and ease. I grabbed a quick interview with Dolph, who was gracious enough to give me a few minutes on the red carpet before his handlers whisked him inside. "What's the most fascinating thing about working with Stallone on the *Rocky* franchise and on *Creed II*?" I asked the Swede, who, before he became an actor, had a dream of pursing a boxing career (he had revealed this to me in a conversation I had with him a decade earlier)."Well, I think the *Rocky* movies are very special for me because it's not only entertaining and about sport, but it's about life, it's about family, it's about things you love, what you want to fight for. It's about some deep issues that touch many people around the world, and even if you don't know anything about boxing, you can resonate with it. It's really changed my life, and now, almost 35 years later, it has changed my life a little bit again. I think because this film was a great chance for me to play a dramatic role. I had some good reviews the first time I worked on *Rocky* with Stallone, and I'm very pleased, and I want to thank Stallone to have given me the opportunity again by transporting me back into the franchise. I never thought I'd do this role again."

I asked him, "Can you give me a funny anecdote with Stallone while working on *Creed II*?"

"One thing I won't forget is that we both look older in the film," he said. "We both are wearing makeup, we've actually got gray hair and wrinkles in real life, and we—the characters—do interviews in the movie, and Stallone keeps wiping his makeup off. Then in the end he goes, 'You tell the people back home this is just make up, we don't look like this.'" The man is in his early seventies now, but his motivation to keep in the best shape possible has never waned.

30

Bruce Lee

Enter the Ring

The beauty of Bruce Lee is how he transcends martial arts and has a crossover appeal. Numerous boxing champions that I have interviewed over the years were not shy to concur that this 135-pound Chinese man left an indelible impression on them. I painstakingly researched a piece relating to Bruce Lee's Western boxing connection, aptly titled "Bruce Lee: The Western Boxing Connection," and submitted this feature to an editor at a leading boxing magazine in November 2015. The piece reflected on what, how, and who in the sweet science game had inspired and influenced him and his art and whether he would have triumphed in the squared ring. If you're well-read on the subject of Bruce Lee, it won't come as a surprise that boxing theories and concepts were an integral part of his personal form of combat he devised, which he labeled jeet kune do. The great pugilist champions I had personally spoken to (and others I had seen quoted) adulated this lightweight fighter. These men actually fought at the highest level in the squared ring. These were world champions, fighters whose life revolved around a competitive arena.

However, if I thought the boxing editor was going to embrace my opinions with open arms, then I was gravely mistaken. The piece drew sharp criticism from the editor via his assistant. "Fiaz says that the 135-pound Lee could hit harder than a man twice his size due to the speed of his punch," the editor wrote in his response message. "How does Fiaz know this? Pure conjecture! So, Lee hit harder than the 160-pound Gennady Golovkin; the 175-pound Sergey Kovalev; the 225-pound Mike Tyson; the 190-pound Jack Dempsey; the 195-pound

Joe Louis? Really? I can't get my brain around that one." Maybe this editor had been hit far too many times in the head. Perhaps he was in need of edification. Those were my immediate thoughts.

I also advocated that had Bruce turned to boxing on a professional level, he would at the absolute least have been an overwhelming force in his weight division. This was a viewpoint shared by Bruce's closest training partner and a man who has widely been acknowledged as the world's greatest martial artist, Dan Inosanto. "At the absolute least, really?" the editor responded, "up against lightweight champs such as Roberto Duran, Alexis Arguello, and Esteban DeJesus?" Speaking of training partners, there was a period in Bruce's life when he was surrounded by boxers and street fighters who were his personal students, who admitted that Bruce would tie them up in knots and they couldn't touch him. "The last paragraph of Fiaz' piece quotes Ricky Hatton," he continued in his assault. "I've interviewed Ricky, and the quote just doesn't sound like Ricky talking. I'm not flat out saying Ricky never used the words used in the quote, but that's another quote I'd like to see backed up." I had interviewed Ricky myself twice, once for the martial arts magazine and the other time for the documentary on Bruce Lee.

Furthermore, Ricky, in his own autobiography, revealed the influence the late great martial arts master had on him. Maybe the editor needed to do his own homework and acquire the opinions from some of the best boxers. I'm sure he would have been in a state of shock by the response. "To me, there were too many loose ends, plus conjecture and inaccuracies in the piece," the editor wrote. "I respect Fiaz' knowledge of martial arts, but the Bruce Lee piece, to me, doesn't quite make the transition. We can't be publishing pieces that would have the pugilist-specialist readers shaking their heads. It's a piece that could work but not quite in its present form."

On a more constructive note, he admitted that the Muay Thai fighters often did very well in Western-style boxing and that some had even won titles very early in their boxing careers. He said these fighters used a lot of punching in their Muay Thai bouts and were accustomed to bruising, punishing, and bone-on-bone contact. But he wasn't sure that Bruce, who was a wonderful athlete and skilled fighter, had that sort of hard-grinding background. After this verbal assault, I happened to mention the situation to my good friend Ronnie Green, the five-time world Thai boxing champion. This man had beaten the champions of the sport in Thailand and is the pioneer of Thai boxing in that country. Needless to say, Ronnie, who I feel has a better grasp on reality, couldn't get his head around the editor's opinions.

Certainly, boxers experience full-contact blows and are able to dish out and absorb punishment. It's a full-contact sport just as wrestling is a body-contact sport. But based on the fact Bruce was a lightweight and hence would've unlikely been a force to be reckoned with in the ring is debatable, fair enough. Be that as it may, when you look at lighter-weight champions who prevailed, you would think that had Bruce pursued boxing, it is quite plausible he could triumph. There are ambiguous statements that he didn't spar full contact all-out, while others documented that he emphasized full-contact sparring. Being the intelligent man that he was, he implemented realistic training methods according to his personal students. Let's get one thing straight here: to make it in boxing on a professional level, even the amateur level, I feel you have to train in pure boxing. Otherwise, it's like trying to become a 100-meter runner by playing soccer or in the NFL just because a lot of running is involved—one must comprehend the clear distinction between the two.

Personally, having been a student of the martial arts—particularly grappling, and any striking was devoid of full-contact sparring—I never did get a taste of pure boxing until many years later when I entered a boxing gym in the hope of acclimatizing myself with sparring in the ring. This was the sole reason. It didn't take long to grasp reality, as the urge for "flight" was really strong. The heavy bag combinations that you mastered for many years just fly out of the window as you struggle to find your target, an overwhelming tendency to flinch as you are bombarded with big bombs. In the process, you're being out-smarted—and in my case by skinny teenagers who had been boxing for some time and looked thin as a stick. Much to my surprise, their ability to hit me and not get hit was both somewhat embarrassing and frustrating. Although the punches didn't hurt or knock me down, it taught me a lesson, and a reality check was in order. Besides, I always had a glove phobia and found it extremely uncomfortable with pillowcases on my hands trying to punch and move.

Once you clear that first monster hurdle, you begin to feel more confident. So, learning a martial art, which within its framework doesn't implement full-contact sparring, is one thing, but getting into the boxing ring is a completely different experience. The sweet science allows you to experience the brutality of a fight, the rawness, in a somewhat controlled environment. I think any serious martial artist should experience, to a fair degree, some sort of boxing sparring to really appreciate getting hit and experience full contact on the move. Otherwise, you will never know the reality of your own limitations—

and true potential. But these boxers wouldn't last in a grappling gym. It's befitting to mention that Bruce's only real experience in the confines of a boxing ring was when he laced up gloves in Hong Kong and competed in the Inter Boxing Competition as a teenager. He knocked out Gary Elmes, winning the championship. I was told by his best friend William Cheung he had used wing chun straight punches in the fight.

After taking criticism, which was hard to swallow, and contemplation, I came to terms with the fact that the critic had several valid points. And to be fair to him, he had the right to his opinion. I even came to value his critical feedback even though I did not agree with most parts. But my primary support for my arguments was that some of the biggest names in boxing had shared opinions that were parallel to my own. The champions Sugar Ray Leonard—who gorged his passion on the likes of Muhammad Ali and Bruce Lee—Evander Holyfield, Ricky Hatton, even the great George Foreman—the latter always happy to speak to me whenever I phone him—all great fighters whom I interviewed, seem to share my view. Countless other world boxing champions seem to be running on the same track. They revere Bruce not only for his iconic status but also for his fighting ability. If these fighters thought Bruce was not a great fighter or that he lacked the potential to triumph in the ring should he have pursued this avenue, they wouldn't have gone on record offering colossal praise. "He influenced a lot of people and showed that size didn't matter," Evander Holyfield told me once. Even heavyweights were intrigued by this 135-pound fighter of a diminutive stature. "I don't know anybody that was better," he added. "He was very technical."

I had done my homework and research well. What these champions had to say about a skinny five-foot, seven-inch man was something that I—and most—value. Moreover, one legend in the fight world whose opinion I would value more than most is "Iron" Mike Tyson. I met him once. "Bruce Lee had an awesome philosophy of life, which blew me away," Tyson once openly declared in Roots of Fight promo video. "Bruce Lee is a killer! You do as much damage as you can and get out without being hurt, less damage to yourself as possible. I have so much respect for his philosophy." When you managed to influence the most ferocious fighter in the boxing game, you know you've done something right.

"Bruce Lee, he didn't believe in fighting in tournaments and stuff," Tyson said. "He basically believed in, 'let's do it right now.' But Bruce Lee was really a street fighter, like an MMA fighter for real." Tyson himself built a notorious reputation for being a ferocious fighter in and out of the ring. Tyson and I have a mutual friend, Joe Egan. They lived and trained together when they were teenagers in New York at the famous Catskill training camp for two years before we witnessed the jam-packed arenas where Tyson fought his fiercest foes. I got a thrill when Joe would tell me how both of them used to watch Bruce Lee movies at the house where they lived. Both teenagers would try to mimic Bruce, replicating the sounds that he became famous for. Tyson was a huge fan of kung fu classics and would fork out thousands of dollars on kung fu flicks. He went as far as watching *Enter the Dragon* to learn explosiveness. And we all know how explosive Tyson became—he was dynamite!

Tyson, a man who loves all styles of combat and is a huge fan of the UFC, believes that Bruce was a real-life ferocious fighter. "No one talked about MMA before that or grappling," Tyson said of Bruce's innovative approach in an interview with *MAXIM* in 2016. "He said, 'I don't believe in grappling because I equate grappling with being on the floor and I equate being on the floor with being stomped on.' And they said, 'What do you mean?' And he said, 'One guy maybe, but I'm fighting five or six guys, but I can't be on the floor wrestling around.' Is that deep or what? That just totally opened my head. We talk about killing, not any championship." Tyson understood that Bruce's approach was not fighting to see who is better but fighting for survival in a street encounter.

Bruce has had more than his fair share of critics, but equally, he has garnered profound respect from some of the toughest combatants.

31

Enter the Octagon

Around the same time, I was talking to an editor of a martial arts magazine in Sweden. I had dealt with this individual in the past but didn't find him very instrumental at all. By then, I had ventured into working with magazines around the globe from America, Australia, Dubai, and Europe while still holding the position of columnist for the martial arts magazine domestically. On a personal level, being recognized for your work around the world and promoting the sports and athletes gave me a great sense of achievement.

I had submitted a piece on Bruce Lee to this Swedish magazine, reflecting on his influence on a new brutal sport and his impact on the MMA scene. I didn't hear back from the editor, so I picked up the phone and resorted to the old-fashioned approach. I was oblivious to what lay in wait. I was in for another unexpected shock. The editor told me that he wasn't keen on covering movie martial artists and wanted to promote only "real" fighters. He made it clear that Bruce Lee wasn't good enough to be in his magazine. What? Almost five decades after his demise, this icon continues to grace the covers of magazines all over the world, from specialist magazines to more major mainstream periodicals, such as *Time*.

The editor went on and on as I listened to his criticism, keeping composed. This magazine had transitioned into a reality-based MMA publication after years of focusing on traditional martial arts. Bruce, according to the editor, was merely a movie actor. Bruce didn't compete or prove himself, but the MMA fighters had proved themselves, he further argued. I wasn't thrilled at what I was hearing.

I tried to refrain from letting my personal feelings take over. Controlling my emotions, I clung on to my professional attitude. But inside, my stomach was turning faster than a washing machine on its final cycle, spinning like mad. Again, I did feel that he was entitled to his opinion. I had to be fair and think with a rational mind. However, just as with the boxing authority I mentioned earlier, I did have top UFC fighters on my side.

Let's look at this with a partial eye. I had spoken with a plethora of top UFC fighters and champions who had a very different take on the martial arts innovator. With the advent of the UFC, a whole new generation of hybrid fighters rose to prominence. Randy Couture, Rashad Evans, Ken Shamrock, Jon Jones, and Conor McGregor, to name a few, were all influenced by the late martial arts exponent. When I met Rickson at his academy in West Los Angeles in 2002, I was dying to chuck the Bruce Lee question at him. With his humble yet dignified bearing, Rickson acknowledged Bruce as being the greatest martial artist of our time. When it comes to fighting, Rickson knows what he's talking about. He has this aura about him; when you're in his presence, you feel this gigantic energy.

Now, MMA is no Mickey Mouse sport; it's one of the toughest sports around. So, I valued the opinions of the gladiators who fought in the Octagon more than most. These men's achievements and experience fighting in a brutal sport were admirable. Again, on the surface, someone may feel that because of Bruce's rather diminutive stature, he may have been butchered in an MMA setting. McGregor (Bruce's weight) is a perfect example of a light fighter who managed to rule the UFC. It's interesting to note that his strength is in striking, and there are plenty of fighters who are more experienced in submission grappling than he is. "I think he could have competed in the 145-pound weight class," Randy once told me when I was researching the life and legacy of the late fighter and movie star. "Sure, he could have got himself in that weight class and done well, there's no doubt about it."

I feel, as part of the argument, it's vital to go to the original source—grappling masters, martial arts champions, and personal students who had trained with the man himself. Essentially, they are the only ones who really witnessed Bruce's true abilities, to whatever degree, firsthand. During his lifetime, Bruce did work out with several world-class grappling experts, notably jiu-jitsu master Wally Jay and pan-American judo champion Hayward Nishioka, who slot into this category very nicely. So, it's crucial to take their opinions on board. After all, these men were world-class grappling competitors and champions. Hayward and Wally were impressed by Bruce's martial arts abilities, and they were in awe of his striking skills and overall pedigree.

Furthermore—and this is the crucial point—when assessing Bruce's ability, most people, including even some modern-day MMA champions and boxers, can't come to grips with the fact you have to separate the theatrical art from reality. A lot of people's perception is based on what they see on celluloid—good or bad. Most view Bruce as the fighter beating up 20 men on-screen, coming out unscathed. In this light, the unforgettable opening scene from *Enter the Dragon* epitomizes true MMA. This scene accurately captures the true essence of MMA in action. This projected exactly what MMA is based on: two competitors attempt to defeat each other by utilizing a variety of techniques, ranging from striking vertical to ground grappling. Bruce is wearing fingerless gloves, which became the precursor of UFC, and black underpants. It's a testament to Bruce's innovative genius.

Very few would doubt that Bruce was revolutionary in not only bringing the fighting arts into the spotlight in the West but also accentuating the need for adaptability and a more realistic training approach. As Bruce embraced American culture and Western combat sports, he kicked martial arts tradition into smithereens in pursuit of devising the ultimate fighting art. His hybrid style encapsulated a composite of techniques and methods that at the time received criticism from the traditionalists. This approach made him somewhat of an outcast in the martial arts fraternity. In modern-day martial arts, we have seen cross-training being embraced and advocated. The MMA movement has catapulted the martial arts to the forefront of combat.

The golden question remains to be answered. Could Bruce have emerged victorious if he locked horns with the likes of Royce Gracie or Conor McGregor? I had thought long and hard about how he would have fared in today's MMA environment. I personally believe that if a frail-looking Royce Gracie tore through no-holds-barred competitions with his technical supremacy, it is plausible Bruce could've whooped asses with his devastating kicks, chokes, strangles, and ground-and-pound provided he spent an inordinate amount of time with a good coach. This is my honest opinion. It goes without saying that he would have had to attain a high level of grappling skills, including ground work, which Bruce's art was completely devoid of given his assiduous approach.

According to one of Bruce's personal training partners, "As far as no-holds-barred tournaments like the Ultimate Fighting Championship, I don't think Bruce would enter something like that." However, all this talk is speculative at best. What is apparent is that his popularity continues to grow. He is the fighter who has been chosen more than any other UFC fighter in the EA Sports *UFC* game, 3.41 million times in the game's first month of availability. This is an accomplishment given the fact Bruce never fought in the UFC, nor did he compete competitively. Both GSP and Jon Jones have been played 3.4 million times, and from there, it's a big drop-off to the next fighters selected.

Based on the response from a plethora of UFC champions and warriors as well as boxers, it's safe to conclude Bruce had the *potential* to become a force to be reckoned with in the squared ring or the Octagon. In conclusion, there's not ample evidence to substantiate this, and, by the same token, there's little to disprove it. There are just too many variables involved to make any meaningful prediction. This debate will always be surrounded by great criticism and speculation. Many credit Bruce Lee as the godfather of the MMA movement, while others are, understandably, reticent about handing this "title" to the late master.

About the piece? Needless to say, it never got into the Swedish magazine. Instead, I wrote the piece in *Fighters Only* magazine.

32

Old School Meets New

Royce Gracie was fighting his old nemesis Ken Shamrock. I was shocked to hear this. I immediately got in touch with Royce to get this validated and also conduct an interview with him. It was always great to talk to Royce and have a laugh with him. Ken had tasted defeat at the hands of UFC's first-ever champion in the first-ever tournament when the Brazilian choked him out in a mere 50 seconds. In their second outing at UFC 5, they fought to a draw in a fight that lasted 30 minutes. The famous rivalry began. Ken was always eager to avenge his defeats and had long desired to add another chapter to their rivalry.

I said to Royce that I was surprised to hear about his upcoming fight. I asked him why he was stepping into the arena again because he had retired years ago. He didn't need to fight any more. This man had started a revolution in combat sports and made a name globally when he sent shockwaves into the fight world, paving the way for promising MMA fighters. Every man wants to be the toughest guy. It's an alpha male thing and a subconscious dream whether we admit to it or not. Royce had become a global phenomenon. He had the world at his feet and had fame and fortune in abundance. So, why return to fight in the world's most brutal sport and put everything on the line when he could stay within his comfort zone? It was time to find out from the man himself.

According to Royce, his nemesis kept pestering Scott Coker, promoter of Bellator. "Man, he wants to fight you, he wants you," Coker told the Brazilian. Royce thought to himself, *Man, I'm a fighter, let's do it—might as well.* When you're a professional fighter and have fought for so many years at the highest level, fighting is in your blood. It's hard to blank it out. When you've dedicated your whole life to something, a cause or a craft, once you retire, you miss that element of your life that gave you that buzz, a meaning to life.

After Muhammad Ali hung up his gloves for good, he also missed the fight. George Kalinsky, the famous American sports photographer who worked with Ali numerous times, once shared an anecdote with me. "At one time in the early 80s, prior to the buildup for Wrestle-Mania, they had a lot of celebrities that were honorary referees," the photographer told me. "They had people like Pete Rose, a diverse group of people. And Ali was one of the referees. I was looking at him and it was the first time that I realized—it was a couple of years after his final fight—and feeling sad because you could see he wasn't the Ali that I was used to seeing. I felt really bad. I remember back when Ali said to me that the ring is his life and everything and the ring is his opportunity to be famous. Here he is in the ring but not necessarily the star. Hulk Hogan was the star that day, and Ali was just one of the supporting athletes." Once you've been in the public limelight but then fade into obscurity, you're sometimes itching to be adulated again.

Still, for Royce I think, like I said, fighting is in his blood—it wasn't that he craved to be in the limelight. Royce told me that other people let age dictate things to them, but that has never been his mentality. "A guy like him who is 220 pounds and a guy like me who is 176 pounds, he still can't understand, I guess," Royce said of Ken's fresh challenge. "He's been losing sleep in the last 20 years."

Ken was bigger than Royce and in pretty good shape with rippled muscles. Royce was planning to avoid getting hit in the fight. "He's still a good grappler," Royce admitted, "he finished a lot of his fights, so he's dangerous." I thought Ken's versatility might be a threat to Royce. Ken had boasted to the media that his longtime nemesis was living in the past because the sport had evolved and advanced. He broached the subject of being a versatile fighter in the modern-day MMA arena. Having remained resolute in his original fighting philosophy, Royce explained that the Helio Gracie system of self-defense advocates that a small person can overcome somebody who is bigger and stronger. And this is what he had proved to the world when he sliced through his bigger, stronger adversaries in his prime. This tenacious man was sticking to his original fighting style when almost all professional MMA fighters were shrewd enough to evolve.

I had seen Ken fight before at an event when he was on the decline. Although I had perceived Ken to be past his prime, which he was, his physical presence could still intimidate many. But no man could intimidate the Brazilian no matter how big or muscular his adversary was. I guess Royce had already sussed his foe out—either that, or he was taking a huge risk this time putting his reputation on the line. This legacy was on the brink of being potentially tarnished, I feared. At the same time, if Ken lost, this would further tarnish his own reputation, which already had taken a severe beating after tallying up a considerable number of losses in the past few years. Both men had pioneered the sport and were holding onto their reputations. But Royce is one of the most confident fighters I have ever known. Having known him for more than 24 years, I don't think I've seen fear in him. I don't think he's ever been scared of a fighter.

This was like the classic Ali–Frazier rivalry of MMA—outing number three—and Ken would find redemption if he triumphed. Personally, I thought it could go either way. As our conversation progressed, I was inclined to ask Royce about training preparations. "What kind of training are you going to do to prepare yourself?" I asked the UFC Hall of Famer. "I can't tell you about my training, man, you're going to be telling Ken," he joked. That's the last thing I would be doing. I wanted Ken to be choked right out. As it happens, Royce wasn't going to be applying any of his trademark chokes that night; he'd be shocking everyone.

The fight took place on February 19, 2016. In the morning, as soon as my eyelids opened, the first thing I did was check the result on my phone. I'm lying there in my bed with my phone as a nervous tremor of emotion ran through me. And as soon as I read the headline—"Royce Gracie Stops Ken Shamrock, but Not without Controversy"—a sense of relief shot through my body. I felt vicarious excitement coursing through my veins.

During the bout, Royce had allegedly kneed his opponent in the groin. Ken protested in anger, pointing to his victor in the ring after he recovered. "You did this on purpose!" he barked several times. Ken was pissed off and resorted to desperate measures. The Brazilian jiujitsu pioneer had locked into a clinch midway through the first round and traded knees before he took Ken down, following up with a series of hammer fists to his floored opponent's face. This was his first-ever knockout of his professional career. You just couldn't picture Royce knocking someone out with his fists. But he had been training some kickboxing for some years. I guess it paid off.

After the commercial break when the beaten fighter was interviewed, he said, "I got upset. I was wrong for getting upset because it wasn't Royce's fault." Yet, after the fight, Ken sent an open letter in which he strongly urged Royce to "do the right thing." Ironically, Ken later failed the drug test, which made the whole episode even more interesting and fueled further speculation. How can you say Royce cheated when you yourself were cheating in the first place? Regardless, I was over the moon with Royce emerging victorious. The Gracie–Shamrock feud would now be put to bed at last, and the defeat plunged Ken into despair. Gracie: two wins and one draw. Considering his time off and ring rust, Royce proved himself. In my prefight conversation, I had asked him if he had any future fight plans. He had a tendency to sign one fight at a time and said that after this fight, anything is possible.

The year had started with a big bang. The first-ever UFC champion had come out of retirement after nine years to prove he still had it in him at age 49 to compete again. Royce was like Pele—previous and current champions seem to endear to him. But "The Notorious" Conor McGregor was now the biggest name in the UFC. McGregor established himself as a global superstar and has taken the sport that Royce had brought to our attention to another level. No contemporary MMA fighter impinged on the consciousness of the MMA fans and beyond like McGregor—though it is incontestable that Royce's legacy has made him the most influential figure in the sport's history, however notorious any past or current fighter is.

McGregor was preparing for UFC 196, where he was going to be facing Nate Diaz. He pulled up in his Rolls-Royce for a training session at Nano's Hapkido, a small gym run by Royce's friend in Hermosa Beach in Los Angeles. Royce, who was fresh from his win less than two weeks before, happened to be there that day. Would Royce melt away under the glow of the UFC's biggest champion given the latter's current star power? No. "The Notorious" was somewhat speechless when both fighters crossed paths. The Irish sensation, usually boisterous, seemed starstruck, struggling to find words as both men conversed.

The name Conor McGregor has become synonymous with multimillion dollars. He is one of the biggest sports superstars, known for his tailor-made suits and brash talk and looking great dishing out pain in the Octagon. Now this Irish man was talking big money. He'd even mentioned how he was on the verge of accumulating $100 million in the UFC. At first, I must admit, I thought it was all speculative talk.

How can you make $100 million as a UFC fighter? I thought to myself. It soon dawned on me that this was plausible but something only Mc-Gregor could pull off. The whole game has changed. Gone were the days when smaller sponsorships were the only sponsors inclined to get involved in a brutal spectacle sport. The UFC had been breaking pay-per-view records for some years. This is where the big money rolls in. Where did you think boxing accumulated all those millions from? Major sponsors and the medium of pay-per-view played a pivotal role.

I remember many years earlier that some top boxing fight purses were $300,000, topped off with a $1.5 million TV deal. So that's $1.8 million right there. Then some went on to make a lot more per fight, reportedly earning a $3 million purse but pocketing a career-best $13 million, taking into account TV and sponsorship deals. The UFC has not only caught up but also eclipsed boxing in certain respects, and McGregor is responsible to a large degree for this. Comparing pay-per-view figures for the two sports, when Ronda Rousey fought Bethe Correia at UFC 190, the pay-per-view buys hit the 900,000 mark. Furthermore, the UFC had eight events in that time that hit the 1 million mark. Of course, the Mayweather–Pacquiao fight is an exception, which reportedly generated 4.4 million and a revenue of $400 million.

At UFC 194, McGregor had beaten Jose Aldo, knocking him out in 13 seconds and earning $500,000. Adding to that was 1.2 million pay-per-view buys, and he reportedly banked $8 million in total. In the much-anticipated UFC 196 when he was facing Nate Diaz, pay-per-view revenues poured in, a million and half buys, totally eclipsing the UFC 194 numbers. McGregor became the first-ever UFC fighter to earn a million-dollar purse. According to sources, the $5-plus for each buy he received reportedly earned him more than $8 million in total for the bout. Each buy was sold at $50 or $55. Something else that needs to be taken into account, as far as the financial figures are concerned, are sponsorships and postfight bonuses, which are not publicly disclosed. I had always heard Dana White talking robustly about how the UFC broke the record. "We just broke the record," he would announce ebulliently at postfight press conferences. Without a question, his savvy marketing skills have contributed to the organization's immense success.

Just as stars Randy Couture and Chuck Liddell had helped propel the sport into the mainstream prior to McGregor's emergence, this UFC champion was now the new superstar, surpassing his predecessors. Every now and again, someone comes into a sport and changes things for the better, stands out from the rest, and is intoxicating to watch. McGregor has done something that no other UFC fighter has. This fighter was even asking for a stake in the UFC. He generated millions of dollars for this sports organization, so much money that he, being an astute businessman, felt he should have a cut of the profits. Undeniably, McGregor had taken the whole sport into another dimension.

At UFC 196 at the MGM Grand Garden Arena, McGregor, on a 15-fight winning streak, faced one of the biggest tests of his career. For Nate, this was his biggest fight at that point of time. Nate tried countering McGregor at every opportunity. McGregor was aggressive from the word go and looked strong. With 40 seconds left in the first round, Nate took McGregor down by catching his leg as McGregor shot a right kick to the midsection. However, McGregor got into the guard position quickly and tried to get some ground-and-pound in as his opponent was by the fence before the round ended. In round 2, McGregor, throughout the aggressor, continued with his explosive spinning back kicks as he did with his fists. Nate's eye had blood running down as his adversary's shots scored, busting open the cut. He was keeping busy with his jabs and the rear hand cross while sneaking in uppercuts when he could—particularly the left-hand uppercut—while also using various kicks and front hand bate to try to close the distance. McGregor used good head movement. With two minutes and 20 seconds to go, Nate caught him with a left straight to the face, hurting him, and a couple of effective punches, eventually getting into the clinch on the fence as the fighters broke away. McGregor shot for a double leg takedown, which Nate defended with a sprawl. With both fighters on the ground, Nate managed to get on top, mounting "The Notorious." As Nate proceeded to ground and pound his adversary, McGregor was forced to turn over and left his back open, prone to a submission. This presented an opportunity for Nate to apply the classic choke with 48 seconds left on the clock. "The Notorious" tasted his first-ever defeat in the UFC.

In the postfight interview, McGregor was humble in defeat. "I'm humble in victory or defeat. I respect Nate came in and took the fight at short notice and came in at 170 [pounds] and done the job. He was efficient, I wasn't efficient, that's how I feel." He said he would face it like a man and come back and do it again and prevail. He admitted that his adversary could take a hell of a shot. "I was relishing the opportunity to step into there and fight Nate." Nate felt he was the superior striker, martial artist, and jiu-jitsu specialist. He had access to some of the top sparring partners in all aspects of the game.

McGregor's defeat by Nate was perceived as a catastrophe for the UFC promotion. I started to, along with countless others, wonder if the defeat would have a disastrous effect on box-office takings at the UFC. McGregor engaged in two epic battles with Nate Diaz. As the much-anticipated rematch at UFC 202 approached, McGregor's wallet was to get a lot fatter. This time around, he would be pulling in a record purse of $3 million, taking his total earnings for this bout to $10 million, taking into account the 1.2 to 1.5 million pay-per-view buys. He was back!

33

Challenging Conor McGregor

These days, Conor McGregor is such a massive name that any fighter who attaches his name to "The Notorious" naturally attracts attention. Challenges to him weren't surprising, but one in particular caught my attention. A month ahead of McGregor's rematch with Nate Diaz on August 20, 2016, the boxing sensation Amir Khan threw a challenge out, stating that he would be willing to face the UFC champion in the Octagon. When asked about how he would do against McGregor and whether he was serious, he told one interviewer, "I was serious about that MMA fight . . . going into MMA for me would not be a problem." He continued his claims in another interview, boasting that "a good boxer will always win an MMA fight. I've always said that." It's a sentiment that I and many others didn't share.

Ever since the advent of the UFC, I've been interested in how boxing champions perceive the UFC and its warriors. After Amir won the Olympic silver medal and turned professional, he had borrowed my Royce Gracie DVDs through a mutual friend, including the first five UFCs when Royce fought back in the 1990s and there were no gloves, rules, time limits, or weight divisions. The feedback I received was that Amir immensely enjoyed watching Royce and the early UFC fights.

Many years later, I sent Amir a video of Mike Tyson paying homage to the Gracies. This time, it was my way of shoving Royce in his face. "I am a chairman of SFL—the Super Fight League," he messaged me back. He went on to explain that he was part owner of an MMA organization in India, claiming it was the third-largest MMA promotion after the UFC and Bellator. "We do shows in India, Dubai, and are now signing a deal in USA—50-plus events in the year," the boxer enthusiastically shared. Sure enough, SFL is an MMA fight promotion headed by business tycoon Bill Dosanjh, with whom Amir partnered in 2012. Its primary intent is to give MMA fighters in India a platform to compete in addition to attracting fighters from other parts of the globe.

At first, I was somewhat surprised that Amir would be promoting MMA or getting involved. But since he seemed to have embraced the "enemy" sport, I asked him if he would like me to ask Royce Gracie about making appearances in India. It would be a great way to promote SFL and MMA, I told him, and Amir said okay.

I phoned Royce, and he was enthusiastic. I advised Amir that for the league to really prosper, it was imperative to bring in some of the biggest names from America, such as Randy Couture, Royce, and others, as brand ambassadors. These were UFC champions who had pioneered the sport and were readily recognizable despite some of them being retired. I felt that if the league promoted itself with globally recognized names and pioneers of the sport from America, then his MMA adventure had prospects of really making waves. Sadly, this would go into one ear and out the other.

I sensed that Amir's interest in MMA gravitated toward the financial side of things. He'd been ramping up his business interests, and, like astute professional athletes, he was going the right way about it as his career waned. Bankruptcy is not an uncommon scenario for world champion boxers—or sports and entertainment personalities—who retire only to find themselves in dire financial straits. At the highest level, boxers can earn millions in a fight and accumulate tens of millions during the course of their career. But even some of the highest earners find themselves in trouble with the tax man as their earning power fades.

I'm a firm advocate of athletes and entertainment artists investing in business ventures. It is estimated that 78 percent of NFL players end up broke within two years after they retire and that 60 percent of NBA players end up broke within five years after they retire. Financial difficulties can force athletes to resort to desperate measures. I invested in a couple of diverse business ventures (print design, accident claims, and laundrette sectors) while I continued to focus on my combat sports business and professional writing career, and, unfortunately, the sideline businesses failed after a couple of years.

Let me make this clear: India runs on large numbers. Its movie industry thrives because the country has more than 1.3 billion people, so if you make a popular film, you're going to sell a ton of tickets. With this in mind, it's my belief that Amir the entrepreneur couldn't refuse a lucrative offer to set up shop there. It's a poor country, but numbers and masses make up for it.

It was perfect timing for Amir because even Bollywood took a shine to MMA. Actor Akshay Kumar had recently starred in a movie called *Brothers*, which became the first Bollywood MMA movie. After conferring with Amir, I phoned his management team to have a chat about the SFL and see if I could possibly be of assistance. But I was, I felt, snubbed in my efforts to offer guidance. After a phone call to his management, we were going nowhere. This individual told me that the SFL fights in India and Dubai were, in his own words, "crap." Not surprisingly, I was never provided with a contact for the main man behind this MMA promotion. Eventually, I made contact myself, but there was no response. These guys were running an MMA league, but I wondered if they were going about it the right way. I was merely trying to help out given my vast behind-the-scenes experience in the MMA world. But sometimes if someone doesn't want your help, you have to step back, and step back I did.

Nevertheless, I decided to do a short profile piece in *MMA Uncaged* magazine about the SFL. I sent the piece to Amir when it hit the newsstands, and he thanked me for the piece. Amir has never granted me an interview, nor did the management ever arrange one. Once, I messaged Amir explaining that someone who was working on one of his projects wanted me to see if I could interview him to promote his own project. I was reluctant to request an interview but proceeded nevertheless because the individual who had asked me is actually a friend. Sadly, Amir never responded. I went on to conduct prefight interviews with some of his opponents—Phil Greco, Samuel Vargas, and Terence Crawford—but Amir Khan never gave me access.

Following the SFL situation, Amir floated a potential crossover to MMA by challenging McGregor. When I first heard the news, I saw it as a desperate scramble to drum up publicity for his MMA league in India and breathe some life back into his venture. It's all part of a trend—recently, combat sports have gravitated toward WWE-style promotion and have become a circus. It's a tired old routine. The fighters know that they are never going to fight each other but resort to the hype anyway, sending the media and fans into a frenzy and deceiving the fans.

I wasted no time picking up the phone and speaking to Royce—always readily available to me—to get his views surrounding this latest round of hype, which I had frankly had enough of. "Recently, it's been in the news that Amir Khan, the boxer, is willing to face Conor

McGregor in the Octagon," I said to Royce. "Do you feel it's merely another publicity stunt?" Royce, surprisingly, was in favor of the boxer pursuing the sport he had pioneered. "I'm glad that Amir Khan is thinking about the transition," Royce said. "And if he learns some grappling—he's got very good hands and power—then he can do it. Anybody can do MMA, you just have to train for it."

Next, I asked Royce, how long, in his opinion, it would it take for someone of Amir's caliber to prevail because grappling is very intricate—you can't pick it up in three months. What advice would he give to the boxer on his quest to capitalize on MMA? "If there is a good teacher out there that can teach him, he's a professional athlete, he could pick it up very fast," he replied. "So if he puts his mind into it, he can do it. It's hard to give a time frame, but it's doable." Despite Royce's optimistic views, he said that although in a boxing match he'd put his money on Amir against McGregor, in an MMA fight, it would be a totally different ball game. "Amir Khan right now wouldn't stand a chance against McGregor, sorry," the Brazilian jiu-jitsu legend told me. "Not in an MMA match. But, having said that, anything can happen; there's only one way to find out."

Once again, Royce emphasized that there is a big difference between these two sports. "If you make a karate fighter to fight tae kwon do rules or fight boxing rules or a boxer fight tae kwon do rules, it's totally different, man." Was it beyond the realm of possibility that Amir would really face someone like McGregor? I knew Amir would never step into the Octagon. Nevertheless, the boxing champion achieved his objective, linking his name with the number-one UFC star.

I remember watching the 2004 Olympics, one of the first times a Pakistani athlete from Britain was given great media exposure. At age 17, Amir was the only boxer representing his nation. Not only did this kid qualify for the Olympics, but he was fighting adults and beating them up. Seventeen is relatively a very young age. You're still transitioning into an adult and don't always have the strength, power, and maturity that develops as you leave your teens. So, I thought that was a brave thing to do. And, of course, no Asian in Britain ever imagined that we would have an Asian athlete who would rise to prominence and be catapulted to fame. After he won a silver medal, the exposure and media attention he garnered was absolutely phenomenal.

As a young British Asian, like many other Asian kids in the community, I grew up dreaming about doing something unexpected and making it big in life. Little did I suspect that a young man who grew up with social links to an Asian community would dedicate himself so relentlessly to the brutal sport that many of us can only dream of prevailing in. Soon, he was fighting in the M.E.N. Arena, the O2 Arena, and eventually the MGM in Las Vegas, the Staples Center in Los Angeles, and Madison Square Garden in New York. It was surreal. While most young Asians were acting tough, Amir was fighting for real in the ring with some of the best in the professional arena. Boxing is a hard-core contact sport. If you merely have a big mouth, you won't cut it in the ring. You need to be able to do the business and leave the talking outside.

I guess it's inevitable that when someone such as Amir prevails, some people from his own community would resort to making derogatory comments. That's human nature. These armchair experts couldn't get into the ring to save their lives, but they were willing to talk down to an Olympic hero.

If you grew up as an Asian in the United Kingdom, you can probably relate to the sport Amir triumphed in—fighting. He had pursued boxing diligently and made the best of himself. I strongly believe that Amir has had a positive influence on the Asian community in his country. The interest that the Asian community has in boxing has grown because of him. Now you have young boys who visit the boxing gyms and aspire to become boxers. They watch and follow the sport more. He catapulted the sport to new heights.

What also impressed me about Amir is the fact he is a very humble and down-to-earth individual. As I learned in life, the road to success often humbles the top champions, and Amir epitomizes this—contrary to some people's perception of his public persona. As a journalist who has worked with professional athletes, I have the ability to switch on a kind of "attitude radar." I've worked with enough famous people to discern their personalities. Many people apparently get the wrong impression of Amir, but trust me when I say he hasn't let fame go to his head. From what I have seen, by and large, Amir has endeavored to be accommodating when it comes to his fans. He rarely refuses to have a photo taken and is a very approachable guy. Comparatively, he's more accessible than most celebrities. But some from the Asian public expect him to come up to all of them like he owes them something. He doesn't owe you anything.

⌒

While McGregor was being needled by a boxer for all the wrong reasons, "The Notorious" had more serious things to contend with—like his own fighting career. Before his upcoming rematch with Nate Diaz, I approached McGregor via his representative to talk to him about the fight and the Irish sensation's life so far. "At the moment we are not doing much media with him, but I'll keep pushing for you," was the reply I received from Zach, who was handling the press for McGregor.

Since I was already thinking about talking to some of the big UFC names and McGregor wasn't available, Daniel Cormier was the next guy who came to mind. He had earned a decision over Anderson Silva five months earlier and was happy to talk. "How do you control fear being a professional fighter when you step in the Octagon?" I asked once we were into the swing of the conversation, mindful of the terrifying adversaries he'd faced.

"I wouldn't necessarily call it 'fear,'" he replied. "I would call it 'nerves.'" In fact, Daniel proclaimed that he feared nothing and no one. "When it comes to another human being, I don't fear any man. It makes no difference." Sometimes, for sure, a fighter feels too relaxed. Any combatant needs to feel some nerves because it's a natural human instinct. But when Daniel walks into the Octagon, he says, it's an opportunity to represent his team, his coaches, his management, his family, and everybody who has invested in his long, up-to-12-week training camp. "It's a relief when I walk up those steps," he told me. "I do get those competitive nerves, and if I don't, then I start to worry a little bit. But I've never really felt fear."

In the fight game, a lot goes on behind the scenes that the audience is oblivious to. Certain fighters, be it for personal reasons to drum up publicity for a fight or just plain disdain for each other, do get into verbal and, on rare occasions, physical altercations. Daniel's not immune to this, so I asked him if he was willing to share any behind-the-scenes stories about things escalating. "You know, I work not only as a fighter but also in the broadcast side of things," he told me before going on to say that he gets to watch and see a lot of things behind the scenes that most of us know nothing about. As it happened, he explained, Dominick Cruz and Cody Garbrandt, who were about to fight at the end of the year, ran into each other when Cody was about to fight Takeya Mizugaki at UFC 202 in Las Vegas. Daniel and Dominick were actually doing co-commentary right next to the Octagon, and both Dominick and Cody came face-to-face as the latter walked past. "Cody is in a nice suit, and Dominick is in a nice suit," Daniel told me. "And these guys are in each other's faces now. All of our bosses from the UFC and the TV bosses are there, but no one knew what to do. Everyone just kind of stood back because it escalated to the point that I had to get in the middle and go there and separate those two guys." If it wasn't for Daniel at UFC 202, Dominick and Cody would've fought in August, according to Daniel, because none of the UFC bosses and TV crew were willing to actually get in the middle of these two 135-pound men with their adrenaline pumping. "I thought that was funny because these aren't little guys back there backstage." Daniel told me. "But they all stood there with their hands in their pockets not sure how to break it up and stop the fight. And I ended up stopping it. I actually made them wait for UFC 207."

I asked Daniel about his rivalry with Jon Jones. "Obviously, between you and Jon Jones, there has been a well-publicized feud," I said. "Do you feel you can hang onto the belt until you retire, or is your worst nightmare coming for you?" Daniel was brimming with confidence. "Sure, Jon will be coming to fight me to try to claim the championship, but I'm going to be here afterwards," he said. "I'm champion until I retire and then correct the wrong from the third of January 2015." He told me with great conviction that he would retire as champion but also that it wasn't a prerequisite to beat Jon Jones to be content with what he'd achieved. Nevertheless, Daniel felt he needed to be there as the champion when his nemesis returned and was planning on beating him.

Another interviewer had asked Jon if competing in a grappling match with Daniel would be of interest, but Jon remarked that he wouldn't entertain such an opportunity, that he would rather meet Daniel in the Octagon, where he could punish him for real. "Would you ever consider a grappling match with Jones?" I asked Daniel, curious as to his take. "I would prefer to fight him in a cage," he said. "I would grapple him. I would wrestle him. I would play basketball against him. I will swim against him. I will play baseball against him, it does not matter. I just want the opportunity to beat him in every sense and everything, in every competitive field there is in this world. So, I'll wrestle him, I'll fight him, box him, kickbox him. I would do all that, every competition avenue there is. I want to beat him in every single aspect of life."

Another thing fans will know about Daniel is that he looks more on the chubby side than a typical UFC champion. "How important are endurance and stamina for an MMA athlete?" I asked him with the hope that he would reveal his training regime. Cardio, he told me, is the most important element of his preparation, and he doesn't care how he looks. "You can look like an Adonis, but if you cannot endure the pain in the ring, then you're going to get dropped," he said. "I mean, a number of guys that I've fought, they were aesthetically better than I am, but when it's time to fight, I've got the cardio. I can push. I'm durable, and I can actually take those guys into deep water where they fall. So cardio and endurance are the most important things." Much of Daniel's training, then, is based around cardio. Even if he was unable to develop an admirable physique, his entire team was focused on getting him to the Octagon in perfect shape to fight. He is a guy you can't help but admire.

34

Tough Man Tales

At the end of 2016, there was another huge fight on my calendar. Dan Henderson, whom I had met when I was at an event with Randy Couture in St. Louis, Missouri, was set to fight Mike Bisping at UFC 204 on October 9. Dan came across as a nice guy and a man of few words, but he was a veteran of the Pride Fighting Championships and a veteran of the sport who was used to taking on tough opponents outside his weight class. Everyone knew it would be good.

The fight was taking place at the M.E.N. Arena in Manchester. I attended the media press conference, where we had the opportunity to interview the fighters. I bumped into my friend Karl Tanswell, who had a fighter on the card. I've always done exclusive interviews, but this was one time when I didn't get the opportunity. Instead, I asked Mike several questions as media members flocked around him. The media day was okay and more of a day out than anything. I was looking forward to being ringside. Press conferences are often fairly interesting but at other times can be mundane.

The night of the fight, the arena was absolutely packed with a raucous crowd, most of them cheering on the home favorite as he entered with his signature theme music playing. Dan had looked solid as a fighter in his training, and looked focused on his walk to the ring. He is a classic wrestler, forged over years of arduous training and conditioning and thousands of rounds on the mat, but he's also a dangerous striker with one killer weapon. His favorite attack, where he would lead with a left low round kick and immediately follow up with the heavy right hand he was known for, all pretty much in one motion, was dubbed the "H-bomb" by fans, because if you were hit with it, you were probably done. Dan's hands were as dangerous as those of any other fighter, and it goes without saying that the caliber of his wrestling was Olympic level. He was a dangerous fighter, and Mike knew it.

Mike wanted to avenge his crushing defeat at UFC 100 when Dan had scored a devastating knockout using that big right hand, followed up with a diving forearm to the unconscious Bisping that the ref was too late to stop. The rivalry had never really stopped, as people never failed to send video clips of the knockout to Mike on social media. Now their rivalry had reached fever pitch, and it was a fight the fans craved. It was also a very important fight for Mike because he was going to be defending his belt—a title that had eluded him for a long time—in the highly anticipated rematch. This was an opportunity for the Brit to prove that he could prevail against his former nemesis in the Octagon. Mike never needed motivation to come in top shape, but for this fight, I knew he threw himself wholeheartedly into his training to ensure that no stone was left unturned in the preparation process.

Thinking about it now, I recall the electricity of the arena, which kept me on my toes as I sat and then stood ringside waiting to see how the fight would unfold. I, of course, was gunning for Mike. You can't applaud or root for either fighter out loud in the UFC press box, but I knew who I was hoping would win.

Dan was booed in his entrance but came out looking strong. Every time Dan resorted to his low kick/right-hand strategy, which I'm sure Mike had well scouted out, I felt a twinge of nerves. Hendo landed his trademark H-bomb in the very first round, sending Mike to the canvas and bringing the crowd to its feet in support as Mike somehow managed to get up. Mike already had a bad eye from a previous fight, and now the other eye was severely swollen, something that appeared to be affecting Mike's vision. Still, he put on a show, outpointing the wrestler despite being cracked with another H-bomb later in the bout. Dan started to look gassed. He hadn't fought beyond a third round in five years, and this was a five-round title fight. When he was accidentally hit with a low blow, he took the opportunity to recover. The fight was gritty, and both men put on a show that would be entrenched in my head forever as one of my best experiences ringside at a UFC fight.

Dan lost a decision, but I think it could've gone either way. Both men had put on a superb performance. Mike's face was bruised and bloodied, while his adversary's face was more or less intact, but the Brit was victorious. Gracious in victory, the champ told the crowd to give it up for his adversary, and, sure enough, a chant of "Hendo!" for the retiring all-time great nearly lifted the roof off the arena. It was the best possible end to an all-time rivalry.

⌒

Working in the world of sports, I have been extremely fortunate to make some lifelong friends—from the martial arts world in particular. One of my good friends is "Big" Joe Egan. In case you aren't aware of Joe, his claim to fame is he was Mike Tyson's sparring partner for two years, and all that time, Tyson never was able to knock him down—not once. This is when Tyson was up and coming to be crowned the heavyweight champion of the world in the mid-1980s. Joe, a former Golden Gloves champion, had left Ireland to live at the famous Catskill training camp with the then-young Tyson in New York in 1983. That's more than 37 years of friendship there. And I'm not surprised that they got on for so long. One thing that strikes you instantly about this Irishman is his amazingly affable personality; you just can't help but instantly develop an affinity for him.

Before I met Joe for the first time in 2010, I wasn't sure how approachable this monster of a man was going to be. He had a frame wider than most big men, and when you set your eyes on him, you instantly were in awe. His figure resembled the body of the bare-knuckle street-fighting legend Lenny McLean, but, as they say, appearances can be deceiving. When we met, Joe greeted me like he had known me all his life. His welcoming attitude put me at ease immediately. I thought, *What a great guy*. He had loads of charisma and charm by the bucket load and was polite from the start. We swapped numbers and have been good friends ever since.

Apart from the fact that this larger-than-life character makes you feel on top of the world, he is extremely humble. If you ask anyone who knows him, you'd be hard pressed to find anyone murmur a bad word about him. But you'll also be hard pressed to hear him say anything derogatory about anyone else. A man so completely devoid of ego, any hidden agendas, or negative energy seems like he should be more or less nonexistent, but there he is, larger than life. As a mark of how well liked he is, when Joe released his own autobiography, Tyson, who wrote the foreword, personally took time out from his busy schedule and jetted to the United Kingdom to support his friend in front of 5,000 people in Canary Wharf.

Not surprisingly, Joe has a profound passion for combat sports, including the UFC and martial arts. "I like to see two men get in the ring and fight," he once told me. "But I like them to be trained fighters." Joe's not an advocate of violence outside the ring. Like many of the toughest men and longest-lived world champions in the professional fight game, Joe is a good role model. Fighting, Joe believes, first and foremost gives you self-respect, and it gives you respect for your opponent. You can play soccer, basketball, or tennis, but you don't play fighting; fighting isn't a game. He admires courage, and it takes a lot of courage to get into an organized fight, no matter what discipline you choose. It's not like having a cheap pop at someone in a bar or on the street. In the Octagon, of course, there's a combination of all forms of fighting, which Joe loves. "Years ago, a question that always got thrown around was, 'Can a kickboxer beat the boxer? Can the judo man beat the karate man?'" Joe said to me once. "And now, all forms of fighting have come together to make the complete fighter."

Of course, I wanted to pick Joe's brain and learn more about his vicious sparring partner—whether he ever saw fear in his eyes, for example, as I had heard that Tyson used to be very fearful in the dressing room before a bout, and, as their boxing coach Cus D'Amato used to say, "There's a very fine line between the coward and the hero." That walk to the ring and the waiting around before you get into the ring is very daunting for any fighter. Once the bell goes off, sure, the fear leaves you because it's time to fight. But the buildup, the walk to the cage or ring? It's very emotional because you have all sorts of thoughts going on in your head. You don't think about losing; you just don't want to let yourself down. You want to give a good performance. If you give your best and you lose, then you've done all you can. Tyson, Joe told me, felt this way as much as anyone. "He'd say, 'Did I do enough? Have I done enough? Has my opponent done more?'" Joe told me. "Mike's a human being, he's not a machine. He had the same emotions that his opponent had."

What Tyson did have over his opponents was the fear factor he carried based on his apparent invincibility and devastating power. When you've got the concussive power in your punch, everyone's afraid of you, and Tyson had that aura of destructiveness about him throughout his early career. He would fix you with an unwavering stare in the ring, and not everyone could cope. There are two ways to look at the word "fear." Joe told me that you can "face everything and rise," or you can "forget everything and run."

Frank Bruno was once asked about his first-ever experience with Tyson, and his answer stuck with me. "I remember Mike being a savage, aggressive, and violent animal, attacking me in the ring." He was referring to when he first sparred with the notorious heavyweight when Tyson was only 15 and Frank was 20. Both men went on to battle it out for real in the ring twice, and Tyson was just too much for Frank, beating him on both occasions. As for Joe, he has been humble enough to admit that the heavyweight champion made him cry often. Their sparring sessions were brutal and barbaric. Tyson, apparently, could often reduce grown men to tears. I once asked Joe what strategy he would implement against the ferocious Tyson when sparring. He said you had to keep your hands up; if you dropped your guard, Tyson was so rapid that he would take advantage of the smallest opening and nail you with his terrifying combinations.

Hearing Joe talk, I had a newfound admiration for Tyson but also for his sparring partner, who'd gotten in the ring with this most feared of fighters on multiple occasions. I thought I was hungry, motivated, and crazy, but having known Joe for many years, I think he beat me to the gold medal for being crazily ambitious. His drive and motivation are second to none. These days, Joe's phonebook is full of famous celebrity friends from the sports, acting, and entertainment worlds. Now he's an actor, with some of his credits including *Sherlock Holmes I* and *II*, and is having a great life.

๑—

In the late 1980s and 1990s, Joe and Tyson spent some time with Donald Trump. Trump, of course, owned casinos in Atlantic City, New Jersey, where he put on a lot of boxing events—he enjoyed attending a lot of bouts and has many friends from the boxing fraternity. Joe first met Trump in New York, where Tyson had an apartment in Trump Tower on Fifth Avenue in Manhattan.

On the occasions that Joe was in the company of Trump, he found him to be very personable, he told me. "I'm Irish, and he had a lot of time for the Irish because he believes that the Irish contributed immensely to building America," he said. "The Irish were the forefathers of early American settlers. They came in boat loads, and they built America. There were lots of other white Americans—Germans, English, and others—but the Irish, in particular, were people that Donald seemed to have an affinity toward. I had a few conversations with him about this because I'm Irish." Trump was well aware of the Irish history of the boxers, too. Ireland has always had a history of producing great fighters, and Trump was familiar with some of the Irish greats. They spoke about Barry McGuigan. "Mike Tyson was a big fan of Barry, too," Joe recalled. "I spoke to Donald about Barry because Barry was renowned all over the world. He was an ambassador for Ireland in boxing. Irish boxers are legendary because we wear our heart on our sleeves."

He said Trump had an absolutely delightful personality. There were no airs and graces about him. Despite being a billionaire, Joe said Trump didn't have that aura so typical of rich men: *Oh, no, you can't approach me because I'm so rich and powerful.* "I'm sure, him landing the job of president of America, he'd still have the same attitude that he had every time that I was in his company," Joe told me. "He'll enjoy shaking hands with ordinary people, people who voted for him, and even those who voted against him." Joe said with great conviction that Trump would be successful in his quest to make America great.

I wanted to discover if Trump and Tyson's relationship was merely business related or personal. Unfortunately, Joe wasn't privy to any business talk between the two. Most of the times that Joe was in the company of Trump, there was, he said, fun and laughter. "Mike was a young man, and Donald was young at heart," he said. "I think he has an awful lot of affection for Mike Tyson as a friend."

Trump, of course, has made headlines ever since coming into the political spotlight. His derogatory remarks about Muslims even prompted Muhammad Ali's family to respond with a statement that I mentioned in an earlier chapter and discussed with Ali's daughter. Speaking with Joe, I wondered aloud if the public's perception—and even the media's—of the president was somewhat distorted. "Let me tell you something now," Joe said. "I've got a lot of Muslim friends— you're my good friend. It's like the Irish: you can't judge the Irish on the IRA [Irish Republican Army]. The IRA is a small minority of the Irish. It's same with the ISIS and the Taliban, who are a very small minority of the Muslim population."

Joe went on to say that you can't paint all Muslim people with the same brush. There are a lot of wonderful Muslim people. "I'm sure Donald's got a lot of Muslim friends as well. It's just unfortunate that his views are over a minority of Muslim people America is at war with."

Trump would have sanctioned the UFC after it first debuted in America, according to Joe, when it was abhorred by the political fraternity. Trump enjoys the sweet science, so Joe doesn't see any reason why he wouldn't have enjoyed the UFC back then and done his best to make it legal and a legitimate sport. Personally, I feel it would have been a big fight on his hands in the bare-knuckle days—but who knows?

"He's a man!" Joe said of Trump. "He's been a fighter all his life, you know, in business. So he admires the physical prowess of fighters as well." Trump's great resilience is apparent in business, Joe said, and he fought all the way to the White House.

Being an ardent fan of the sweet science, Trump actually went as far as to get involved in MMA by having a hand in the now-defunct Affliction MMA promotion, a direct competitor to the UFC. At the time, Trump declared, "It's really something that I'm doing because I enjoy doing it. If we make money, that's great. I think we will. I think it will be successful." On the flip side, Trump, who had a significant equity stake in the business, once went on Howard Stern's radio show only to be embarrassed by exposing that he lacked knowledge of the game. He didn't even know the surname of the organization's number-one fighter, Fedor Emalianenko, who was widely considered the greatest MMA fighter. Still, Joe liked him. All this talk was, of course, just before Trump became president and caused turmoil.

35

Notorious

Before the UFC gladiators first graced the Octagon, back in the early 1990s, another violent phenomenon had already emerged from obscurity in the form of bare-knuckle boxing. With the mainstream press suddenly offering exposure to this underground movement, the street-fighting brawlers who participated in its bouts became instant celebrities. Suddenly, the life stories of these once-unknown fighters were on bookshelves, and the men themselves were doing interviews and appearing in films. Notorious figures Lenny Mclean, Roy Shaw, and other hard men, many associated with true crime, unexpectedly found themselves on the *Sunday Times* best-seller list.

What was so striking about these men? What was the appeal and interest? *The Guv'nor* by Lenny McLean, an autobiography released in 1998, was one of the first of its kind, kicking off a whole new genre and meeting with resounding success. It told the life story of Britain's hardest man, an unlicensed bare-knuckle boxing fighter or, should I say, "street fighter," who once fought and beat the New York Mob's best fighter and who went on to carve a meaningful career in TV and Hollywood films. Although Lenny died around the release of the book, the media frenzy was in full force. It was no surprise that it landed in the number-one spot. It reminded me of when Bruce Lee died. After all, Bruce's glossy epic *Enter the Dragon* was released five weeks after he died and made a global star out of him.

It was fascinating to see how Lenny met with mass appeal—a nonprofessional fighter who fought in front of a couple of hundred people at a time, not in big arenas with millions more watching on TV. It's safe to say that it was beyond the scope of even Lenny's imagination just how infamous he would become. For me, it would've been a major sin to ignore this movement given my interest in combat. The careers of these lethal street fighters were something I couldn't ignore.

In the early days of the boom, I remember talking to a freelance newspaper journalist who had exploited some of these characters, including Lenny, in prominent tabloids. He told me that the editor of a certain tabloid giant had great relish for these men and their gritty stories, which was why he ran these articles in the paper. I would soon come to realize that when it came to getting a story or client in the press, a lot of the times it depends on the editor's taste and interest as well as the level of interest from the public. No matter how much you felt a story was compelling, you could hit a brick wall if the editor wasn't interested. But if you could find one who shared your passion for combat and the martial arts, you could do great things. Personally, I respected martial artists and professional fighters who had their heads screwed on straight, the kind who exuded respect in and out of the ring, abided by an unwritten code of ethics, downplayed their hard-man image, were humble, and were not labeled "gangsters," as some of the notorious men from the bare-knuckle world were. But, like everyone else, I was also intrigued by these violent street fighters.

In June 2017, a film, *My Name Is Lenny*, based on Lenny's life, was released. Before its release, I had the opportunity to interview Lenny's only son, Jamie, who offered some rare and compelling insights into his late father and who had been involved in casting the lead before the director came on board. Personally, I actually felt that Joe Egan had the perfect size and build to play Lenny, and I'm sure he could've pulled the cockney accent off. Still, an Australian actor by the name of Josh Helman played Lenny and, I must admit, did a commendable job. Josh looked every inch the menacing man Lenny was, pulling off his mannerisms and little nuances to a tee.

Another familiar face played Lenny's most famous rival, Roy "Pretty Boy" Shaw. Mike Bisping, who had landed roles in several top Hollywood movies, had contacted the producers personally because he wanted to play the part of Lenny's well-known nemesis. Jamie, for his part, was oblivious to the fact that the UFC star had done any acting before. The producers, along with Jamie, sat down and talked about it and scanned over some pictures of Roy when he was younger. And the resemblance between the two was pretty remarkable, it was concluded.

Another thing in Mike's favor was that he is very comfortable in front of the camera. When the cameras started rolling, he was doing

15-hour day shoots in really unbearable heat, and he manned up and took it. He perfectly brought out the brutality of his character in front of the camera and did a great job, with only one moment of concern coming when an accident occurred on the set. Mike was playing the drums in the film's dream sequence scene and cut his finger in the process. Luckily, the damage wasn't too bad, as he had a big fight coming up.

I was very curious to learn about Jamie's take on his father's thoughts on the UFC. It was something that, I believe, would definitely have appealed to the big brawler. When Lenny died, the UFC had been going for almost five years. Of course, it was bare-knuckle and with minimal rules back then. "Back in those days, I think he would probably have struggled," Jamie said when I asked him how his father would have done in the Octagon. "But if it was completely a stand-up game and bare-knuckle, he would have done really well." Lenny was in his mid-forties then, but maybe if he was in his twenties when the sport began, he may have taken up the offer to enter the Octagon. At the time, Lenny wasn't that big. He weighed 210 pounds, so he wasn't the huge monster of a man that everyone saw in *Lock, Stock & Two Smoking Barrels*, when he was over 280 pounds. And despite his heavy frame, Lenny was very fast. His hand speed was just phenomenal. I remember watching a documentary in which he was dressed up in a nice light gray suit in a car showroom and demonstrated his hand skills to an up-and-coming bare-knuckle fighter, with added head butts thrown in for good measure. He was absolutely terrifying.

"Yeah, he liked it," Jamie continued. "We used to watch it on the old VHS tapes when it came out after 1993." Furthermore, Lenny told his son that UFC was going to be massive as long as they marketed it right. He was right about that.

Would the British brawler have been inclined to learn a more sophisticated art form in the form of grappling? After all, the street fighting he was accustomed to was fairly simple. "No, I don't think he would have because I can't see him grappling," Jamie said. "I think he was very sort of hard to control. I don't think he had the patience to learn the grappling skills; it's a long process." Lenny had a great tendency to get things over and done with, Jamie told me, his raw physicality and aggression being his greatest assets. Lenny was well aware of the Gracies, though, and I learned that Jamie is cognizant of their history in Brazil. "Their family was involved [in] no-holds-barred fighting but also in learning an art form," he said. "Where my dad grew up, it was a very rough place to survive, and you didn't have time to learn; you had to learn on the street."

Coincidentally, just over two months earlier, I had asked Royce Gracie his views on how someone such as Lenny (or any other bare-knuckle street brawler for that matter) would fare in the Octagon he once ruled. Royce said he had never heard of Lenny or seen him fight but proceeded to explain, "If a guy is just a brawler without technique, they wouldn't last long. Sorry, you're comparing a street footballer playing on the pro team. Just because he's great on the street game kicking coconuts and balls around, it doesn't mean he's going to do great on the soccer field. Yes, he's tough, he plays barefoot on the street, but that's no way to build the technique to play with the big boys on the main field." The same goes with the street fighter—a guy who is a big street fighter with no technique might win one or two brawls, but he's not going to stay on the top for long time, Royce told me.

Lenny, in later years after he stopped fighting, turned his hands to acting and was a natural, getting paid for belting men on-screen instead. Before *My Name Is Lenny* ever saw daylight, there were plans on making another film with Jason Statham in the lead. It was a potential project with a £10 million budget assigned to it. Statham was really eager to play the part, and he had contacted Lenny's son, but the production company went into liquidation, so the deal fell apart. It was five years later that Lenny's life story finally made it onto the big screen. "My friend was driving Liam Neeson the other day, and he was talking about the documentary we did last year," Jamie told me. "He told him he was a big fan of my dad's and that he wanted to play the lead in *My Name Is Lenny*." What these people admire is that Lenny was born on the wrong side of town, and he didn't have an education; he just had to fight for survival. He didn't win the heavyweight title of the world; he won one from the street. He was a unique personality and real-life character.

I was at the red carpet premiere for the movie on June 9, 2017, accompanied by a friend of mine from North London. My friend Mike Bisping was kind enough to do a quick interview with me on the red carpet, as was the lead, Josh Helman. Lenny's brother had flown in all the way from Australia.

As everyone congregated inside the theater, I was paying close attention to the crowd. With East End gangsters in their sharp suits and women dolled up to the nines, it was like being at a speakeasy. As for the film, although I enjoyed it, it would've revived Lenny's legacy further had a major studio produced it. A bigger budget and bigger noise would have definitely done Lenny's life the justice he deserved. It's an amazing story of an incredible man. Nevertheless, Lenny McLean is now a legend, with a massive fan base and a cult following—not bad for a guy who made his name in the underground arena.

⌒⌒

The year 2017 was also one when sporting history was made, as the two biggest stars in combat sports inked a deal to rumble. Conor McGregor had challenged Floyd Mayweather to a super fight during a back-and-forth war of words that had quickly escalated. In the summer, I started writing for the *Sun*, becoming a contributing boxing and UFC writer as well as a showbiz writer. I also started to contribute to most of the other national papers—the *Sunday Mirror*, the *Daily Star Sunday*, the *Sunday Express*, the *Mail on Sunday*, and the *Independent*—and to develop a working relationship with the *Sun*'s sister paper the *Sunday Times*. I spoke to my sports editor at the *Sun* and threw around some names associated with McGregor to secure some prefight exclusives. At this point, I happened to be focusing more on boxing than the UFC. Just before the two went head-to-head in Las Vegas in August, I had locked down several sparring partners from Team McGregor who were preparing the UFC star for the biggest test of his life. Among them was an Irish boxer by the name of Jay Byrne, whom I thought I'd prod for some answers to get an indication of just how McGregor was progressing in his secret training camp.

I asked Jay about the sparring sessions and how the UFC star was transitioning to a hands-only game—whether he was finding it a challenge or naturally adjusting.

"I can't give out an awful lot away because we signed a form saying a lot of information will not be dispensed," Jay told me. I reassured him that I understood, and he revealed that McGregor's most interesting quirk was his ability to throw shots from different angles. That was no secret, but it was interesting to hear from a sparring partner. Apparently, McGregor would throw very unorthodox punches and had a tendency to change his stance an awful lot. Jay also told me that his partner was brimming with confidence in the ring at the training facility, but then again, confidence is McGregor's middle name. Another distinctive quality McGregor possessed was his conditioning. The man is a pristine athlete, and his conditioning was typically top notch, Jay told me. He was also looking very strong in the gym. McGregor wasn't apparently going to cut any corners in his training, though many people expected him to be outclassed. It was an interesting fight. Being primarily a striker, McGregor prevailed in fights largely because of his crisp boxing, though he did use kicks to change distance and was, of course, used to small gloves. Grappling isn't something he uses a lot, but it's a threat that all strikers have to take seriously. So how hard would it be for him to conquer the square ring?

To investigate further, I managed to lock down another sparring partner of McGregor's. I asked professional boxer Louis Adolphe what impressed him the most about the UFC champion. "I like his movement; he's unorthodox and the way he can get behind you," he told me. "He had quite a bit of weight behind his hands, a lot more weight behind his hands than I expected, due to his bodyweight being higher than it used to be." He further went on to compare "The Notorious" to one of the most famous soccer superstars as far as both status and work ethic go. "He's the Cristiano Ronaldo of the fight world, there's no question about it," Louis told me. "He doesn't cut corners."

McGregor was certainly mentally prepared. He has always believed in himself. If you don't believe in yourself, then you don't get anywhere in life, and he's the living embodiment of this philosophy. He believes in everything he's going to do. I was told by multiple people that he was certain of the notion that he would beat Floyd Mayweather. Louis, however, backed up a little, conceding, "He may not, but he believes he's going to do it."

Perhaps strangely, "The Notorious" had insisted on not using a boxing coach when preparing for his first-ever boxing bout. I was perplexed, but his sparring partner explained the reasoning: Mayweather had fought and beaten Olympic Gold medalists and numerous world champions and hall of famers, guys who have been boxing since they were kids and who nobody could really beat. With this in mind, McGregor's approach for the fight had to be unconventional, and a boxing coach would try to mold him into a somewhat different fighter, trying to teach him to box for 10 weeks. McGregor had no delusions about what would happen if he tried to beat Mayweather at his own game. Instead, what McGregor brought to the table was a vision of what he was going to do and a fresh game plan in his mind. The game plan wasn't to outbox Mayweather; McGregor's game plan was do whatever it took, whatever he felt he had to do to beat him. He was ready to rough up the champ, make it into a brawl, and hit him from every angle. When McGregor got into the ring, he was hoping not to go 12 rounds. He was going into battle with great conviction that he could knock Mayweather out well before it hit that point.

Still, for me, it was hard to digest how a man with only MMA experience, even one the caliber of McGregor, would prevail in boxing against such a phenomenal pugilist with a spotless record. The only person whom I spoke to who was really positive about McGregor's chances was revered pugilist Evander Holyfield. Although he conceded that Mayweather was the overwhelming favorite, he also said that McGregor could shock the boxing world. He explained, "The only way he can have a chance of winning is, for example, if it's a dull fight and Mayweather loses his cool and both swing at the same time and McGregor knocks him down." When you get into the ring, he told me, one lucky punch is always a possibility.

᧖

Before I made my final prediction, I felt that the views of a UFC fighter who had shared the Octagon with McGregor were important to take in, and I found the perfect subject. Eddie Alvarez had fought and lost to McGregor nine months earlier in the historic Madison Square Garden arena at UFC 205. Not only that, but McGregor had put on a boxing clinic against the man who was sometimes known as the "King of the Underground"—at one point putting his hands behind his back to taunt Eddie into throwing a punch.

"Conor has this Muhammad Ali persona, where what he does outside the ring is all part of the show," I said to him. "What can you tell me about the experience of fighting him?"

"I think some people think they're not in a fight—they don't treat it as a fight until the day when the actual fight happens," Eddie said to me. "For Conor, the fight actually begins the first time you meet, whether it's on a press tour or week of the fight, that's when the fight will actually begin then for him. All confrontation and the bickering, it will begin the minute he meets you, not in the cage. If you're new to the sport or you don't really understand or you don't deal with the bickering stuff, then it can go bad for you. Most of Conor's fights begin way before he enters the ring."

This made sense and was reflected in the way McGregor was trash-talking and taunting his opponent—and in its popularity. The McGregor–Mayweather road show caught the attention of the media and the public alike. Billed as the biggest fight in history, it generated 4.3 million pay-per-view buys and $600 million overall. This was no fight—it was an event. As I was doing my own thing surrounding this fight, I remember watching prefight press conferences where they did a city-to-city tour, and, let me tell you, it was cringeworthy—two men trying to upstage each other with Oscar-winning performances. Not surprisingly, the public bought it, but I wasn't enamored with the prefight spiel. I know that McGregor's an entertainer, and his trash talk, psychological warfare, and pre-match predictions have often led to comparisons to the late Muhammad Ali. Yes, his popularity is due in part to his big mouth, and it's an identity he relishes.

Did the fight live up to the hype? Some certainly think McGregor acquitted himself well, and I think he left many fans surprised. He asserted his physicality, landing a few punches on Mayweather in the early rounds, including one uppercut that landed clean. Sure, he lost after gassing out, but the majority of the UFC fans knew the loss wouldn't put a dent in the UFC organization or, by and large, in McGregor's reputation as a fighter. After all, it wasn't an MMA-rules fight, nor was it a title fight. But there were others who weren't exactly impressed with McGregor's punching ability, and some believed his adversary could have gone for an early knockout had he so desired. I think most commentators knew the fight had been arranged merely for financial gain for both parties and to fatten the bank accounts of anyone else associated with the event. Had Mayweather lost, that would have been the end of boxing, but I don't think there was a real risk of that happening.

Both superstar athletes laughed all the way to the bank with a huge amount of money, while a few fans were left dismayed. McGregor, meanwhile, received a mixed response from the fighting fraternity. While some former boxing champions commended him for enduring 10 rounds, others had less favorable opinions to offer. What was most frustrating was when the teams tried to start talking up a rematch. It wasn't a fight, I felt, that people would want to watch again. We had seen it all—everything that both men had to offer. These days, I feel the whole thing about a boxer fighting a UFC champion is absurd; we know that both athletes will triumph in their own arenas. What we learned from this was that such a bout isn't necessarily going to be interesting unless you want to watch someone be outclassed.

This highly hyped sporting event, something that I had previously thought might not even manifest into a reality, undeniably further catapulted the UFC superstar's name beyond the confines of the combat sports sphere. Suddenly, your average person on the street was aware of Conor McGregor's existence, and this could only be a good sign for the UFC. As for the number of UFC champions who have since then called out boxers, I've lost count. And even boxers are not shy to get in on the act. But my personal opinion? *No thanks! Never again.*

36

Meeting with an Underworld Figure

Tales about people overcoming insurmountable odds, growing up amid crime or poverty, or having had to fight and finding a light at the end of the tunnel are stories that can be deeply personal, candid, and shocking at the same time. It's a category many UFC fighters fit perfectly into. Tamer Hassan, an actor with a portfolio of Hollywood blockbusters, is one of those characters, as I learned several months after the McGregor–Mayweather fight. Tamer has appeared on a number of high-profile TV shows, including *Game of Thrones*, which he told me was probably the toughest job he has done. The actor had been used to doing movies where the talent gets treated like luxury, where it's more relaxed and the stars have privileges, he told me, but on *Game of Thrones*, it was an absolute nightmare. He was half naked, he told me, constantly shooting without even time to have lunch. It was all work, work, work, he said, not only for the actors but for the crew as well. Furthermore, the writer would be writing as the scenes were being shot. It was just constant, nonstop action. Nevertheless, it was a joy for the hard man turned actor to be part of this series with an ensemble cast; he loved every minute of it.

Tamer's credits are quite impressive and include an appearance alongside Curtis "50 Cent" Jackson in the crime comedy *Dead Man Running* and the action film *Blood Out*, which starred Val Kilmer and Luke Goss. It was *Dead Man Running* that both collaborated on first. 50 Cent, of course, is a music icon, an ex-gangster who started dealing in drugs before he turned a teenager during the 1980s crack epidemic.

The man has obviously been through the mill. I mean, he's been shot, he's from the street—all things Tamer could relate to.

Before the music star turned up on set, Tamer told me, Alex, the director, flew to New York to meet him to pitch the project and explain his role. It was kind of the beginning of his acting career, and he was very happy to do this gangster flick. Tamer had the perception of a man of 50 Cent's reputation of being hard-spoken, tough, very to the point, and very demanding. However, when 50 Cent turned up and greeted Tamer, shaking hands for the first time, Tamer immediately found the former gangster to be very soft-spoken, very in control, very generous, and sincere to a fault. A friendship between the two quickly ensued. The Grammy Award–winning musician, according to Tamer, is always willing to learn, doesn't have any ego, and is an absolutely wonderful human being.

I'm always up for being treated to interesting anecdotes when it comes to major stars. Besides, 50 Cent's passion for combat sports is no secret, so I find him fascinating. When he was younger, he was a frequent visitor to a boxing gym where he learned the sweet science, and after dabbling in boxing promotion when his career took off, 50 Cent got involved with MMA. He's currently involved with the second-largest MMA promoter in the world, Bellator. Considering that Tamer was brought up and fought in the streets, I asked what Tamer thought of no-holds-barred fighting and the UFC. "To be fair with you, being a boxer, I hated the UFC," he told me. "Back when I first watched it, it was kind of an undisciplined gladiatorial street fight. And I kind of still have certain reservations about it. For me, to have someone's head on the ground and you're ground-and-pounding them into the canvas and they can't move—that's not a safe sport." I was somewhat surprised with the response, but he conceded he now had huge respect for UFC and MMA fighters—especially after rules changed to make it safer.

The Cypriot was born in the late 1960s in London, so he grew up in the 1970s and 1980s. Back then, London wasn't like it is today—one of the world's most cosmopolitan and culturally diverse cities. It was a very racist society, especially in the inner city, where the Hassan family grew up in a council flat in a tower block. If you were black, Turkish, or Irish in those days, you were subjected to intense racial abuse.

"I'm six feet, three inches now, but back then, I was a very short and tubby little Turk kid," Tamer said. "The bullying, the racial and physical abuse that we'd get for just walking down the street was horrendous. No one wanted to be your friend." At the time, there weren't a lot of Turks living in South West London, so life was isolated for Tamer and his brother, and they would get bullied all the time. The brothers were never fearful, but they weren't big enough to defend themselves when older kids and grown men were nasty to them. For Tamer, it was worse, as his own brother used to bully him, too, he told me.

Getting a broken nose, black eye, or cut on the arm or leg was not unusual for Tamer. So to try to change things, he had to find his own path. First, his mother encouraged him to take up martial arts. He first took up judo and did well, but it wasn't enough for him to defend himself. He found that it's very difficult to grab someone on their lapel and arm and throw them over your shoulder when you are getting abused. Next, though, his mother introduced her young son to a dear friend of hers who became a kind of second dad to her children. This gentleman took the young boy and his brother under his wing, and both youngsters then pursued boxing by attending All Saint's Boxing Gym in a church hall in New Cross. "I ended up breaking my brother's nose on the first day there," recalls Tamer. His new father figure saw potential in the young man and disciplined him, educating him about life and being there for the family as a pillar of support.

When he started boxing, little did he know how it would change his life for the better. He recalls the moment at which he came to understand how respect was earned. "I won my first fight, then won the second," Tamer told me. "As soon as I had several fights and was winning, people started leaving me alone. It was quite funny because in my day, all the girls liked the boxers. It was kind of cool to be a boxer at the time."

It wasn't long before Tamer started building a reputation for himself. Eventually, the bullying and the abuse faded away. "Those who verbally or physically abuse you, they're actually cowards," he told me. "They have a problem with themselves, and I learned that quite quickly because once I started to become a boxer, people showed you respect and became afraid of you." After 12 to 18 months of boxing and competing, there was no more bullying—quite a lesson for a young man to learn.

∽

Unlike the gangsters in movies, the real-life gangster fraternity who had an insatiable appetite for violence had never invoked my interest or influenced me—especially when a generation of youth seem to heavily be influenced by such characters. Money, fame, and power, sure, these elements are synonymous with gangsters, but I've never been interested in them.

There was an exception, though. When a documentary based on the Godfather of British crime was set for release, I received a message from the same publicist who was responsible for *My Name Is Lenny*, and I was interested in taking the interview he suggested. The next thing I knew, I was on a train bound for the capital to meet and chat with the Underworld's Freddie Foreman, famous for being the Kray twins' enforcer and hit man. This was going to be an interesting meeting and experience, I thought. Just how interesting I'd soon find out.

In April 2018, I met the publicist, and we rushed to Freddie's flat. The publicist said Freddie would be impressed by the fact I had made an effort to look good in a suit—a good sign, I thought. Freddie, a bespectacled short man, had a cream-colored short-sleeve polo shirt on, was very welcoming, and greeted me with a warm smile and a handshake. Although he was in his mid-eighties, he looked pretty solid. We sat down, and he made me feel comfortable. I casually opened up the conversation with the topic of martial arts and UFC. Freddie, I learned, had been a boxer back in the 1940s and 1950s. He talked me through some photos that adorned the wall, including a shot of him as a boxer and some shorts that actor Stuart Granger had given him with initials engraved on them. He even dined with the Queen Mother back in the day, I was surprised to learn.

Here I was with one of the most feared and notorious men at the heart of London's Underworld, and yet you couldn't have found a more perfect gentleman. This was a man who had allegedly been involved with murder and some of the most brutal criminals of his era, but you'd never have known it by looking at him. I had always perceived Lenny McLean as kind of mean—his stern demeanor was such that you'd tremble in your boots just looking at a photograph of him. I once heard Lenny say that if you're nice to someone, let's say, if you're telling a group of young men, "Please don't do that," they will take that approach as a weakness. Lenny would always use the hard-nosed approach. I came to realize why he used the rough approach instead of the more mild one, and I think his philosophy was spot on.

With this in mind, I asked Freddie for his take on niceness, and his answer somewhat surprised me. "Civility costs nothing. My parents taught me to be polite and well-mannered. It doesn't mean you're weak or you're not strong just because you're polite and you treat people fairly and you don't cause any trouble—whether it's business or at home or wherever you are." Bullies and ignorant people might make the mistake thinking you are soft, he said, because you're polite, but you can deal with bullies. Old courtesy, Freddie felt, seemed to be going out of the window.

The Kray twins, who were behind plenty of nefarious activity in their time, had been amateur and professional boxers in their youth, I knew. They even entertained Sonny Liston at one time. Since their story had been done to death, I asked Freddie if he had anything to share with me that he hadn't revealed before, and he shared a story that was brand new to me. Apparently, the twins would send out four of their firm's guys to round up anyone who they wanted to speak with. These men were 280-pound giants, and they used to go out and pick up—kidnap might be the correct term—certain people whom Ronnie wanted to meet and fetch them back to him. One of these people was musician Cliff Richard. The Krays sent out three guys to pick him up and bring back the music star for a chat. Fortunately for Sir Cliff, the crew didn't go through with it. "He was appearing at a theater nearby, but these three henchmen didn't have the heart to do it, so they never bothered," Freddie revealed. "If they had done it, I don't know how it would've turned out, but it wouldn't have been very pleasant for Cliff for sure. It wasn't fair on him." As a result, Ronnie got very annoyed.

The key story that emerged from my captivating conversation with this aging Underworld figure was the one of how he had turned his life around, even if he left it a little late. "I want to tell the youth of today, don't miss out on your education," he conceded. "I missed out because I was an evacuee. Schools were closed down; they didn't even open them in the war because of the bombing." You've got to go out and get a decent job and make a living, and you have to have the knowledge and intelligence, he told me. Otherwise, you're going to end up doing heavy labor all your life—scaffolding, meat poultry, hard-labor jobs, all of which he had gone through—or be plunged into a life of crime. It's harder and harder to commit crime now (or at least to get away with it) with all the cameras in the streets everywhere in the city, he told me. Some of the criminal activities Freddie took part in you simply couldn't get away with now, and you'd be throwing your life away the first time you tried.

Next, Freddie said something that stunned me. This reformed character revealed he was proud of the fact that none of the people he dealt with ever went to the hospital or was injured badly. He too was apparently always treated fairly and carefully and not injured in any way. In contrast, he told me, with all these stabbings now among the young people, it's a complete waste of life, and one just can't see where it's leading.

Another interesting thing Freddie shared with me was that he had been the technical adviser to Tom Hardy for the film *Legend* directed by American director Brian Helgeland. Tom, who played both of the Kray twins, told Freddie it was one of his most difficult roles because the twins were so alike yet different, and the only way you could separate and make out the two characters was by little mannerisms and patterns of speech. Freddie, of course, knew this more than most. According to the ex-gangster, of the two, Ronnie was the nuttiest one—but he preferred him since Ronnie was more true to his word than Reggie was. Reggie used to sit on the fence and see what way it went before he decided whom he was going to agree with, whom he'd side with. With Ronnie, Freddie revealed, if he was with you, he'd be with you regardless. Reggie had the quizzical look on his face all the time. You could tell he had all sorts of thoughts swirling around in his head when you were talking to him. He wasn't listening to you; his mind was elsewhere. If you asked him, "Did you get what I said?" he'd say, "Oh, yeah, yeah." But with Ronnie, he'd listen to you and was more genuine as a person. That's what Freddie brought to Tom's attention: a simple way to separate the two of them in the way he played each character.

According to Freddie, he was the only non–crew person invited on set by Tom Hardy because it was a closed set, which means there are restrictions in terms of who can be present. "Tom wanted to speak to me about how he was portraying the Krays," Freddie told me. "I was there to guide him personally. He felt I was the one person who could really offer him a true insight into the characters." Interestingly Tom had starred in the MMA movie *Warrior*. These days, the Hollywood actor keeps in touch with the former Kray enforcer. It was refreshing to meet this man, who is part of criminal history. I left that day not only with great insights into the workings of the Underworld but also with a newfound respect for a man whom I had heard of only from afar, a notorious figure who once ruled the streets of London, a convicted criminal and associated with murders. Once again, preconceived perceptions of people often don't tell you the full story.

Later, the publicist told me that Freddie had liked me. I was invited by one of the producers of the documentary to the premiere, but it was Ramadan, the month of fasting, and I just couldn't make it to London's Soho, so I regretfully declined. It would've been an experience to see which characters showed up.

37

The Perils of Sports Fame

Although my forte is combat sports and entertainment, I'm not unwilling to cross over into other territory on rare occasions—as long as it doesn't become a habit and is in an area I would find somewhat interesting or the individual I'm interviewing is a high-profile personality. I have interviewed athletes ranging from track and field and swimming Olympians to NFL and NBA superstars. Soccer is the world's most popular sport, and its popularity, in both participation and interest, in the United States has increased. According to a Gallup survey, almost 25 million people play soccer in America. It is the third most watched team sport behind only American football and basketball. Also, according to an ESPN poll, soccer is the second most popular sport in America for the 12- to 24-year-olds.

So, as I looked for more interview opportunities, it was the natural place to start. George Best was top of my list. Sometimes known as the "fifth Beatle," treated like a pop icon and a pinup, he was an emblematic figure, the first true celebrity soccer player, well before the emergence of David Beckham. I had long admired the soccer sensation—alongside Pelé, he was my favorite player—and had crossed over to the United States himself. He was one of the first stars who came to America in the 1970s, joining the Los Angeles Aztecs. But it was after years of trying to persuade Pelé to join the North American Soccer League (NASL) that George became the focus. Pelé signed up with the New York Cosmos to a three-year $7 million contract to help promote the sport in the United States. More recently, I got in touch with Pelé's daughter who resides in Florida. I sent her a WhatsApp message because she was working on a documentary focusing on women's soccer, now a global phenomenon. FIFA ranked the U.S. national team number one in the world after its back-to-back World Cup victories in 2015 and 2019.

Eventually, I learned more about George from his ex-wife, Angie Best, who had had a roller coaster of a life with George, who was an alcoholic. In 2018, I spoke to Angie after she became a reality TV star—not that she wasn't well known previously. What intrigues me about George, as well as a chunk of the wider public, are his antics off the field as well as his dazzling skills on it. He epitomized the soccer superstar.

"You see, that's the problem, that's the difference between George and everyone else," Angie told me when I asked her about her ex-husband's party life and the glitz and glamour that have been attached to his name. "He hated celebrities. He didn't hang out."

I was astounded. I had always perceived the soccer player as a party animal, a real reveler. On the contrary, apparently George and Angie didn't frequent any fancy restaurants or attend any parties when they were residing in Los Angeles. They lived in Hermosa Beach—a place where I had on several occasions trained with a UFC champion friend of mine more than two decades later—where they had a modest apartment. "We weren't grandiose, we didn't have fancy cars," Angie recalled. "We had each other and his soccer. And, of course, his Bestie's Bar, which was the only thing he was interested in. So, the parties and all those things didn't exist in George's life. He wasn't that kind of a person."

Much of the time, it emerged, George was a very subdued individual and kept to himself. When he did party, it was with some of his close friends down at the pub or in his bar by himself. Angie had lived with Cher before she moved in with George, so she and Cher would frequent parties, but George would snub them.

George was reticent about opening up about anything, and it was really very difficult to get anything out of him, Angie told me. "But he used to say to me that it was enough that he knew he was the best," Angie said. "He didn't talk about being George. I think the George that the public knew was the George that he put out there for them, but the real George was a completely different person. He was a shy, sweet, intelligent, humorous drunk."

I asked her whether she could compare David Beckham, who became a superstar beyond the confines of the field and a pop culture icon, to George off the field.

"Let me say something before I forget," she proceeded to tell me. "That was all about timing and people managing the player. If George had been managed properly and had a proper agent and manager, he would have been able to make millions, and he would have been looked after." David was not quite the player George was, in Angie's opinion (far from it), but Beckham had a team of handlers behind him. They groomed him, looked after him, and went to great measures to make sure he didn't derail himself and that he went down the right path. They secured lucrative sponsorship deals and took care of his financial affairs. "And he was treated the way celebrities and stars should be treated," Angie said. "George wasn't. Because George was the first of his kind, and people didn't know how to manage him, they didn't know what to do. Then of course if you had tried to tell George anything, what to do, he would have just laughed in their face."

When George and Angie returned to England, George started drinking again. Angie had left America and her job there to come home to England with George when he started to play for an English club again, and this left her feeling dispirited. "I was very unhappy with him because he would go with Tim Adams—his agent—and Billy Connelly out boozing," remembers Angie. "I would be really unhappy because I'd be left at home doing my needlepoint. I had my own flat, so I left his place." One evening, Cher called Angie, saying, "Angie, please come back. I'm going back on the road, and I need you. There's a ticket for you at the airport." On hearing the good news, Angie went to see George in the hospital—he had had an accident outside Harrods while driving drunk—to tell him she was going back to America. "I walked into his room, and some girl, a random stranger or a nurse probably, was pleasuring George," recalls Angie. "I was horrified and rushed straight out. I took off and got on the plane to America. I got ready to go on tour with Cher there, and I was staying at her house."

While staying with Cher, she was inundated with calls from her mother, who would call Cher's house to persuade her daughter to call George. He didn't know where Angie was staying. "He didn't have Cher's number," Angie recalls. "We didn't have mobile numbers in those days. So my mum used to call me and say to me, 'Darling, you must call this boy. He calls every day. Have you spoken to him?' Eventually, after two months of this nonsense, I said okay. I got on the phone to him: 'Hi George.' And he said, 'Don't hang up! Will you marry me?' I said yes. This was in the late 70s."

The marriage, sadly, wouldn't flourish. George would drift into depression. While Angie was with him, she didn't know anything about depression. In the 1970s and early 1980s, it wasn't talked about in the open like it is today. She came to the conclusion that he just needed somebody to settle him down, cook him dinner, have a nice house, and keep him happy. She made the effort and tried all that, but years later when she looked back on their life together and how things evolved, she saw what had happened. "I would see George would go very quiet," she told me. "He'd sleep late. He'd start to grow a beard, and he'd eat food that was full of sugar. That would happen for a couple of weeks before he went on a bender. Now when I look back on it, I can see how the picture evolved. But at the time, I was clueless about his depression."

George left his mark on both English and U.S. soccer, changing the landscape of the game. Americans first fell in love with the world's most popular sport back when he and Pelé were playing there. George would open the gates for future soccer superstars who would, at the end of their storied careers, play and promote the game across the Atlantic. It's a shame he wasn't able to enjoy the fruits of his labors himself.

⌀

A later soccer star who also became the subject of controversy and often appeared in newspaper headlines for all the wrong reasons is former Manchester United star Wayne Rooney, who would follow in the footsteps of George Best and teammate David Beckham by going over to the United States to play for D.C. United. Wayne had a connection to a couple of my interviewees—Joe Egan once told me that when Mike Tyson was in the United Kingdom, he wanted to meet Wayne. According to Joe, Tyson had a great deal of admiration for the soccer player, who, much like Tyson himself, had been catapulted to fame at a young age. "Iron" Mike had a lot of respect and concern for Wayne because the former heavyweight champion was cognizant of the pressure on his young shoulders. So, when the notorious boxer was over for an after-dinner speech in Manchester, Joe planned to introduce him to the young star. In fact, it was Joe and our mutual friend Charlie Hale who first suggested Tyson do these dinner events. At this particular event, a table that had been reserved for the Manchester United team was given to the Carrington training ground staff because the team was stuck in traffic after an away match. On another table, there was Wayne's wife, Coleen, and her family. Tyson had prepared a presentation for Wayne, but he presented it to Coleen's brother—Wayne's brother-in-law—instead.

Despite Wayne and the team not making it to the event, Joe introduced the soccer sensation to Tyson in a restaurant in Manchester called Lounge Ten later that same night. This place has a high-profile clientele and a pedigree of attracting the region's celebrities, including many A-list sports stars. As it happened, a mutual friend of Wayne and Tyson owned this restaurant and hosted a private, intimate dinner for the former heavyweight champion.

"Wayne was over the moon to meet Mike, and the latter was over the moon to meet Wayne," Joe told me. "An ex-boxer himself, Wayne loves and follows the sport of boxing, and he's a very good fighter himself. Because they're both superstars, Mike wanted to speak to Wayne about the perils of global fame, pitfalls, and the problems that all young superstars encounter. Mike imparted a little bit of advice and gave him some inside knowledge on things to watch out for when you're a rising superstar."

Wayne, I'm told, really appreciated Tyson's advice and concern. Everybody's aware of what's happened in Tyson's life, the pitfalls he's faced, and the people who took liberties with him during and after his career. Lawsuits, thieving promoters, personal and social problems in a life spiraling out of control, multiple trials, and bad investments—Tyson has experienced it all. Although he enjoyed a legendary career, he battled bankruptcy after a frivolous lifestyle that culminated in his downfall. Wayne, who used to box as an amateur, has been around boxers all his life, and some of his best friends are pugilists. All three men talked about boxing as the evening unfolded.

Since then, Wayne has apparently managed to keep his head screwed on as far as his finances are concerned, though how much of an effect the former heavyweight champion had on him is anyone's guess. Tyson continues to do multiple gigs to rake in money, from his Las Vegas show to autograph signings to offering personalized birthday messages for fans who are willing to part with their hard-earned money for a celebrity messaging service. Still, Tyson may have lost it all, but what he achieved one can only envy. And he still has time to become rich again—in more ways than one.

38

Michael, Matt, and Martial Arts

When it comes to musical royalty, you can't get bigger than Michael Jackson. The late pop star's life was plagued with controversy, but even since his demise, Michael Jackson continues to make headlines and make the front-page news. So, naturally, when I heard his brother Tito Jackson was going to be visiting the United Kingdom, I jumped at the chance to meet and interview the former Jackson Five member, a founding member of a group that has sold over 100 million records, making them one of the best selling of all time. I think anyone would have, but I had one special motivation in mind—finding out more about his brother's interest in martial arts.

When we first sat down to chat, Tito seemed very down to earth. He had been coming to the United Kingdom since the early 1970s, and he easily recalled the very first time the band was on tour on these shores. Heathrow airport, he told me, was swamped with 10,000 fans there to welcome the Jacksons. They followed the brothers to their hotel, bringing traffic to a standstill and singing Jackson Five songs in the street. This was the beginning of a special relationship between the Jacksons and the devoted fans across the pond. Tito told me that ever since then, the United Kingdom has been in their corner, as fans in the United Kingdom seem to, as he put it, "get it."

The dedication, love, and support these fans gave the Jacksons are the main reason Tito has continued to show a lot of love and dedication to them also, he told me—to try to give back the same feeling. "In America, sometimes you can be a little skeptical about certain situations," he told me. "With policemen in America, you feel inferior to them. It's that kind of place." It sounds simple, but in the United Kingdom, the policemen are nice, he said. They talk to you properly, and so does everyone else. At the time, I didn't quiz him on whether he had experienced police brutality. Perhaps he had because African Americans often are victims of racism, and despite their fame, I knew that back in the old days, the Jacksons also suffered racism in its ugliest form.

Michael's relationship with Tito was great. They had a special love for each other. "I always felt that he was there for me and I was there for him," Tito said. "We talked about everything from when we were children to when we grew into adults. However, Michael wasn't a sports person, so we didn't talk about sports or things of that nature." Tito was a little different from all the other brothers because he enjoyed working on cars, making furniture, and getting his hands dirty. Michael appreciated those types of qualities. He often showed interest in them, although he didn't get involved in them practically.

It was a fairly clear day when I interviewed Tito, and we were sitting outside of a countryside hotel. Our chat continued as a light breeze turned to a rather stronger one. I changed the subject matter slightly, as I wanted to slip in a question pertaining to something that, I would say, had been somewhat of a close-guarded secret, something one of Michael's friends had divulged to me: the fact that I had been told that Michael wanted to marry Bruce Lee's daughter. *How can I pass on a golden opportunity like this—after all, it's Michael's close family member*, I thought. I was desperate to dispense with any speculation and discern just how much substance this claim held. So, I worked my way up to the question gradually because I felt if I started to probe into deeply personal matters about his brother, it could derail the whole interview. It was, I felt, too much of a risk to take. One thing I've learned over the years is that if you have a controversial or personal question for your subject that you feel could upset the person, then you leave it to the end of an interview. Still, if I approached things delicately, with a little humor thrown in for good measure, I felt I could squeeze something out of Tito.

"It's interesting that Michael did martial arts and you did, too," I said to warm him up a little before hitting him with the big knockout blow.

"Yes, there was a time when we all took up kung fu—starting back in the 70s—for a little while with a gentleman called Kam Yeun," Tito said. "Michael was very good at it."

Despite the Jacksons' interest in martial arts, they were unable to continue because of the simple fact they were constantly traveling around the world. Despite that, Tito said, it was a great time in their lives. "We all loved Bruce Lee," he continued. "He's one of our heroes. Michael had conversations about him all the time with us. When I watched *Enter the Dragon*, what I noticed about his style was it was so different and unique. He had just so much 'style.' He's just a hero." Tito went on to tell me that all the Jackson brothers wanted to have the Bruce Lee body, like many other kids of the time.

This was my opening. Still hesitant, I felt another warm-up question was required before the final assault. I asked if he felt Bruce influenced Michael as far as his mastery of body movement and dancing went.

"I wouldn't say he owes his style to Bruce Lee," he explained. "But I would give Bruce Lee credit for some of the attitude that Michael had and came to embrace." I felt that now was the perfect time to chuck in the golden question. Whether it would catch him off guard or not I wasn't sure, but I could no longer hold back.

"Is it true that Michael wanted to meet Bruce Lee's daughter Shannon Lee and marry her?" the question was sprung on him, as a smile crept across my face. Tito seemed a little apprehensive, but he didn't walk away.

"Probably, knowing Michael, yeah, he probably did want to marry her," he said. "We all wanted to meet Bruce Lee; he was our hero. I don't know if Michael ever got the opportunity to meet Bruce or his daughter, but it would've been a great situation for that to have happened."

Now, Matt Fiddes, who never fails to astonish me, had told me this a year before. Matt was Michael's bodyguard for 10 years and is a friend of mine who claims to be the owner of the biggest martial arts franchise schools in the world. A friendship between Matt and I ensued a couple of years before I met Tito. Matt once disclosed to me that at every music store they went to, Michael would purchase the whole Bruce Lee film collection. Michael was a Bruce Lee fanatic, he told me, adding that Michael had begged him to connect him to Shannon Lee and Bruce's widow. Yes, begged him! According to Matt, this was the late pop star's dream.

Michael had also given Matt some advice on business matters. I had once quizzed Matt on how he managed to build what he claims was a £30 million empire with just £100 to his name as he started out. "What happened was, Fiaz, if it was not for him, I would just have five martial arts schools now," he proceeded to explain. As much as Michael was an extremely gifted musician and an exceptional dancer, Matt told me, he was also a very shrewd businessman, very intelligent—people forget that. They see him as the man behind the makeup, the mask, and all that fake stuff, but behind all that, there was a lot of intelligence.

"Michael once said to me, 'How's business?" Matt told me. "I said, 'Good, Michael, but, I've gone as far as I can go.' He said, 'What do you mean?' I said, 'Well, I've got five schools and the next town is 50 miles away.' He said, 'Oh, poor you. If I can sell albums all around the world and have the biggest albums and be a billionaire'—which he was on paper because of the Beatles catalog and his other assets—'you can find a way to get someone to travel 50 miles to open a school. I'm going to call you every week from wherever I am in the world.'" According to Matt, that's exactly what Michael did. Using a napkin, he wrote down a list of things to do for Matt, starting with the basics. Look for an instructor. Plan this out. Do this by this day.

Michael would call Matt up to check on his progress. The conversation, Matt told me, would often be funny. "Matt, how many schools have you opened lately?" Michael would ask. Matt would say, "Four, Michael. What have you been up to?" He'd say, "I've just closed a deal for $80 million." Matt would feel like crap. It was another level. During one conversation, the pop star revealed something to his friend that would forever change the young man's life for the better. He said, "There's a thing called franchising. That's what you need." Matt's response was less than enthusiastic. He said, "Well, no one has done this before in martial arts." Michael said, "Well, that's exactly what you've got to do." And that stuck in Matt's head. No one had done it before, especially in the United Kingdom, as far as martial arts schools are concerned. But, amazingly enough, a year later, the martial arts entrepreneur allegedly had 600 martial arts schools to his name.

❧

I learned a lot from Matt about Michael Jackson—revelations about the world's greatest entertainer in all his complexity, passions, unhealthy obsessions, eccentricities, flawed personal life, and failed ventures and personal relationships. Matt had traveled with the late pop star not only whenever he visited the United Kingdom but also around the world, including staying over at Neverland in California.

From the way Matt told it, it sometimes seemed that Michael wanted to marry literally every famous woman. Before he pursued the daughter of the world's greatest martial artist, he had another woman on his mind. Matt revealed to me that Michael wanted to marry Princess Diana and was absolutely besotted with her. "He was always telling me that Diana would be his ideal wife, but they (the establishment) wouldn't let him meet her again," he said. "I think in his head, there were two things swirling around. Firstly, it was a way to be bigger than the King of Pop. He would have a royal connection. Secondly, he also wanted to be a father to her children. He did that with Lisa Presley's kids wonderfully, and he desperately wanted children at the time. I think with Princess Diana, he was just in love with her completely. I mean, they both were very similar people. He always told me she was his ideal wife. He said to me, 'I wish she was alive so I would've tried harder, we belong together.'"

Above all, the one thing the pop star shared with Matt that stuck with him forever is that when Diana was part of the royal family, she might have been the only person in the world who could understand his life. Michael was the most misunderstood person Matt had ever met, my friend said. No amount of fame or stardom can act as a replacement for healthy relationships, but perhaps these two misunderstood souls really were made for each other. A caring, compassionate, wonderful person, Diana endeared herself to the pop star by her elevated character and indefatigable benevolence. Michael spent hours and hours talking on the phone with the late princess, spending thousands and thousands of dollars on phone bills as they spent all night on the phone. After she died, Michael canceled all of his upcoming concerts. He was actually very distressed that he wasn't invited to the funeral. Then again, he understood that if he had attended, it would have turned into a media circus and that the focus, perhaps, would have turned on him. Still, Cliff Richard was there, and so were George Michael and Elton John, and so he felt he should've been at least invited. Instead, he watched it on TV.

The media have long served as organs for exposing and embarrassing famous personalities. In today's media-saturated environment, no story gains traction quite so rapidly as one that tears down a well-known public figure. And Michael wasn't immune. He certainly had the ability to say some outrageous things on TV shows. When Michael married Lisa-Marie Presley, one of the first things he did was a TV chat show with her to put the record straight, and the world tuned in. So Michael was of the opinion that Charles saw him as a threat, according to Matt, and the late-night phone calls Michael and Diana shared would allegedly aggravate Charles. Diana had revealed a great deal to her friend during their phone sessions, but Matt refrained from divulging everything to me. What he did tell me, though, was that the King of Pop and the princess had developed the kind of trust that enabled them to talk about anything and everything.

Michael also wasn't against using the media. "He would take advantage of the paparazzi and tip them off when he stayed in hotels," Matt said. "He had a couple of fans he was very close to, and we'd use them, and he'd say, 'Hey, can you tell them I'm going to be at this hotel.'" Sure enough, the press would turn up. On other occasions, Michael got banned from hotels because the fans resorted to spraying graffiti on the walls, tipped off to his presence by the press. Essentially, Michael had a love–hate relationship with the press. He would be deeply upset if he was in public and no paparazzi turned up, just like Diana. Then again, when he wanted his private space, he would stay at the actor Mark Lester's house, where they would do deals with fans to help out in creating publicity.

The King of Pop's story is definitely a complex but fascinating one.

39

A New Direction

New World

While I was mingling with pop royalty, things were reaching fever pitch on the political front. On July 26, 2018, I met with Reham Khan, the ex-wife of former sportsman and current prime minister of Pakistan Imran Khan. If I'm honest, I had ambivalent feelings about interviewing her, as I felt it could have deplorable consequences. Yet I didn't want to pass on the opportunity either. If anything, I just wanted to meet her.

The conversation leaned toward her motives for writing her highly controversial self-titled memoir, which had garnered equal parts publicity and notoriety. I said to her that it was alleged that certain individuals, the opposition party, offered her lots of money to actually put together a book to defame Imran Khan. Dismissing the rumors, Reham claimed she had a very different viewpoint as to why she needed to tell her story.

"For example, I've got 18 things happening in my life, and the chances are that someone from your family or you yourself will have experienced some of them," she said. "I've led a very interesting and challenging life, and I've experienced many different lifestyles, cultures, and continents. People who don't know who I am."

Reham told me with great conviction that she isn't the sort of a person who can be derailed; she makes her own decisions as a strong-minded woman.

"Nobody can bully me," she continued. "A lot of people have tried to contain me, and a lot of people have tried to bully me. I'm a very free-spirited person who pretty much cannot be dictated to. People try, but I'm not going to let them change my mind." It was apparent that she was on a mission to pursue her objective knowing full well death threats lay at her doorstep, something she claimed.

I must make it explicitly clear that there had already been countless derogatory stories relating to Imran Khan floating around at the time out in the open. I wanted to get her to shed light on her own views and be able to discern the validity of these other claims.

"Can you clear up the allegations about the stories which basically said you wanted to take over the party?" I asked.

"When they say I want to be part of the party, I say there's nothing wrong with being ambitious," Reham said. "But being a British national, I couldn't take a risk of leaving my British nationality because I have kids here." Her prime responsibility was and is with her children from her first marriage, in which she suffered extreme domestic abuse. "I came here because of the death threats in Pakistan. How can I give up my nationality? When they started these accusations, which were in September, which was before the wedding was announced, I didn't pay too much attention to them." This woman couldn't have, in a hundred years, imagined that these were serious—that's what she told me. According to her, she didn't attend the meetings that she was rumored to have spoken at, further claiming that she was being framed, something that had started well before the wedding. Some regarded her as a bad influence on the sportsman-turned-politician who ran the country, but she told me differently. If you are not facilitating their agenda, she said, they get rid of you in that government.

The never-ending string of rumors and salacious allegations surrounding Reham, which I had ambiguous feelings about, left me somewhat perturbed. They painted the prime minister in a very bad light. I had, in the past, avoided the sensationalist journalist route, as I had spent the bulk of my career in sports, and it wasn't something that I gravitated toward. Then again, writing about Hollywood definitely opens you up to the sensationalist showbiz world, and I must admit, to an extent, it has rubbed off on me. Having said this, I endeavor to avoid sensationalism. Any attempts to derail her ex-husband were certainly a failure, as he was embraced by the public, and the media essentially refused to entertain the allegations.

Reham seemed very approachable, confident, and intelligent. She spoke about her time at the BBC and said she wanted to get involved with community programs where martial arts would help young women with self-defense. My friend, a martial arts instructor, was present that day, so they talked about that further, but nothing came to fruition.

None of the conversations I had with Reham ever made it into the papers. Needless to say, I was relieved, as I had no intention of vilifying Prime Minister Imran Khan, who is perceived by most a hero in his country—a country the United States has worked closely with on a wide array of issues—and has done more for his country than any prime minister before him.

⌒

When I was done hobnobbing with the wives of prime ministers, talking politics, and having to sit through sordid revelations, it was time to get back to focusing on my forte—combat sports. Deontay Wilder was facing Tyson Fury in what was going to be Tyson's meal ticket into America and the consciousness of American fans. The fight was to take place on December 1, 2018, at the Staples Center in Los Angeles, and I spoke to Deontay on October 17.

I learned, for a start, that he was a late starter as far as boxing is concerned. So why was he inclined to pursue a bloody sport when there are less dangerous vocations? Some fighters get into boxing or martial arts because of being bullied when they were growing up—it's pretty common—but for Deontay, the reason he pursued the sport so relentlessly was none other than his young daughter. She had been diagnosed with life-threatening spina bifida, which is a condition affecting the baby's spine, and he was fighting for her.

"My daughter inspires me to come to the gym," he told me. "She inspired me to change my profession. I was just a guy in college, on the basketball team. It was a job. I'd do it all over again if I had to for my daughter."

The heavyweight was willing to do whatever it took to take care of his child. Deontay had pledged to his daughter that Daddy would be a world champion one day and be able to support her. The "Brown Bomber" did just that as he swept the heavyweight division, undefeated for 40 fights. He further added that he did this not only for his daughter but for all his children as well. "It's such a great motivation and a blessing to have those little ones in my life," Deontay said. "They're so intelligent and amazing. I just love them." *Very touching, indeed, a softer side to the big giant*, I thought.

Before I hit him with any questions about his upcoming fight, I asked, "Will we see you fight Anthony Joshua before both of you retire?"

"Anything can happen, especially with a potential Joshua fight," was the reply. Even so, he said that the biggest fight in the world right now was with Tyson Fury, a hulking six-foot, nine-inch boxing beast. His mind was focused on the Gypsy King, but the AJ fight was certainly something that had his interest, he made it clear.

According to Deontay, AJ's team had their reservations and that the only way the fight could potentially materialize is if the fans were vocal enough.

"And stop all the bullshit that Eddie Hearn always keeps on talking about," Deontay said. "If this continues, then there won't be a Joshua–Wilder fight. You will never see he and I getting in the ring together. They will never see me knock Joshua out." He claimed the reason behind the reluctance from AJ's end was that his team feared Deontay, the most dangerous man in the boxing game. "It's one of those fights that it might one day happen, or maybe it never will," he concluded. "It's uncertain. Not because of Deontay Wilder but because of the other side."

Two years later, I asked promoter Eddie Hearn what his thoughts were on Deontay's comments. "Those comments look silly now, because all we ever received was an e-mail from Deontay Wilder's Hotmail account asking about numbers," he said to me. "We asked for contract details, but they were never sent. But Wilder and his team are showing their true colors. He fought Tyson Fury and lost his belts. So he's now irrelevant to our picture."

Taking Deontay in another direction, I said to him that certain boxers are fans of the UFC and MMA.

"What's your opinion on Khabib wanting to fight Mayweather?" I asked. Khabib had beaten his bitter rival Conor McGregor in their classic UFC 229 fight exactly a year earlier. "Do you think this crossover from UFC champions wanting to test themselves with boxing's best has gone too far?" Deontay confirmed that, yes, he feels everyone should definitely stay in their own lane. Yet he added, "But I also feel that if it makes a lot of money, then yes. If people want to see such a fight, then it should happen. People love seeing fantasy matchups, those fight that make you think, *Man, that would be amazing*. That's why people do it."

With Khabib challenging Mayweather, the former, he stated, could make a lot of money out of the bout. If people want to see such a matchup, if there's great interest in it, then there would be no stopping anyone. Money is a great motivator. "I'd do [a crossover fight] one day if it makes money," Deontay conceded. "At the end of the day, whether it's boxing, MMA, or UFC, whatever you want to call it, it's all combat sports." Deontay has some friends who fight in MMA, but his focus has been on boxing, a sport that has always taken control of everything for him. MMA fighters work just as hard as anyone else, he admitted to me, and he wished them all well and said he hopes they make as much money as possible.

Going back to his opponent, Tyson had been subjected to harsh criticism ever since he became the world champion. His views were often perceived as abhorrent, and everything that came out of his mouth seemed to attract the wrong kind of attention. Consequently, he became so disillusioned that he once announced he was going to move to Los Angeles, where the public and fans treated their sport stars with great reverence. I asked Deontay if he felt Tyson hasn't received the respect he deserves in the boxing world.

"People are just weird sometimes and will make certain remarks that I just don't understand," he said of Tyson. "But I do understand Fury. Currently, he's only getting negative feedback, and people are like that because he's fighting me. They say, 'He needs more warm-up fights if Fury wants to fight Deontay Wilder.' You would not hear that he needs more time to fight, he's out of shape, and so on if he wasn't fighting me."

Deontay also added that when people come back from a dark situation to perform, some people will always want to see them fail again. "There are a lot of things that people want to say, that they really have nothing good to say but just want to discredit you." People didn't want Deontay to succeed either, he told me; they don't want him to prevail and do the things that he said he'd accomplish. "I think I'm also a victim in that people give me a lot of criticism, especially right now. The only reason they give me criticism is because they don't want me to succeed."

Next, Deontay revealed his strategy: he was going for a knockout. He was confident—and with good reason. Known for his heavy fists, he had given many an opponent the beating of a lifetime. When fans go out to watch a boxing match at an arena, he explained, they don't want to be there all night, and they certainly don't want to sit around watching the fight go the distance. The fans, he told me, want the thrill of seeing someone get knocked out so they can go about their business and enjoy their night out. That's what the "Brown Bomber" had made his name doing, and that was what he planned to do again.

As you probably know by now, the fight ended up a draw— though it was one of the most exciting draws the world had ever seen.

It was inevitable it would lead to a rematch, which would once again generate millions for all concerned. The Gypsy King went on to beat the "Brown Bomber" in their rematch just over a year later and again in October 2021, solidifying his status on the worldwide stage. Tyson has become a household name, the American public has embraced him, and the heavyweight champion's charity donations have been truly inspiring. Tyson's appeal has gone beyond the confines of the ring: his struggle with mental health and defying the odds is something that resonates with the wider public.

⌒⌒

While the Gypsy King was in the limelight, so was the world's most famous royal family. Princess Meghan Markle was the talk of the town, and her estranged family garnered endless public attention from the moment it was revealed the Hollywood actress was going to wed Prince Harry.

One of the most bizarre characters I have ever come across and interviewed for the papers is Meghan Markle's estranged brother, Thomas Markle Jr. No introduction required there—he's probably more famous now by association than some A-listers. It wasn't long before I was speaking to the brother of a princess. He had just fought in the ring in a celebrity boxing match and was fairly chatty. He had been scheduled to fight Mark Wahlberg's best friend Henry "Nachco" Luan at the Showboat Casino in Atlantic City, New Jersey, but Luan failed to show up. Nevertheless, the fight went ahead, and Thomas was awarded a decision over a boxing radio host. Amidst our conversation, though, he suddenly claimed his promoter had shortchanged him, and he had a story that I should run, disparaging the promoter. Alarm bells started ringing. Thomas had a reputation for bad behavior, stemming from his run-ins with the law and general drunken behavior. I wasn't going to get into this. Thomas has long been a fan of boxing and the martial arts and enjoyed the training, so instead we discussed some of the boxers of the 1980s and 1990s. He had followed the sport with a close eye, I could tell, even if on a casual level.

He also wanted money to be interviewed for the *Sun*. I can count on one hand the number of people I've interviewed over the years who have asked for payment for granting me an interview—and I've interviewed hundreds of famous personalities over the years. I told him that I'd have to confer with my editor and got in touch with my showbiz contact. She e-mailed me back: if the story makes a spread, then we will pay £2,000 ($2,600); if it's a lead, then we will pay £800 ($1,000); and if it's a splash, then we could pay more like £3,000 (almost $4,000). She said that they would pay him only if the story went to print and that payment would be delivered two weeks after the date of publication.

Okay, I thought, great. Once Meghan's brother was convinced and satisfied with the sum being offered, he wasn't hesitant to talk. And, boy, did he rip into Meghan. His disdain for her was all too apparent. Still, we got off to a civil enough start.

"How did you and your father perceive Meghan's future had she not met and married Prince Harry?" I asked.

"She was on her way to being a successful actress; being in *Suits* was a big stepping-stone for her," he said. "It was a good move on her part, but I think if for some reason her career failed and never met Prince Harry, she would still have a family—us."

Since the courtship, though, the rift between Meghan and her father and family had deepened, and her brother's detachment was all too apparent. To add further conflict, Meghan didn't visit her father when he was hospitalized after he suffered a heart attack.

"What would your feelings be should your father pass away or find himself in critical condition and Meghan never gets to see or speak to him?" I asked.

"That's a good question, actually," Thomas replied. "I thought about this the other day. That would probably be the saddest thing on the planet. If something critical happens to our father, would she show up? I honestly don't think she would. Would it be too late at that point? The thing about this is, God forbid she's not that heartless, because she would have to live with that her entire life." He felt nobody could live like that or carry that burden on their shoulders for the rest of their life.

"Do you think the royal family is finding all this quite bizarre?" I asked, referring to Meghan's rift with her family.

"I think any normal family would find it bizarre that you ignore your entire family and don't give a real explanation," Thomas said, further adding it doesn't matter if you're royal family or just run-of-the-mill family anywhere. "I don't know if they're just siding with Meghan or giving Meghan what she wants. I'm sure they've opened their arms to Meghan, but they must be wondering, *What kind of family is this? Why won't she talk to them?* I'm sure it's come up in their conversation." Thomas believes that Hollywood changes people. Being an actress and starring in a show, you become psychologically programmed to believe that you are better than people. Some people let it go to their heads, while it doesn't affect others, he told me. "And Meghan let it get to her head that she's better than everyone else and that she's better than her family and her friends," he said. "That's pretty obvious to me."

Thomas wasn't shy about expressing his disdain for Meghan. In fact, that was the whole point of him speaking to the press. He thrived on it. I soon realized that, for him—and for some of his other family members—it was a mechanism for making money. I mean, there was no class. There was no dignity. Ever since Meghan's relationship with Harry was announced, Thomas had been hounded by the press, yet he has used the press for his own financial gain. I ended up interviewing Thomas three times, and it wasn't unusual to receive a message from him asking when he was getting paid by the newspaper. Despite being aware of the process, he was always anxious. He would invariably say that he was in desperate need of money, he was going to get evicted, or he had bills piling up. He also apparently had arthritis issues come up the year before, which had had hit him pretty hard. It was very bizarre.

Soon it became apparent that he had, by and large, virtually nothing new to disclose: the record was always the same, Meghan needs to make amends with their father, and she's abandoned the family. I mean, if you truthfully have sincere intentions and want to express something, make a point, but if your motivation is money and you're willing to do media only if you get paid, that shows your true intentions. It raises the question of just how close some of the family members were to Meghan and even raises doubts about the credibility of some of the allegations. Of course, her father had spent a lot of time with Meghan and was close to her, but as for the other family members, who knows? I recall that when Muhammad Ali died, several women came forward claiming he was their father. It was bizarre, but this sort of thing happens with celebrities.

On October 2, 2019, I spoke to Thomas again. This time, his sentiments hadn't changed and he did everything he could to defame her again. I thought, *Here we go again*. I often stressed I needed new material in order to convince the editors to pay him, and although he had some generic stories of Meghan's childhood, I was somewhat dubious as to just how much time he actually spent with his sister in adulthood. What I found disturbing is that he would sometimes tell me to add my own depth and color to the feature with a halfhearted laugh, saying, "Make it a really interesting piece." That just validated my suspicions of his true motives. Again, he messaged me from his cell phone: *I could really use the money*.

Thomas next told me that nobody in his family knows the Meghan whom they knew. She's pretending to be something she's not, was his argument. Meghan's father had invested hundreds of thousands of dollars in her, he told me. Growing up, Meghan had been pampered with everything she ever asked for from her father—clothes, cars, money, and love. Whatever she wanted, she apparently received. Thomas told me that their father has the receipts to prove it. Soon enough, what Thomas had to say had dried up, and the papers were less enthusiastic about speaking to him.

40

Flying High

In early 2018, I finally managed to make a start on one of my dream projects—collaborating with Muhammad Ali's brother, Rahaman Ali, on the definitive biography of his late brother. No one knew The Greatest better than his only sibling. There existed an unbreakable bond between the two, with Ali's death leaving his brother bereft. Not only was Rahaman the family member Ali was closest to, but he was his best friend, best sparring partner, and a constant companion to Ali on his travels all over the world. They dined together with presidents, rubbed shoulders with celebrities, you name it. This monumental memoir/biography, I felt, would be arguably the most important perspective on one of the twentieth century's most iconic figures.

In October 2019, I visited Rahaman in his hometown of Louisville, Kentucky. I had also arranged to meet up with his manager Ron Brashear, who flew over from Atlanta the next morning. Ron and I had made other plans. After two nights in Louisville, the itinerary included flying over to Los Angeles and then to Sin City, Las Vegas. Ron picked me up in the late morning to drive me to Rahaman's home. I could hardly wait, as I was really looking forward to meeting Ali's brother. We arrived at the house and Rahaman, whose health had deteriorated considerably, was dressed up in a sharp dark navy suit, looking very smart indeed. He had on his trademark hat.

He was feeling elated and was in good spirits, which was, to be honest, a great relief and solace. I experienced him to take things lightly, but apparently, he has a somewhat serious side, too. We all drove to the Ali Center, including his wife.

"Your home is my home," Rahaman said to me. "Come visit me often." Now Louisville is out of my way and hardly on my radar whenever I visit the United States. I routinely hit the West Coast and Los Angeles, where several friends live, and I endeavor to see Rahaman's niece Rasheda in Las Vegas. And if I fancy the East Coast, then New York is to my taste. Nevertheless, I had to make this trip to Ali's hometown and meet his closest family member. Besides, we had cowritten a book, so it was imperative we met before one of us left this Earth.

Several years before I met Rahaman, I had plans to meet Ali himself. I was going to call Ali's daughter, whom I have been friends with for many years, and we'd go to the Arizona home with several of my close friends. That was the big plan. Unfortunately, since my visa had expired and I had other things going on, I didn't get around to renewing the visa on time. To my great regret, Ali passed away before I could make good on my plan, and I never was able achieve my goal. When I later revealed the plan to his daughter, she said her father would've liked me and would've even done an interview with me.

When we got to the historical Ali Center, Ron had arranged to do a short advance announcement about our landmark project. After lunch at a restaurant, we settled in back at the house, where we spent some quality time with Rahaman. This man had had it all—money, cars, homes—but now all that had vanished. Ali had taken care of his only sibling when they were together, but when Ali's health deteriorated in later years in his ripe old age, something of a wedge grew between various Ali family members.

I felt wretched about the state of affairs. There is no doubt that had Ali been in charge of his senses, he would have never neglected his own brother, whom he had grown up with and loved more than anyone else, alongside their parents. There had been rumors circulating for years about the family feud. Ali's family had certainly garnered some negative press, something that I refrained from involving myself in despite being a journalist who typically has considerable latitude in criticizing public figures. Sure, a few family members had been in the spotlight prior to and after Ali's passing, but family problems are nothing unusual. We all experience them at one time or another in our lives. Ali's family had their own share of problems and inner battles to contend with, but I didn't want to get involved. If anything disparaging was attached to any press that I was doing, I would never want to attach my name to it. I simply would never want to get involved.

Ron gave some copies of the book to Rahaman to sign for some very distinguished personalities. He signed copies for Bill Clinton,

Barack Obama, Will Smith, and Clint Eastwood, to name just a few. Speaking of Clinton, he had actually been approached by us to write a foreword. The former president acknowledged our request and said that he'd do anything to help and support Ali's brother and that Ali was a good friend of his and he loved him. Rahaman had actually met the former president. Unfortunately, Clinton's agreement with his literary agent prevented him from endorsing a third party's book in the form of a foreword. NFL great Jim Brown, a man who had been a close friend of the three-time heavyweight champion, wasted no time in stepping up.

༂

We arrived in Los Angeles a few days later. I rang Paul Heller, who produced *Enter the Dragon*, and Ron and I went to see him at his home in Beverly Hills. Paul had been an executive at Warner Bros. studios and had worked with the likes of Clint Eastwood and Elizabeth Taylor. I had a short discussion about his thoughts in relation to Hollywood producing a new Ali biopic—after Will Smith's portrayal almost 20 years earlier didn't quite hit the mark. I told Paul that the ultimate goal would be to have a major Hollywood movie made based on our book. Paul said with great conviction that it was perfect timing, even suggesting Robert De Niro as being the ideal man to potentially produce such a film. "I think De Niro is your man," Paul said. "He understands boxing. He's done *Raging Bull*." The producer showed a lot of optimism, and given his stature and experience in Hollywood, it was advice that I would be embracing seriously.

I've had the pleasure of interviewing Paul twice, including two years earlier when I first visited him at his home—a nice bungalow tucked away in a quiet street. Sitting down with the man who was pretty much responsible for catapulting Bruce Lee to superstardom on a global level was a great experience. Paul, who is one of the most affable people I've ever met, was 92 but looked well for his age. It was wonderful to be treated to some fascinating anecdotes by this Hollywood legend, and I was rather impressed by the fact his memory hadn't lapsed at all. He told me that *Enter the Dragon* originally had a modest budget of $250,000 assigned to it, which then went up to $400,000, but once they were done, it was inflated to $800,000, including costs for music and so on. Nevertheless, it became one of the most profitable movies in the history of cinema as far as budget-to-profit ratio goes.

Paul told me that Bruce would often visit him at the house and once sent him flying with his famous one-inch punch in the same room we were sitting in. I learned how the producer, of all people, would paint the famous red scars on Bruce's body because the Hong Kong makeup artists didn't quite grasp the importance of continuity, leaving the American producer to take up the task himself. I asked him what Bruce was like. He said, "I've never met anyone in my life who wanted to become a star more than him." After our conversation, he showed me some photos, but what I really wanted to get my hands on was the original script for *Enter the Dragon*, so I asked if he had it. He showed me one, saying, "It's not the original, but it's my copy." It was one of the original ones. That day, I was in a rush, as I had arranged to meet up with Muhammad Ali's son-in-law Kevin Casey, an MMA fighter who fought in the UFC; otherwise, I'd have enjoyed spending more time with Paul.

One of the highlights of this trip to Los Angeles was that I was going to be meeting an American sporting legend who, although he had retired many decades earlier, is still a massive name—the one and only Jim Brown. The running back and hall of famer held several NFL records and is lauded by many as the greatest American football player in history. Besides having an illustrious, storied sports career, in the late 1960s, he pursued a movie career, appearing in several cult classics. Moreover, we were going to meet him at his home in Hollywood Hills. We drove up to Jim's house, passing some very nice homes. We were greeted by Jim and his lovely wife Monique, who were welcoming. All of us congregated in their beautiful living room, where everything was cream colored. *Very nice*, I thought to myself. From the see-through glass doors, you could see the swimming pool. And there it was: the balcony, where you had the best view of Los Angeles and Hollywood I could have imagined.

Jim had been living in the four-bedroom, four-bathroom home for many years. His health had somewhat deteriorated, and he had a walking stick, but one glance at this 83-year-old athlete's face, and you'd think he didn't look a day older than 49. He must be the youngest-looking 83-year-old I have ever seen in my life. One thing that did not escape my notice was the sheer size of his forearms. They were like massive baseballs. These guns were huge as a bodybuilder's forearm.

We gathered in the room that Jim used as his office because the lights were too dim in the living room. Having a casual chat with an NFL great was an experience I'll forever cherish. I found him to be very approachable, and humility radiated from him. Despite his fame, this is a man who has his feet firmly on the ground. I said to him that he was humble considering his status.

"We, me and Monique, we don't do the bullshit," he said. Jim is someone who, even though he's a superstar who's rubbed shoulders with the biggest names, disliked attending certain events where egos are running around loosely and where it's all about who sits in the big chair and all that eccentric stuff Hollywood is known for. He spoke to you like he had known you for a good while, like you weren't a stranger.

Jim's friendship with Ali can be traced back to the mid-1960s. Both men were at the top of their respective sports and had something else in common: achieving justice and equality for African Americans. Jim had spent an inordinate amount of time with Ali and Rahaman in the 1960s and 1970s, and a deep friendship had ensued, especially between Muhammad and Jim. Ali's brother had always taken a backseat, being in the shadow, while Ali's polar opposite brash personality won millions over. Jim said that Ali's brother deserved success and acknowledgment and that he was the ideal person to tell the Muhammad Ali story.

Of course, being an MMA journalist, naturally the conversation was going to gravitate toward the UFC for me. This isn't known by some modern-day UFC fans, but Jim was involved with the UFC after its creator Rorion Gracie—both men were friends—approached him in the early 1990s to come on board. After Chuck Norris and John Saxon declined work as commentators because they felt the event was just too raw and too gritty for them to be involved with, Jim was easier to persuade and ended up co-commentating ringside.

Naturally, I wanted to ask Jim what his thoughts were on those two diminutive-looking men, Royce Gracie and Bruce Lee, who had revolutionized the martial arts world in two different eras. "Those two unique individuals are both awesome," he said. "Bruce was very unique and very effective in movies, but Royce was the real deal! They don't say 'cut' in the UFC." Ron let out a laugh.

"Royce was a great, great person, unbelievable fighter," the NFL legend said. "He was fully responsible for the whole mixed martial arts thing, being recognized by whole the world. Because he was not a big guy, but he could beat big men, and he was a champion fighter and a nice human being."

I said, "He changed the world of fighting in a sense because they had been doing no-holds-barred in Brazil, his father, and it took off in America the whole concept, but people were shocked, but now it's a sport."

Jim replied, "For me I look at it this way: to me he was a scientist. He could beat people twice his size. He knew and understood what I might call 'martial arts,' and he had an attitude that nobody in the world could beat him. Boxers can only use their fists, but in the sport that Royce excelled in, you had to know how to do all these other things [grappling and ground fighting] that were strange in this country at the time. He was a pioneer, in my opinion. He created a whole way of inspiring fighters, and size didn't matter; it didn't matter if you were a lightweight or heavyweight, you could be as heavy as you wanted to be, and this guy could whoop you." Jim laughed out loud, adding, "He was the most influential MMA fighter, and he presented himself in a certain way. And at the time, I think the promoters understood the value of his style of fighting. It was amazing for me, sitting ringside and commentating. I'm looking at this little guy, so slender. The least-looking-tough guy. I had so much respect for his style, people would go," he tapped his hand three times on the desk, "I give up,' and that would be it." Again, he let out a laugh.

I had interviewed Jim nine years earlier over the phone, but this was even better. A man of his caliber who has had a stellar multidimensional career? You don't get bigger than Jim Brown in the world of American sport. It's a moment I savor.

⌒

In Las Vegas, we had a meeting lined up with one of Muhammad Ali's closest entourage members from his heyday. I have met many people in the fame game and experienced some outlandish situations, but meeting this particular individual, whom I shall refer to as "Mr. B," turned out to be a horrible experience. This guy, in his late seventies, had been right by Ali's side primarily throughout the 1970s. He had been part of sporting history by association. Now he was living a modest life. He was on welfare amounting to $30,000 a year, he told me, but he was content.

We met him at a diner, where it was so quiet you could hear a pin drop. When we arrived, he didn't even bother to welcome us. That set the tone for the day.

One of the most amusing things that happened that sunny afternoon was that I practically choked to death when I was sipping water. I was sitting directly in front of Mr. B when he made a sudden derogatory remark about Ron's little camera that was parked on the table. I burst out laughing while sipping water from a glass, which prompted me to jump up and swiftly move several feet away because I didn't want to give Mr. B the impression I was laughing at him. This guy didn't even blink. I thought I was going to fall over on the floor laughing and make a real scene. Eventually, I sat down, still out of breath, and I was trying so hard to settle myself. Trying to keep a serious face. Mr. B asked, "Are you okay?" Gasping, I said, "Yes, I just almost choked on water."

This man didn't seem to have a nice word to say about anyone. He was just a constant naysayer who tried to cast gloom on everything. We came to learn that numerous people had parted ways with this Ali entourage member over the years. It wasn't surprising because his attitude was absolutely abhorrent.

Why were we there to meet him? Ron had set up a meeting with this man primarily to discuss business. Being an inner-circle member of Ali's team in the old days, he'd had dealings with many important and famous individuals. His contact list, no doubt, must have been a who's who of the celebrity world. He had convinced Ron to meet because he said that he would not only ask but also "make" Eastwood produce a movie based on Rahaman and my new book. It soon became clear that this would never happen.

When Ron and I got back to our hotel, next thing you know, Mr. B phoned Ron, upset that a certain individual who had trained with Ali had been given a substantial amount of coverage. So, the next day, we met up with Mr. B again. It was going to be round 2.

The next day, I sat in front of him on the right, and Ron was sitting to my left, directly in front of Mr. B. The day before, I had asked Mr. B if Muhammad Ali ever met Bruce Lee. I already knew the answer to the question. I knew with absolute certainty that both legends never crossed paths. After all, I'm a biographer of both. Still, I just couldn't help but see if Mr. B would say otherwise. It left me stunned when he said, "Yes, we met him." I responded with, "They never met." My response was met by an incensed glare as he barked, "Yes, we did! He was a very nice man." I was disorientated. For a split second, he almost had me doubting myself. Next, I revealed to him that I'm a close friend of Bruce Lee's goddaughter, whom I'd known for many years, to give him a little taste of the fact I knew what I was talking about. Suddenly, his face fell, but he stuck to his guns, refusing to backtrack.

I had interviewed and spoken with countless individuals who were around Bruce and close to him—and I think I told him this—and I had put the same question to several. Not one said that Bruce had met Ali. Not even has Bruce's immediate family been documented saying this, ever! Bruce's daughter Shannon Lee did say to me a year later in October 2020 in an interview when I asked her about Ali, "I think my father was and would have continued to be a huge fan of Muhammad Ali's, and so are we. There are two names that are mentioned together in the same breath often. I think that's wonderful, it's a beautiful thing." In fact, no human on Earth has come forward proclaiming both legends ever met other than Mr. B. Moreover, I had questioned several people who had been mutual friends of Bruce Lee and Muhammad Ali. One particular individual, the same person Mr. B abhorred for some reason, tried to connect the two icons, but Bruce died in 1973 before a meeting could materialize. But what was his motive then? I have no idea.

The fact of the matter is that nowhere will you find anything whatsoever documented that even remotely confirms that Ali and Bruce ever met. I thought maybe Mr. B and Ali met one of the Bruce Lee impersonators in the 1970s, as there were many imposters cashing in on the name with cheesy movies at the heart of the kung fu boom after Bruce's untimely demise. That would explain it. This was the only plausible answer. I did learn something new. Andre Morgan, one of the producers of *Game of Death*, revealed to me that there were discussions at the studio about inviting Ali to costar in *Game of Death*. But Bruce died before they could make contact with Ali. Sometime later, the producers—Andre Morgan and Raymond Chow—did have a lunch meeting with soccer legend Pele in Hong Kong to ask him whether he would appear in the film.

As we spoke about Ali, Mr. B looked me right in the eyes, tensed up with his fist clenched on the table, and made it clear that no one knew Ali better than him. He complained that I should have interviewed him about Ali when I was doing my research. Sure, he was around Ali as one of the more prominent members of his team, but it was clearly stretching it by making the claim of "best friend." I can't remember what I said, but I triggered something because he suddenly barked, "Don't put words in my mouth!"

The day before, Mr. B had his own little digital camera with him and had taken photos of us with him posing like he was a celebrity. On the table was a cream-colored A4 envelope. He opened this and took out two enlarged photos. I asked, "Is this for us?" He calmly said, "Yes." Next thing you know, he's personally autographing both photos to Ron and I. *What an egoist*, I thought to myself. He had gone to all that trouble to take photographs and then autograph them so apparently we can go away with piece of a souvenir and hang his mug in our home or office.

What further stunned me was that despite claiming to be Ali's best friend, he bad-mouthed the heavyweight champion on several occasions in my presence. One Ali family member who is a good friend of mine told me that Mr. B on numerous occasions had talked trash even in front of strangers, divulging to them how Ali's family didn't help Ali's brother and so on.

Meeting this old man is an experience I would never forget. Despite the fact that the meeting was far from amicable, however, it was still an experience. And despite having differing opinions, we all left that day being civilized and moving on.

While in Vegas, Ron and I had lunch with Floyd Mayweather Sr., who is a friend of Ron. Anytime Ron's in Las Vegas, he stays at his home. I found Mayweather Sr. affable, a down-to-earth guy always up for a laugh and joke. Also, visiting Vegas and not having lunch or dinner with my good friend Rasheda Ali is never going to happen. I had dinner with her, accompanied by Ron. It was a pleasant evening, and I brought up my horrific experience with one of her father's close entourage members.

41

A Tumultuous Year

The year 2020 was total chaos. From March on, as the whole world battled COVID-19, our world was turned upside down. The crisis has had a dramatic effect on how we live our lives, the economy, and every industry from tourism to theater and cinema as the world was forced to socially distance. As we managed through the unprecedented impact of the pandemic, though, the combat sports world was hit as hard as almost any other industry, with fights being canceled, some promotional companies thrown into financial trouble, and fans left disappointed.

There was, however, the hope of a comeback for the world's biggest MMA organization. As the pandemic gripped entire nations, UFC president Dana White insisted the UFC would overcome the forces that had slammed the brakes on virtually every other sporting league and event. As the United States locked down, he went into negotiations to buy an island in international waters that could host fights without legal repercussions, like something from *Enter the Dragon*. Despite the demands of social distancing, professional fighters started to get back to training and fighting, though their cornermen would have to wear masks and the crowds couldn't attend fights.

Meanwhile, it was an incredibly exciting time for UFC. Stepping up to welterweight for the third time in his career, Conor McGregor had emerged victorious against Donald "Cowboy" Cerrone at UFC 246, which took place on January 18 before most people were aware of the seriousness of COVID. It only took "The Notorious" a mere 40 seconds to dispatch his foe, using a blistering array of techniques.

After sprawling from a flying knee, McGregor landed some surprisingly effective shoulder whips from the clinch, wobbling his opponent before finishing him with pinpoint striking and ground-and-pound. While McGregor was laughing all the way to the bank, UFC fans were left hoping to see a rematch with McGregor's old adversary Khabib, though the latter was to face another opponent—Tony Ferguson—at UFC 249 on April 18 at the Barclays Center in Brooklyn, New York. In the event, COVID struck again, Khabib was under quarantine in his home country, the event was pushed forward to May 9 in Florida, and Khabib was replaced by Justin Gaethje.

Nevertheless, Khabib—at the time lightweight champion and the dominant force in the division—would finally defend his crown against Justin—crowned the interim champion—at UFC 254 on October 24 on Yas Island in Abu Dhabi for the UFC lightweight championship unification bout. In Russia, the fight was aired on REN TV and drew almost 11 million viewers in the country, though, interestingly, it garnered only 675,000 pay-per-view buys.

It's incontestable that Khabib is an awesome fighter. He is a draw, no doubt. Still, had this been a rematch with McGregor, it's my belief that the pay-per-view figures would have skyrocketed. McGregor's fights will always attract bigger pay-per-view buys. This is likely to change only if the star gets derailed to a point where he is no longer relevant, and his performance against Cerrone had many convinced that he was a better fighter than ever. Still, Khabib pocketed a McGregor-sized pay packet of his own on that occasion, earning a staggering $6 million, excluding bonuses.

It was a fight that some people thought would be one sided. Typically, Justin is a big hitter, using chopping leg kicks and tight boxing to turn every bout into a brawl. He's not against getting up close and taking punishment, something that many thought would play into Khabib's hands, as Khabib is something of a pressure fighter who wants nothing more than to drag you to the mat and punch you until you make a mistake.

In the event, though, Justin had improved his game and was mobile from the start, making himself a moving target as opposed to a stationary one. Khabib, meanwhile, put pressure on his adversary, showcasing his punching skills. He still managed to take Justin down, and though Justin fought admirably, the gap in skills on the ground was clear. In round 2, Khabib slapped on a triangle choke, forcing Justin to tap out in one minute, 34 seconds.

After the fight, during the traditional post-bout interview in the Octagon, Khabib shocked the MMA world as he announced his retirement from the sport. He had tallied up a 29–0 professional MMA record. His father, who was also his longtime coach, had passed away from COVID-19 in July at the age of only 57, leaving him bereft. He made an oath to his mother, he explained, that he would never fight again after his final title defense, and he was going to follow through with his promise. The UFC's latest big commodity was leaving the sport that had spread his name around the globe after coming to prominence just two and half years earlier when he won the UFC lightweight belt in April 2018. It was six months after winning the title that Khabib would come to be known by virtually every combat sports fan after a bout with McGregor that had been clouded by controversy. The war of words had escalated into a series of real-life assaults, with McGregor attacking a bus that Khabib was on after Khabib confronted his teammate Artem.

Ever since beating "The Notorious," Khabib garnered a much bigger following, especially from the Muslim world, while McGregor received disdain from many. I always stayed impartial as certain people and fans continued their vilification of the Irish sensation, but when he was accused of making anti-Muslim remarks after talking about Khabib's religion and his wife, I wasn't thrilled either.

Khabib leaves an impressive legacy behind him. He will forever be remembered as a UFC great, one of very few fighters to never taste defeat. Among MMA fans, you will always have differences of opinion as far as the greatest of all time is concerned, but he's certainly in contention. I had spoken to Khabib's manager several times pertaining to working with the UFC champion, but nothing came to fruition.

Khabib may have retired, but there was another fighting legend who had been at the forefront of the sporting press. And I was going to be taking note. I was busy juggling publicity demands and promoting a couple of biographies I had released. I was going on prominent radio stations—talkSPORT, talk radio in the United Kingdom, and a radio station in the New York area—on both sides of the Atlantic and packing in media interviews talking about my favorite subjects: Muhammad Ali and Bruce Lee. I wasn't going to be sidetracked by reveling in the media as I filled my diary with famous personalities who were part of their own press junkets to interview for the newspaper. Michael Parkinson, David Arquette (who had had a stint with professional wrestling amidst his Hollywood career), Terence Crawford, Eddie Hearn, Shannon Lee, and even former Miss World Priyanka Chopra

Jonas were all on my list, and I was working flat out. The pandemic really affected even the papers I write for, with most staff working from home, not mentioning budget cuts.

⌒⌒

So, who was making these headlines? Amidst the pandemic, it was Mike Tyson who was splashed across the sports pages. Although "Iron" Mike was in his fifties, rumors started to circulate that the former heavyweight champion was making a comeback and ready for the ring. He was training with a Brazilian MMA coach Rafael Cordeiro at Kings MMA—the well-established Huntington Beach MMA gym. But he wasn't planning on entering the Octagon, not at all. It was rumored that the retired boxing champion was coming out of retirement to face a potential former champion. Soon enough, the sporting press was in a frenzy. Several years earlier, I had been assigned by the *Sunday Times* to interview Tyson in Las Vegas. Although I made the trip—I had other meetings and people to see there—I was disappointed that the chat with Tyson didn't materialize. Now, of course, a plan quickly formed in my mind. I was going to reach out to former champions myself to ask what their thoughts were and whether Tyson was doing the right thing.

One of the first names that cropped up was Evander "The Real Deal" Holyfield, who had beaten Tyson in their two high-profile fights. I had always found Evander affable. I often call him directly if I want to interview him for the newspaper sports pages, and he always obliges with no hesitation whatsoever.

In the end, I had two conversations with Evander, both relating to a potential comeback fight with his old foe. Our first conversation took place in May. I asked him, "Recently, you've announced a comeback. Are you doing this because Mike Tyson's announced a comeback?" Evander replied, "No, no, no. My whole thing is doing something for my foundation. Exhibition fights even with people who don't even box. That's the idea." He made it clear that he had already contemplated pursuing an exhibition fight before Tyson announced his return. Tyson wasn't the one who invoked his interest in lacing up the gloves again, he said.

I asked, "Would you be interested in fighting Mike Tyson for a charity?" He said, "I would do that! Yes, I want to fight Mike Tyson. My whole thing is I'm open. And I know that I want to do well for myself at age 57. The thing is, I can protect myself well, I know that. I can definitely handle him." I probed him further, arguing that he was

57 years old and asking if his age would not be a factor in the risk of getting badly hurt. He told me that he was taking care of his body, regularly hitting the gym. Next, I asked him to tell me what kind of training regimen he would go through if he were seriously contemplating a comeback. He was already physically in good condition, judging by the images that were circulating online. "I know my reflexes aren't as good as they used to be," he conceded. "But it depends who I go against and if I'm to go three rounds of two to three minutes a round."

A third fight between the two legendary pugilists would, without a doubt, provoke immense interest. It's something that I would be interested in for sure. Tyson has captured the world's imagination for more than 35 years, and I believe fans will always be drawn to him far more than any other boxer alive, active or inactive. I was somewhat surprised at what he told me next, though. "We have to come up with something that explains that this is not a knockout grudge match," Evander told me with a mild laugh. "It's not about who can beat who but to show people we were some of the greatest fighters in our era and we've come together as men to do something for others now. Not, 'I'm still mad at you! I'm still this, I'm still that.'" He continued, "I can still shoot the jab. I can still shoot the shots, but not like a killing thing, *I'm going to hurt you, I'm going to show you that I can knock him out.*" I wasn't sure that keeping things safe and sanitized would be the right attitude forward if the potential fight was to leave an indelible impact on the fans. But that's Evander for you, a gentle giant with an affable personality. How can you not like the guy? He was aware of how sharp Tyson was looking but insisted he was also in very good condition and shape physically and mentally.

Tyson had suddenly been inundated with offers after he had initially released a clip of himself hitting the pads with ferocious power. It was almost a throwback to the prime Mike Tyson as he literally ripped the pads out of the coach's hands. Bear in mind that Tyson had been inactive for 15-plus years, during which time he had essentially turned his back on any boxing training. Now everyone wanted a shot at the former champ. In fact, I also managed to speak to Tito Ortiz, who in the past had also been coached by Mike's current trainer, who had jumped on the bandwagon to try to entice the boxer into fighting him in a boxing match and not MMA rules. "Since we have both announced a comeback, a fight between me and Mike would definitely be the fight people want to see," Evander added. "I don't have anything against Mike personally. The thing is, I think it would be good for the sport, and even though boxing is a rough sport, we can show people we come together."

But Evander's idea was shattered. It was Roy Jones Jr. whom eventually Tyson would be locking horns with. When I spoke to Evander again, as the date of the fight neared, I wondered if he had given up all hope of facing his foe one final time. I asked whether, if they offered him and Tyson the right money, regardless of whether Tyson won or lost against Roy Jones Jr., would he still fight? Would Tyson want to really face Evander again and be willing to get in the ring for the third time with the man who gave him much trouble in their previous legendary encounters? Evander was adamant, saying that while he was open to fighting him, Tyson would really want to do it as well. I asked "The Real Deal," "Why did Mike choose to accept a fight with Roy Jones Jr. while there were a lot of other fighters lining up offers, including you?" I think some felt Tyson had a better chance of beating Roy Jones Jr., and so he accepted the easier fight instead of facing the likes of Evander Holyfield, and I wanted to get Evander's opinion and see if he felt Tyson was ducking him. "Of course that's the whole point of asking yourself when you're going into something how comfortable you want to be," he answered. "If you fight somebody on your level, then you both stand a chance to lose, but I don't go in with that mentality nor plan on losing." Evander would never fight anyone if he felt he was going in to lose, but he respected Tyson's decision to fight Roy. "It's a decision Mike made," he told me. That was enough.

I did learn something else from Evander. He was on a mission to help boxers and youngsters alike. As far as boxing went, he had plans to help the sport and the fighters who put their lives on the line in what is a brutal sport for the long-term health of its participants. "What I'd like to say about boxing is it's one of the only sports that don't have a pension plan for participants when they get older," he said, diverting his attention from all the Mike Tyson talk. "So, a few have ideas about how I can help other fighters who become champions when their boxing careers are over, to help them decide what kind of plan are they going to have to take care of themselves, including healthwise." Evander, who had made a staggering $300 million in his career, didn't have problems personally. Despite losing most of his wealth, he'd taken care of himself and made a lot of money back, but he understands a lot of fighters out there didn't take care of themselves. "So people like Mike, myself, and some other people, we should look at how do we make this game better for these younger people who are doing the same thing careerwise that we did. People who came up like us in life who didn't have other avenues to do real well other than pursuing boxing."

On November 29, Tyson and Roy Jones Jr. fought for eight two-minute rounds in an empty arena, sharing an engaging draw. Several days before the fight, rules were made public, which basically stipulated the following: no knockouts, no winners or losers, and no betting on the exhibition fight. Some fans were infuriated, thinking that the pair should have fought to the finish, and others were confused, placing bets with companies that were later forced to refund them. Still, it was a great bout. Tyson looked in good shape as he used his physicality and forward pressure. He landed with lots of body shots and power, but I think he was holding back somewhat. His opponent was being cautious, and Roy looked a little out of shape, trying to keep Tyson away with the jab but not looking as fast on his feet as he did during the prime of his career.

After the fight, the presenter asked Tyson if he was happy with the decision. He asked him, "Mr. Tyson, what do you think about that?" Tyson, without hesitation, blurted out, "I'm good with that." Then he was asked, "Do you think you won the fight?" He responded, "I'm good with the draw." The presenter asked, "Why?" Tyson said, "Because I entertained the crowd. The crowd was happy with it."

Early the next year, I spoke to Evander again, and he told me his team was working out a deal with Tyson's team to finally make the third fight happen, which will generate $100 million.

Mike Tyson was back, UFC's superstar Khabib had retired, and a tumultuous year was coming to an end. I was working on a compilation of interviews with some of the top UFC champions in history. From the pioneers of the sport and hall of famers to current champions who have captured the hearts and minds of the millions making the UFC a dominant force and the biggest sports company in the world, I wanted to talk to the people who made it happen. I feel that these challenging times have given people a chance to reflect and that the sports world will continue to flourish and mesmerize fans who crave seeing skilled men put all their talent on the line, whether it's beating the living daylights out of each other or appreciating the little nuances of a grappling match. The future is bright for fighting, and I can't wait to see it.

Epilogue

On more than one occasion, I recall my close friend, the editor at the martial arts magazine, saying to me, "We are lucky to be doing what we love. We could've been working in a factory or somewhere." He was right. In life, if an individual is fortunate enough to have a hobby manifest into a professional career, then, believe me, it's one of the greatest feelings in the world. For me, earning a living doing something you relish in a professional capacity, whether you're a fighter, an actor, a musician, a writer, a sports athlete, or an agent or a manager of an artist, is a dream come true.

You have to savor what you do. I have, almost without exception, immensely enjoyed my work over the years. It has, by and large, felt like playing instead of working. And, whenever I feel dejected, I look back on the good times in my profession—a beacon of hope, status, and something to fall back on and give solace in my darkest days. It has been an absolute pleasure being part of diverse fields, somewhat interlinked, in a behind-the-scenes capacity, seeing things other people can't and meeting people who many would treasure the chance to just say hello to. In hindsight, it was a constant progression up the ladder. I reached a point where I always knew in the back of my mind that any goal I set I would achieve. There would no longer be doubt clouding my mind.

Recently, it dawned on me that further goals are still waiting to be conquered. When you've ticked off your goals, where do you go from there? You can either fade away into obscurity or put your motivational cap back on and set new challenges. Well, my love affair with sport and the Hollywood fraternity is far from over. I'm too obsessed to call it a day. I plan on being part of this for a long time. As I was finishing writing this memoir, my agent—who also represents Rahaman Ali—has started pitching to Hollywood arguably the most intimate biography ever written on Muhammad Ali, the greatest sportsman and one of the most adulated figures of the past century, in our quest to nail down a deal with a major Hollywood studio, potentially to have them produce a biopic film based on our book. This, if it sees daylight, will be monumental.

Life is what you make it. I have been reaching for the stars ever since I was a small boy. And when I reached the top, I learned a lot about people and life. Despite the immense obstacles I've encountered, it will never dispel the memory of the enjoyment of the journey and the ultimate contentment and experiences.

If I could tell anyone reading this one thing, it's simple: have high ambitions because the sky is the limit. I always say there are three vital ingredients that are the backbone of anyone's success, indeed my own success: obsession, motivation, and tenaciousness. Like all successful people who had hurdles to overcome, you have to defy the odds and prevail.

Afterword

Looking back on my life, some of my most awkward moments have come from trying to explain and convince members in the community of my profession in the literary world. Finding it somewhat taboo, I had a tendency to be reticent from broaching the subject. When we are growing up and maturing, some of us are often inclined to boast or sugarcoat our achievements. But that mentality soon faded when I became a bona fide professional. Indeed, humility set in, and I no longer felt the need to prove myself or crave validation.

As I mentioned earlier in the book, *Sunday Times* best-selling author, martial arts innovator, and former doorman Geoff Thompson, who left school with no qualifications, was told that people like him don't write books. People like us are destined for the factory floor, according to many people, but Geoff would partly dispel this myth for me. I can also vividly recall Eunice Huthart, the martial artist who parlayed her success into a lucrative stunt career in Hollywood, once saying how she had a hard time convincing other mothers of what she did for a living. When picking up her kids from school, the martial arts champion would have to stand there for 20 minutes explaining to parents what she did for a career. I could understand her struggle, even though I had little interest in convincing outsiders of my worth at the time.

One afternoon when I was at my sibling's house, we had visitors—family friends we had known for decades—and I decided to break my oath. The man of the family, several years older than me, whom I had known almost all my life, a nice guy, had somehow got on the wrong side of me. Amidst our small talk, he asked me what I did for a living. Oh, yeah, this was the golden question.

Now, me, I had ventured into an unconventional career. So simply explaining myself, as I said earlier, always put me in a dilemma. Who in their right mind who knew me growing up was going to believe that I was a professional writer and author? Taking into account that I had left school with no real qualifications and on the surface I was devoid of any impressive exterior, I felt like the lie detector would come out with the vain hope of tripping me up. Often, I got the impression that some people thought I was either lying or just sugarcoating what I did for work.

I told this man that I was a writer and had written several biographies on high-profile personalities, one being Muhammad Ali. Suddenly, this guy went into deaf mode. I realized I was talking to myself, as his interest in listening to me faded faster than you could blink.

Truth be told, I had run-ins with a lot of these types. When I initially embarked on my first literary adventure at the tender age of 21, freshly back from my first trip to America—having fulfilled my initial dream of training with an original student of Bruce Lee and Royce Gracie—I was ready to start another chapter in my life, looking to penetrate the combat sports world via the medium that involved the mighty pen. On this occasion, another associate of our family who was visiting our home tried to mock me for the sheer pleasure of it. The conversation shifted to me, as it typically would in these social gatherings. "You write books?" this guy sarcastically questioned with the typical smirk that I was only too familiar with. Ironically, it was one of his family members who had first taped the movie *Enter the Dragon*, which I had watched as a kid at someone else's house and which was my introduction to Bruce Lee that planted a seed for all the success that followed.

What does valuing a person or something actually mean? It means that you appreciate them, you see how amazing they are (for example, in their job and their qualities), and you find them of high worth. Appreciation is to recognize the full worth of someone or something. Respecting someone means you have a feeling of deep admiration for that individual, elicited by their qualities, abilities, or achievements—and due regard for others. It's that simple.

In my early years, I had to learn the trade while making mistakes. I can relate to controversial film director Quentin Tarantino in more than one way. The movie buff's first film was shot on a camcorder. Working in a video rental store, he was very passionate about making a film.

The only difference between the director and me was that I wanted to convey my message via the medium of print, while he wanted to utilize celluloid. A lot of people who make it professionally as artists, actors, writers, and musicians look back at their first attempts—the initial amateur phase—and they cringe. Years later, when I achieved the status of a professional writer, a bona fide authority, I realized it was acceptable to go through the amateur learning phase that I went through, and it wasn't just me that had sunk into the trap. In fact, the editor of the number-one martial arts magazine once told me that he didn't think much of the first-ever issue he edited.

I'm a firm believer in the philosophy "If you want to learn to swim, you must get into the water." First, you will learn to drown. Then you will hold your own. Eventually, you will learn to swim. And if you're persistent and unleash your potential, you'll become a champion swimmer. This example perfectly resonates with most things we pursue in life. I went through the swimming pool scenario myself in my quest to prevail in my career, getting wet in the pool, almost drowning. But no way was I going to drown. If you think you can sail through life perfectly, you're not venturing into life but merely existing. Soon, I developed a fastidious approach as I learned from my mistakes.

Still, the negative mind-set of those around me left an indelible stain on me. I have, by and large, endeavored to be a positive person, but I have grown up with both positive and negative people, and the latter will always drag you down if you let them.

Being defined wrongly and having people telling me my worth was a constant battle. When people I knew took a potshot disguised under light banter and I would laugh it off, they equated it to weakness. Because of my friendly and unpretentious, warm exterior, this more often than not gave others artillery as they relegated me into the "unimposing" category. There's a saying: "Don't mistake kindness for weakness." It took me several decades to consciously come to terms with these facts, concluding with "in life, if you keep your hands down, you're going to get hit." You have to keep your hands up as a defensive mechanism. Imagine leaving yourself open in a boxing ring or the UFC Octagon—you're inviting your partner to tag you in the face.

I can attest to the fact that the most pessimistic individuals, in most cases, are the "talkers," and to make themselves feel better, they have to drag down the "achievers" regardless of the endeavor you're in. The contrast between the two, the person defining and the person being defined, may be worlds apart. Another saying I like is "Opinion is really the lowest form of human knowledge." It requires no accountability and no understanding necessarily. I found that the most dangerous "talker" is the one who will make you believe you're worthless. This is the type who will wrongly tell you your self-worth.

I've always found that professional personalities, well-educated individuals, and essentially those who have gone on to achieve things in life are less prone to having a negative aura about them. I have always been held in high esteem by friends and associates who were professionals. One of my friends, Lance Lewis, who actually is, to an extent, one of the inspirations behind me writing my memoir, was the first non-American member of legendary Thomas Hearns's world-famous boxing gym in Detroit. Lance had joined the gym at a relatively young age. He had boxed professionally and could have gone on to carve out a lucrative career in the sport, but there was a scandal that prevented him from continuing his boxing career, even if he did win the world title in kickboxing. Lance's encouragement to me was optimistic. He told me that I was an Asian of Pakistani descent growing up in a Western country and that maybe I didn't make it in education, but my drive, passion, and determination propelled me to achieve what I ultimately did. People in communities are often of the notion that it can't happen to people like us, but you have to defy the odds and grab your dreams. Lance said it's an inspiring story. The encouragement he offered certainly got me thinking.

We are fighting all our lives. Whether it's for a new job, more money, recognition, acceptance, power, or whatever, life is a constant fight. It's a daily fight for survival for some. That said, you have to recognize that the biggest adversary in your life is you. Yes, that's right: you are your biggest opponent. I learned early in my own life that the mind is the most powerful tool. Martial arts teach you about life and tackling problems, overcoming hurdles, and developing certain character traits. They made me into the man I became, teaching me to master myself—and even if I nowhere near pursued them to the extent my interviewees and subjects have as far as physical level is concerned, I'll always be grateful to them for that as I learned more as a professional writer.

Acknowledgments

A huge thank-you to the staff of *Martial Arts Illustrated* and *Impact* magazines: Moira, Martin, Neal, John, Roy, and especially editor Bob Sykes for giving me the opportunity and embracing me earlier on my writing career. Our 15-year working relationship was a lot of fun. Another thank-you to all my editors at the magazines—*Impact, Men's Fitness, Muscle & Fitness, MMA Uncaged,* and *Fighters Only*—and national newspapers—the *Sun,* the *Sunday Mirror,* the *Daily Mirror,* the *Daily Star Sunday,* the *Sunday Express,* the *Independent,* the *Mail on Sunday,* and the *Sunday Times*—whose help and support have contributed to my success in my professional writing career. Also, I would like to thank the personalities I have interviewed over the years from the sports and entertainment worlds—you were, of course, an integral part of my success.

I would like to thank my longtime personal friends Diana Lee Inosanto, Royce Gracie, Rasheda Ali, Ron Balicki, Bob Sykes, Ronnie Green, Lance Lewis, Seyfi Shevket, Joe Egan, and Peter Consterdine for their countless years of support and encouragement.

I would also like to thank Muhammad Ali's brother, Rahaman Ali, who gave me the opportunity to make history. I would like to thank my agent Charlie Brotherstone. I would like to thank Joel Snape for editing the manuscript. Thanks to Daz Chadwick for taking several photos. I would like to thank my editor at Rowman & Littlefield publishers, Christen Karniski, who believed in me and found my story fascinating and fought in my corner. Also thank you to Nicole Carty and the staff at Rowman & Littlefield who worked on this book.

I would like to thank my friends in the industry, in both the United States and the United Kingdom, who have enriched my life and supported me.

I must mention some of those who have influenced me as a writer. Some of my earliest influences, first and foremost, include Bruce Lee biographer John Little. Considered to be one of the world's foremost authorities on martial arts masters and action film stars, he was selected by the Lee family to review the entirety of Lee's personal notes, sketches, and reading annotations and to compile books on the late icon, including the philosophies of Lee. He inspired me profoundly, culminating in my being selected by Muhammad Ali's closest family member to collaborate on the definitive biography of The Greatest. Other inspirations of mine include my friend and best-selling author Geoff Thompson, who had an indelible influence on me as a writer. I was inspired by his story of becoming a writer after leaving school with no qualifications. Other inspirations include Davis Miller—a Bruce Lee and Muhammad Ali biographer whose part biography, part memoirs received acclaim—and Matthew Polly—another Bruce Lee biographer who also wrote his own memoirs on Shaolin kung fu and MMA. When I was a lot younger, the Canadian bodybuilding writer Robert Kennedy also inspired me.

In life, we strive to elevate ourselves. Some of us take our passion to the extreme and become totally consumed by it. Of course, to succeed and realize our dreams, we must endeavor to pursue our passion wholeheartedly and be dedicated. Achievements and accolades and acclaim are all great, of course, but sooner or later, we may—or should—realize that the core happiness and meaning of life lies in not merely fulfilling our ambitions and achievements but also cherishing those who are close to us and appreciating the simple things in life, to achieve contentment.

About the Author

Fiaz Rafiq is a sports and entertainment journalist and author. After two decades of working in publishing, including 15 years writing for best-selling magazine *Martial Arts Illustrated* and contributing to magazines such as *Impact: The Global Action Movie Magazine, MMA Uncaged,* and *Men's Fitness,* he became a contributing writer for multiple national newspapers, including the *Sun.* An acclaimed biographer of some of the most towering figures in sports and Hollywood, his books include *Muhammad Ali: The Life of a Legend, Bruce Lee: The Life of a Legend, Arnold Schwarzenegger: The Life of a Legend,* and *Champions of the Octagon: One-on-One with MMA and UFC Greats.* Rafiq is the coauthor of *My Brother, Muhammad Ali: The Definitive Biography* with Ali's brother Rahaman Ali—a *Sunday Times* Book of the Year published in seven languages. He also qualified as a professional bodyguard and enjoyed a career in Close Protection.